WORLD CLASS SPEAKING

*The Ultimate Guide
to Presenting, Marketing
and Profiting like a Champion*

CRAIG VALENTINE
and MITCH MEYERSON

MORGAN JAMES PUBLISHING • NEW YORK

WORLD CLASS SPEAKING

ISBN: 978-1-60037-474-6 (Paperback)
ISBN: 978-1-60037-473-9 (Hardback)
Library of Congress Control Number: 2008929794

Published by:

MORGAN · JAMES
THE ENTREPRENEURIAL PUBLISHER ™
www.morganjamespublishing.com

Morgan James Publishing, LLC
1225 Franklin Ave Ste 32
Garden City, NY 11530-1693
Toll Free 800-485-4943
www.MorganJamesPublishing.com

Cover/Interior Design by:
Rachel Lopez
rachel@r2cdesign.com

Habitat
for Humanity®
Peninsula
Building Partner

ACC Library Services
Austin, Texas

CONTENTS

PART I

How to Master the Art of Public Speaking

PART II

How to Generate Leads, Customers, and Huge Profits from Your Presentations

PART III

How to Use Virtual Speaking to Reach Thousands and Make Six Figures without Leaving Home!

ACKNOWLEDGEMENTS

From Craig

Special thanks to Mitch Meyerson for his vision, encouragement, and valuable co-authorship for this book. Thank you also to:

Darren LaCroix, Patricia Fripp, Ed Tate, David Brooks, Mark Brown, Cynthia Lay, and Gregory Lay for being so understanding as I immersed myself into this project

And finally to all the Champion's Edge members and my speaking students around the globe for acting on the tools found in this book and proving over and over again that they work.

From Mitch

Special thanks to David Hancock for his tremendous support for this project from the beginning.

To my partner, Craig Valentine for his insights, amazing energy, friendship and fantastic contributions to this book.

And to the Certified Guerrilla Marketing Coaches and my many friends and fellow entrepreneurs all over the world.

FOREWORD

by Patricia Fripp
Past President of the National Speakers Association,
Hall of Fame Speaker

You may be interested to know the first work on the subject of public speaking was written over two thousand five hundred years ago! The principles were drawn from the practices and experience of orators in ancient Greece.

Since those early beginnings, great speakers and presenters have: inspired us to work harder; motivated us to set and achieve higher goals; lead us to follow them to war; persuaded us to vote for them; and convinced us they are exactly who we want to do business with.

My own journey into the world of public speaking started with Dale Carnegie, Toastmasters, and my first National Speakers Association convention in 1977.

At the time I owned San Francisco financial district's most exclusive men's hairstyling salon and spoke to promote my business at service clubs. After my first free speech I realized people who heard me speak said, "If her staff cuts hair as well as she speaks, I'm going there!" It was the most fun and least expensive way to promote my salon.

Fast forward a few years…little did I know I would become the National Speakers Association's first woman president, a *Hall of Fame* speaker, an executive speech coach, and be invited to address audiences on four continents. For this young woman who emigrated from England at twenty as a hairstylist I thought, "Wow! Only in America and the speaking profession!"

Largely through the efforts of NSA the profession of public speaking has become established. Since then "experts who speak" have been in demand and can earn a very comfortable living. Because of technology and the Internet, the ways to communicate and promote have expanded.

In the early 1970s one of my hairstyling clients took me to hear Venita Van Caspel, the "First Lady of Financial Planning" and author of *The New Money Dynamics*. You can imagine my excitement ten years later to share the platform with Venita at a well-attended conference and get to know her personally.

As a new stock broker, and the only woman, Venita was told, "There is your desk, phone and phone book; start dialing for dollars!" After three hours of cold-calling, she realized it would be more effective to invite people who were interested in money to a seminar.

She was right! History was created. Since then professionals in all industries realize that when you stand up and speak eloquently about your industry, you are perceived as a greater expert than one who has equal skills and can't speak. Also, if you present to thirty people at one time, you are often more effective in marketing than initiating thirty appointments. Not to mention the time savings.

By now you realize the benefits of speaking effectively and using those skills to market yourself. Therefore, your next question should be, "Where do I get advice? Who is the best person to listen to?"

Based on thirty plus years experience, my best advice is "Look at who has already accomplished what you want to do, preferably one who enjoys world-wide credentials to prove it. You can't go wrong reading what my friends, speaking and marketing heroes Craig Valentine and Mitch Meyerson, have to say."

Don't reinvent the wheel! Follow their advice and you will cut years off your learning curve...and feed your family exceptionally well doing so!

INTRODUCTION

MASTERING THE ART OF PUBLIC SPEAKING: CRAIG VALENTINE

At ten years old, something disturbing happened to me. Walking through the mall by myself, I ran into my friend's father. He asked about my family. I don't remember what I said, but I never forgot his response. He fixed me in his gaze and said, "Do you know you have a serious lisp? Craigy, if I were you, I wouldn't talk anymore, because every time you open your mouth, you remind me of Daffy Duck!"

My heart dropped. My confidence and esteem plummeted, and for the next five years, you couldn't get a word out of me. By age fifteen, though, I was sick of voluntarily muting myself, so I started striving to become empowered—rather than embarrassed—as a communicator.

Eighteen years later, on August 21, 1999, I stood on stage in Chicago, being crowned as Toastmasters International's 1999 World Champion of Public Speaking. That's a long way from Daffy Duck! Out of twenty-five thousand contestants in fourteen countries, I came home with the first-prize trophy.

Since 1999, I have used the art of public speaking in many ways. I used presentations to become the three-time salesperson of the year for the Mid-Atlantic Division of Glencoe/McGraw-Hill, to become an award-winning management trainer for one of the largest seminar-training firms in the

United States, and to become a full-time professional speaker delivering hundreds of speeches per year, all around the globe.

However, my biggest surprise after winning the world championship was getting a phone call from Wade Randolph. I hadn't heard of Wade, but he had heard of me! He said, "Craig, I'm from down in Richmond, Virginia, and I was wondering if you'd be willing to coach me in speaking?" I said, "Wade, I don't coach speakers," to which he replied, "I'll pay you good money." I responded, "Wade, let me get my whistle!" Little did I know that Wade would be one of thousands of speakers, from Toronto to Taipei, that I would eventually coach or teach.

I then wrote the book *The Nuts and Bolts of Public Speaking*, produced the *Edge of Their Seats Storytelling Home-Study Course for Speakers*, cofounded *The World Champion's Edge*, conducted speaking boot camps around the country, and created many other speaking-related products and services. Through this consistent combination of coaching sessions, speaking engagements, and product development, *World Class Speaking* was born. Once I met Mitch Meyerson, *World Class Speaking* exploded into what it is today: a life-changing tool for you and your next audience.

Today, people say, "Craig, you're a natural speaker." Nothing can be further from the truth. You know my humble beginnings. If I can become a world-class speaker, anybody can. There's nothing special about me, but there's something very special about the speaking tools I've uncovered. Put them to use, and you will change your life for the better—in every possible way. You'll have more money, freedom, and control over the lifestyle you want to lead. The best part is that you'll touch many lives along the way. All these special tools are in this book waiting to be uncovered by you. Use them and become a World Class Speaker.

INTRODUCTION

Creating a Lucrative Virtual-Speaking Business:
Mitch Meyerson

S peaking and presenting has always come naturally to me. Whether it is to a group of three people or as a guest expert on Oprah Winfrey's show, I enjoy the opportunity to communicate clearly on topics that I am passionate about. Yet, even a natural speaker can grow to become a *world-class* speaker through the principles clearly outlined in this book.

My early experience came in an unusual way: in my twenties, I performed in a rock 'n' roll band four to five nights a week. I'll admit that while it didn't make me a lot of money, I did learn how to feel more comfortable presenting my talents in front of a group of people. This transferred very nicely into my entrepreneurial ventures later in life.

However, there is one problem I've always had that has stood in the way of developing a thriving speaking career, and that is this: I'm not a big fan of traveling. The thought of driving to an airport, battling security, and then flying hours to a destination just hasn't ever fit into what I've considered my ideal lifestyle. As a result, I've passed on many lucrative speaking engagements and business-building opportunities. All of that changed for me, in the late 1990s, with the growth and expansion of the Internet.

In 1999, with three psychology books (*When Parents Love Too Much, When Is Enough Enough?* and *Six Keys to Creating the Life You Desire*) under my belt, and with years of running a successful brick-and-mortar psychotherapy practice, I became tired of Chicago winters and began looking on the Internet for a way to transition my skills into a virtual business that I could run from any location, including the warm, sunny climate I dreamed of.

So, after research and a strong, new business idea in 1999, I developed the Guerrilla Marketing Coaching program, which was delivered to dozens of people at a time, exclusively over the phone and the Internet. Tapping, over the net, a global market of entrepreneurs looking to enhance their marketing skills, I soon had clients and students all over the world in my virtual classroom. My business exploded, and I followed this with more books (*Success Secrets of the Online Marketing Superstars, Mastering Online Marketing, Guerrilla Marketing on the Front Lines,* and *Guerrilla Marketing on the Internet*) and three other online courses, including the 90 Day Product Factory, the Online Traffic School, and the Master Business Building Club.

As we speak, over 95 percent of my income is done virtually over the phone and Internet, and now I fly only to destinations that are desirable. In section three of this book, I will be sharing the keys to developing a six-figure virtual-speaking business by mastering online-marketing skills (the title of my most recent book) and using cutting-edge technology to reach tens of thousands of prospects and customers all over the world.

As an emerging world-class speaker, I invite you to integrate your live presentations with a strong program of teleseminars and Internet-based communications systems. If you do, you will not only dramatically increase your income, but you will spend more time working out of your home (or any location you choose) and truly develop the life you desire.

WORLD CLASS SPEAKING

A few years back, I called a lady who was supposed to be one of the best public-speaking coaches in the country. I said, "I need a coach, and I need to be coached by you." She asked, "Are you sure?" I replied, "Yes. I did my research, and I know you're the one I want to coach me." She asked if I knew how much she charged. Shrugging it off, I responded, "It doesn't matter." She paused and then said, "Great! That's a wonderful attitude. That will be four thousand dollars per day." I shot back, "I'm pretty happy with the skills that I have."

Often, we look at the price of doing something, but we don't look at the cost of not. With this realization, I decided to get coached by her, and guess what happened? Even though I was already the World Champion of Public Speaking, I realized that I was nowhere near where I needed to be as a speaker. I came face-to-face with the following fundamental truth: "What got me here won't get me there."

What got me here as a speaker won't get me to that next level. What got you here as a speaker won't get you to that next level. It always takes new strategies, new understandings, and new tools. *World Class Speaking* is about these new tools. When it comes to giving captivating speeches, turning them into profits, and reaching thousands of people with your message, please understand that what got you here won't get you there. So how do you get there? *World Class Speaking* is the way!

WHAT *WORLD CLASS SPEAKING* IS NOT

World Class Speaking is your future. Let's start off by understanding what *World Class Speaking* is not. It's *not* about

- striving for paid speaking engagements, only to feel unemployed after each speech
- being dependent on fee-based engagements
- having to constantly travel around the world (unless you want to) on extended road trips that would break up even the Huxtable family
- living a life of business success, only to realize that you don't know your own kids
- sending in proposals that compete with dozens of other speakers, which results in many more disappointments than appointments
- having just one, two, or even three streams of income. If you don't gather at least ten streams, you will not be practicing *World Class Speaking*
- having initials after your name
- being anything less than stellar on the speaking platform

WHAT WORLD CLASS SPEAKING IS

World Class Speaking is about

- turning your ideas into captivating presentations
- turning your presentations into multiple income streams
- mastering the art of public speaking so that you can keep your audiences on the edges of their seats, leaning on your every word
- taking advantage of the technological tools you can use to speak to thousands and make at least six figures each year, without even having to leave the comfort of your own home (unless you so desire)
- living the lifestyle you want without sacrificing the income you deserve

World Class Speaking is about having it all!

Do you remember quizzes that had multiple-choice questions? Here's one for you. How would you answer it?

As a speaker, I would like to

A. Keep my audiences on the edges of their seats with spellbinding, content-rich presentations

B. Master marketing so that I can turn my speeches into multiple lucrative income streams

C. Have control over my life so that I can spend my time where I want, while still touching thousands of lives with my message

D. All of the above

For *World Class Speaking,* the correct answer is D.

There are many resources that will help you become a better speaker. There are a few resources that will help you get paid to speak. There are even resources to help you use technology to make presentations. However, *World Class Speaking* is *the* system you need to profit by putting it all together. Plus—and this is the best part—you will immensely enjoy the process. Many speakers struggle throughout their entire careers. While they're struggling, you'll be thriving. With *World Class Speaking,* you can have it all.

The book is laid out into the following three distinct parts:

PART I: Mastering the Art of Public Speaking

PART II: Making Huge Profits from Your Presentations

PART III: Using Technology to Reach Thousands and Earn Six Figures without Leaving Home

Mastering the Art of Public Speaking (Part I)

There is a definite process for keeping your audiences on the edges of their seats. It is not easy to come by, and it is not easy to use. However, once you master it, you will find doors opening for you that you never even knew existed. The great news is that behind those doors live the kinds of profits that most speakers will never see. *You* will.

In this book, you will pick throngs of tools that you can use to keep your audiences leaning on your every word, while you give them a message they won't soon forget. How do I know? These tools helped me win the Toastmasters International 1999 World Champion of Public Speaking, out of more than 170,000 Toastmasters in 68 countries and over 25,000 contestants. They also helped me become the three-time salesperson of the year for a division of Glencoe/McGraw-Hill and reach unheard-of heights of up to 233 percent of goal while selling more than 8 million dollars in educational resources in a single year. The process works, but it's up to you to work it. Part I of this book is divided into four tool-loaded chapters to help you become the kind of speaker others will travel far and wide to see.

Chapter 1:   Dos and Don't of Masterful Speaking

This chapter sheds light on the seventeen mistakes most speakers make and shows you how to avoid making them. You will also come to understand the core essence of public speaking and your real core value as a speaker.

Chapter 2:   How to Structure a Presentation to Keep Your Audience Hooked

This chapter provides you with a step-by-step structure (the "Construct Your World Class Speech" Structure Model) you can use for any speech up to ninety minutes in length. You'll see how to build your speech on benefits, while most speakers build theirs on processes. Any great speech starts with a great structure. A great structure is what you will pick up in this chapter.

CHAPTER 3:   How to Develop Content That Keeps Them Thirsting for More

This chapter provides you with the special PARTS formula for making an unbreakable connection—even with the toughest of audiences.

CHAPTER 4:   How to Deliver a Speech that Keeps Your Audience Enthralled

This chapter provides you with the ten most critical delivery skills you must possess to avoid looking out on an unfulfilled audience staring back at you with uninterested eyes. You'll learn how to quickly build trust, confidence, and credibility before you say even one word!

By the end of these four chapters, you will have all the tools you need to be, by far, the best speaker in your neck of the woods! When you employ these tools, you will master the *art* of public speaking.

MAKING HUGE PROFITS FROM YOUR PRESENTATIONS (PART II)

This is the best time in the history of the world to use your presentations to create multiple income streams. It's easier now than ever, due to the relative ease you have in reaching your market and, better yet, having your ideal customers flock to you. If you're ready to turn these spellbinding presentations into mind-blowing profits, *World Class Speaking* is for you. It will feel good to have income approaching you from all angles. Imagine checking your bank account and seeing ongoing deposits that add up to true financial freedom. You will have the security others long for. Your biggest problem will be keeping track of it all. Don't let that stop you! Part II is divided into four chapters that will help you generate leads, customers, and huge profits from your presentations.

Chapter 5: **Begin with a Profitable Marketing Mindset**

Even if you don't like marketing, this chapter shows you how to lay down the plan that will bring in active, passive, and recurring income. As the saying goes, "Failing to prepare is preparing to fail." Once you finish this chapter, you will have a six-step marketing plan in place to meet with massive success.

Chapter 6: **Become a Master Storyteller and Profit from Their Buy-In**

When people buy into your story, you can consider your products and services as sold. The most important tool you can use to master both the art and the business of speaking for profit is storytelling. You will walk away with the five-part model you need to become a masterful storyteller.

Chapter 7: **How to Systematically Generate Leads with Your Presentations**

In this chapter, you will put a plan in place to keep your funnel full so that you feel the security that comes from passive, recurring streams of income.

You'll never feel unemployed again, and you will make money while you sleep. You'll also uncover what you need in order to work successfully with speaker bureaus and meeting planners.

Chapter 8: How to Easily Profit from Back-of-the-Room Sales

You'll learn how to make more money in a one-hour speech than most speakers make in one month of struggling. You will also walk away with my special SWAP (Selling Without Annoying People) formula. After all, who wants to become the kind of speaker others run from? You'll learn to sell without turning people off.

By the time you finish Part II, you will have all the tools you need to create multiple income streams without wasting a dime of your money or a minute of your time.

How to Use Virtual Speaking to Reach Thousands and Make Six Figures without Having to Leave Home (Part III)

So often people approach me and say, "Craig, I want to be a professional speaker, but I'm not sure I can disrupt my lifestyle by traveling so much. After all, I do have a family." I completely understand. In fact, I spent a few years as a road warrior, speaking upwards of 160 times per year and being in new cities every week. That can grow old quickly. Plus, if you have a family, then chances are that they are suffering from your absence. Don't fool yourself. Even if they don't come out and tell you, trust me, they are suffering. Far too many speakers have let the road drive them straight into divorce and disappointment. Nowadays it does not have to be that way.

If you practice *World Class Speaking*, you will find yourself using technology to reach your ideal customers from around the world without putting your family up for a sacrifice. From the comfort of your own home, you will be able to speak to more people than most speakers who travel the world can reach. And what is the most exciting part? You'll learn to rake in money even while you sleep. Imagine waking up in the morning (or in the afternoon, if you prefer) and finding that you not only made thousands of dollars overnight, but that your product is automatically already in the hands of your customers. You've just snored yourself into a fortune!

That's what you get form Part III of *World Class Speaking*. Part III is divided into three chapters that will help you speak to thousands and generate a six-figure income without having to leave home. They are

CHAPTER 9:   Create Masterful Teleclasses and Joint Ventures that Generate Profits

This chapter shows you how many speakers currently butcher the art of giving teleclasses and destroy any confidence their prospects and customers once had in them. You'll find the keys to creating the best learning environment for turning suspects into prospects, prospects into customers, and customers into great gossipers (viral marketing). Then you'll see how to join forces with others (even with your competition) to explode your business opportunities and your income.

CHAPTER 10:   How to Master Online Marketing

This chapter demystifies the process for making the Internet work for you.

You'll find out how to become a true internationally known speaker and build an empire that reaches a global market. You'll understand the six strategies for making money online.

CHAPTER 11: How to Automate Systems to Rake In Money while You Sleep

This chapter shows you how to put your system on autopilot, so that it keeps working even when *you're* not. You'll get the tools necessary for creating ongoing passive, recurring income from multiple income streams. You'll also see how you can use your greatest employee (it's not a person) to automatically send consistent communications to your market, thereby generating more interest and more income. Finally, you'll walk away with a system to take money online while delivering your products and services to your market.

By the time you reach the end of Part III, you will know how to reach thousands of people and generate thousands upon thousands of dollars without sacrificing what's most important to you in life. You'll feel the relief from having much more control over your schedule and hence, over your *life*.

FINAL WORD ON *WORLD CLASS SPEAKING*

My good friend and 2000 World Champion of Public Speaking, Ed Tate, once said to me, "Craig, there is a difference between an investment and an expense." You know what he did next? He invoiced me! Seriously, though, Ed inspires me, because he never rests on his laurels of being a great speaker. Years ago, I traveled to Las Vegas for a two-day workshop, intending to learn new marketing skills for small businesses. I figured I would not know anyone there other than the trainers. I wish you could have been there when I entered the training room, glanced up to the front, and saw Ed Tate sitting in the first row. Ed was already taking notes. Why? It's because Ed knows the same fundamental truth I picked up when I was coached: what got me here won't get me there. That's why Ed is a world-class speaker in high demand. What about you?

Now it's your turn! You've invested your money and now it's time to invest your time. It's a fact that most people don't read past the first chapter in most books. I challenge you not only to read all of *World Class Speaking*, but also to practice the tools you find in each chapter. When this happens, you'll find yourself looking at more opportunities in one month than most speakers might see in a lifetime. You will become a world-class speaker. But don't stop there. Wannabe speakers get to a certain level and feel comfortable. World-class speakers *commit to being uncomfortable* by stretching and growing past their comfort zones. Will Rogers once said, "You might be on the right track, but if you just stand there, you'll be run over." Are you standing still as a speaker? If so, always remember this: what got you here won't get you there.

The Most Important Idea

Finally, once you get to the end of this book, there is a path you should jump on immediately to take your speaking and income to unbelievable heights. It's our free 7-Part World Class Speaking Toolkit. Valued at $97, this resource (free for you) will not only turn you into the best speaker in your neck of the woods, it will also help you get paid handsomely for your new ability.

Get your free 7-Part World Class Speaking Toolkit at www.WCSpeaking.com

PART I

*How to Master
the Art of Public Speaking*

Chapter 1

Dos and Don'ts of Effective Public Speaking

Avoid Making These Seventeen Costly Mistakes in Public Speaking

Let's begin our journey by understanding the difference between wannabe speakers and world-class speakers when it comes to the art of public speaking. Wannabe speakers generally make the following seventeen mistakes. World-class speakers avoid these mistakes and reap the rewards for doing so. Here are the seventeen common mistakes speakers make:

1. **They don't master the essence of public speaking.** The essence of public speaking is to tell a story and sell a point. Wannabe speakers

how too many speakers begin their speeches, and then you will pick up tools to start with the kind of bang that makes your audiences say, "I'm so glad I'm here, and I can't wait to see the rest of this!"

8. **They force-fit.** Force-fitting means they try to get too much information into too little time. There is an old speaker's proverb that states, "If you squeeze your information in, you squeeze your audience out." There is no time to engage, to play, and to connect with your audience. Later you will discover a rule-of-thumb formula you can use to include just enough information but not too much. When you do this correctly, you will be able to watch your audience walk away with satisfied smiles on their faces. It will be as though they've just finished a great meal.

9. **They don't build their speech on benefits.** Wannabe speakers, if they use benefits at all, sprinkle them on at the end of each point—or worse, at the end of each presentation. They think this will motivate people to act. That won't get it. The structure of the presentation has to actually be built on benefits, and very few speakers do this. Once you do, you will keep your audiences on the edges of their seats, and when they get up, they'll take your next step. Later, you will see just how you can build a benefits-laden speech from the ground up. This is *World Class Speaking* at its best.

10. **They have an "I" or "we" focus.** The most important word in speaking is "*you*." It needs to be used with an 80:20 ratio with the words "I" and "we." Whether setting up your structure, doing check-ins and questions with your audience, or driving home your points, you need to use "you" and "your" as often as possible. Later, you will

uncover the most effective ways to do this. When you do, you'll find it almost effortless to keep them leaning on your every word.

11. **Their delivery is not truly dynamic.** If you get mail delivered to your house and it's destroyed by the rain, chances are that whatever that mail contains will be affected. That's because content is directly tied to delivery, and being ineffective with one leads to a destroyed speech. What you say is not enough to make an impact. How you say it is critical. It's not about bouncing off the walls. It's not about being dynamic the entire time. It's not about simply changing your stress, rate, pitch, and volume. It's not about the powerful pause. What is it about? You will find out in chapter four, which is on delivery.

12. **They lip-synch.** If you use PowerPoint slides to say the same thing visually that you say verbally, you are lip-synching your presentation; you are the Milli Vanilli of public speaking. Abuse of slides has destroyed more presentations than any other device in history. Speakers who use slides improperly compete with themselves, and their audience members lose. The audience must choose among watching the screen, reading their handouts, and watching you. Do you know what they usually decide to do? They mentally check out of your presentation and just leave the shell of the body there for you to bore to death. Later, you will get the tools you can use to make slides work *for* you rather than weaken you.

13. **They use Ditch-digging introductions.** Most speakers understand that you should always give a written introduction to the person introducing you. However, they don't understand what makes a good introduction. Instead, their introductions are just a tweaking

of their bio. This is horrible when it comes to speaking and the audience already starts thinking, "Enough already. Okay, so he has done this and that. What's in it for me to be here?" Later, you will learn a foolproof method for writing an introduction that makes your audience members say, "Great! I'm in the right place."

14. **They don't get their audiences involved.** Involvement breathes life into a speech, but wannabe speakers leave audiences gasping for air, because they don't get them involved. If they do get them involved, they don't do it early enough. Waiting until the end of your presentation to ask, "Are there any questions?" does not suffice as good audience involvement. There are so many ways to get and keep them involved, it ought to be a crime not to. Later, you will pick up tools to keep them involved, engrossed, and engaged throughout your entire presentation and beyond. You will see eyes wide open rather than glazed over. Remember that audiences like to be heard too. Get them involved, and do it early.

15. **They forget about the floor.** They don't own the stage. Wannabe speakers take the stage, but World-Class Speakers own it. You have the ability to add clarity, great emotion, and impact to your speech just by using the stage in masterful, purposeful ways. Later, you will discover how to use this speaking platform to spark an unbreakable connection between you and your audience members.

16. **They don't connect.** If you do not connect, you cannot affect. Connection is about energy, but it is not about bouncing off the walls. Later, you will see how to match the energy of your audience so that they feel connected to you within the first few moments of your speech.

17. **They speak for standing ovations.** Too many speakers strive to get a standing ovation instead of what they should strive for: standing *invitations*.

WHAT IS THE CORE ESSENCE OF WORLD CLASS SPEAKING?

If you know anything about me, you know I'm all about the nuts and bolts. Theory has its place and is an important backdrop, but the practical and tangible tools you pick up in this book are what will make the difference in your future and fortune as a speaker. However, there *is* one strategy that's at the heart of *World Class Speaking*, and it goes back thousands of years. Therefore, before we jump into all the tangible tools, starting in chapter two, wrap your mind around what you're about to read. It will make all the difference in your failure or vast success as a world-class speaker and will lead you to see significant profits!

The Heart of Public Speaking

At the heart of public speaking is a story. Bill Gove, the first President of the National Speakers Association, summed it up best with his advice to

"Tell a story and make a point!"

That is the core essence of public speaking. We speak to be remembered, right? Well, what better way is there to be remembered than to tell a story? Think about it: When people remember your story, what will they also remember? That's right; they'll remember your point.

Think back to when you were a kid. Did you ever say to your parents, "Mommy, Daddy, please tell me a story"? Do *your* kids ever ask *you* for a story? I know mine do every night. Stories drive life. Believe it or not, many of our values and our understanding of life came from those early stories.

For example, do you remember the story of the tortoise and the hare? What was the moral of that story? Slow and steady wins the race. How about *The Wizard of Oz*? It reminded us that there is no place like home and that the strength we might need has been in us the whole time. Finally, how about the story of Goldilocks and the three bears? This is the interesting thing about stories. They can provide you with several different messages based on where you are in your life. Each person can take something different from them. When I was young, I felt that Goldilocks was an innocent little girl who wandered into a house and made herself comfortable. Now, of course, I think Goldilocks should be locked up for breaking and entering! After all, who breaks into a house and then complains that the owner's bed is not comfortable enough? But I digress … Stories breathe life into your speech and captivate the audience, all while slipping in a message that can change their lives. When you master storytelling, you'll be well on your way to mastering the art of public speaking.

WHAT IS THE CORE VALUE OF WORLD CLASS SPEAKING?

Now that you understand the core essence of public speaking, there's one more theoretical concept you must grasp before moving into the tangible tools in chapters two through eleven. It's the core value of public speaking. What is the actual value *you* bring to the table as a speaker? How do you measure it?

What do we really bring to the table?

Years ago, I had a speaker friend named Tim who regularly called to say, "Craig, I killed with my last audience. They loved me!" Although I never claimed to "kill with my audience," I, too, have walked away from some speeches feeling awfully good.

Then, one day, it happened. One of my speaking mentors called me on one of those good days and asked, "Craig, how did your speech go?" I said, "It went great. I really connected and they walked away with great information. I know I made a difference." He said, "Really. How do you know that?" I proudly responded, "Because I could feel it. Plus, they gave me a rousing standing ovation at the end." Expecting him to approve, I was shocked to hear him repeat his question. He asked, "So, how do you know you made a difference?" At this point, I knew I probably shouldn't answer, so I didn't. He then went on to explain in the following conversation:

He said, "Craig, there is only one surefire way to know whether or not we made a difference." I said, "What's that?" He said, "You'll know you made a difference when they bring you back again. It has nothing to do with standing ovations. It has nothing to do with how good you feel you did. It has everything to do with what happens after you leave the platform." He went on to explain the real value in what we do as speakers. "The real value you offer is in what happens three days, three weeks, or even three months after you have left the platform. What changes do they make with the tools you provided for them? If they make no changes, you make no difference."

Wow. All this time, I'd thought I could measure my success by the standing ovations—come to find out they don't matter at all. It took me a while to adjust to this, but eventually it removed a great weight from my shoulders. Now, I no longer had to worry whether they would stand.

Eventually, I stopped caring altogether. When you get to that point, you can truly have a tremendous selfless impact on their lives. Over time, I have come to summarize this in the following statement that I coined: Don't speak for standing ovations; speak for standing *invitations*.

You want to speak so they invite you back. You want to provide so much value that they want to see what else you have to offer. Perhaps they hire you for coaching, buy your products, join your newsletter, put you on a retainer agreement, or give you some other kind of invitation. Who cares how long they clap; it's how long they call that matters.

My speaker friend Tim called me again about a year ago, and once again, he said, "Craig, I blew them away this weekend. I really made an impact." This time, I was able to gather my thoughts and ask him, "How do you know?"

So, how do you provide this long-term value? There are several tools you can use to get called back time and time again, and you will pick these up in the remainder of this book.

How Do You Start Putting Together a Great Speech?

Can you imagine what a person with no bones looks like? Pretty gross, right? What about a high-rise building that stands on one skinny stilt? Pretty dangerous, right? People without bones won't live, and buildings without strong foundations won't stand. In fact, whatever you build needs a solid foundation. You're probably saying, "Craig, I've heard this a thousand times before. Why are you bringing this up now?" I'm glad you asked. If people understand this fact of life so well, why do so many speakers assume this does not apply to what they build? In other words, when building a speech, why don't they start by building a structure?

Wannabe speakers still make the mistake of building their speeches on either a weak or no foundation. They have nothing to hold the speech together, give it proper support, and help it function to meet its purpose. The answer to where to start creating your speech is: with the *structure*. The structure is your skeleton (bones) and your foundation (support). What most wannabe speakers do not know is that it's a well-thought-out structure that helps drive a message home and make it stick. So while most speakers start creating their speeches by toiling away at the content and practicing the delivery, you make sure you start in the right place. Tend to your structure. A speech is like a building: the stronger the foundation, the higher it can rise. Take your speech higher!

Now that we understand the "Dos and Don'ts of Masterful Speaking," let's dig into chapter two, with the all-important starting place for creating a masterpiece: the structure.

Chapter 2

How to Structure Your Presentation to Keep Your Audience Hooked

Where Do You Start?

I f you were in my audience years ago outside of Montreal, Canada, on a Friday evening, you would have witnessed one of my worst speeches ever. It was *beyond* bad—it was embarrassing. The audience was turning red with anger, and a few of them even left before I finished. Before the event, the person who drove me said, "Craig, this is a wonderful audience. They give standing ovations to everyone out of courtesy."

Well, when I concluded that evening, not only did they refuse to stand, but they barely even clapped. What happened to make this event so dreadful?

KNOW YOUR AUDIENCE

The reason for my demise that evening was simple. I did not know my audience. I had very little idea who would be there. I neglected to do the pre-speech work necessary for aligning my message with the needs of the audience. As a result, I sucked. I later came to understand that nearly everyone in my audience had seen me do that exact presentation a few months earlier. That Friday night, they didn't leave their jobs to travel over to the far side of town to watch me give them the same exact information that was still fresh in their minds. I had no idea I would have the same audience. If I had done the proper pre-speech work to find out where my audience was, I would have prepared something to take them where they wanted to go. You simply cannot even begin structuring your speech until you intimately understand the needs of your audience. This is the first step.

THE TWO LOCATIONS YOU MUST KNOW

Have you ever had car troubles? One day I decided to take my car to the H&H Auto shop to get it fixed. I drove to where I thought the shop was and realized I was in the wrong place. Then I called H&H on the phone and Kelly answered. She said, "H&H Auto Shop, how may I help you?" I asked, "Can you tell me exactly where you are located?" To my surprise, she shot right back with, "Well, where are you calling from?" For a second, I thought, *Am I talking to Socrates?* but I said, "I'm over near the Starbucks off Bobble Road." She said,

"Great. Just take a right out of the complex, go through two lights, and make a left into the next driveway." I got there in no time at all. The key to getting there was in knowing where I was first and then knowing where I wanted to go. These are the same two locations you must know about your audience:

1. Where are they?
2. Where do they want to go?

LOCATION NUMBER ONE: WHERE ARE THEY?

It's absolutely critical to understand where your audience stands at the moment, and the best place to start is with your initial point of contact. Ask the meeting planner, or the person who initially reached out to you, the following questions:

- How did this event come about?
- Who will be in the audience?
- What are some of the challenges they have been wrestling with?
- What are some of the achievements they have had?
- How have you addressed these issues so far?
- Have you had other presenters?
- What did you like about them?
- What would you have wanted them to do differently?
- Where will the event take place?
- What else is happening at the event?

Notice that none of these questions is about you. They are all about them and where they stand. When a doctor diagnoses a patient, she does not say, "Tell me how I can make you feel better." Instead, she asks, "Where do you hurt? What brings you in here today?" Always start with *them*.

When you ask these questions, hush up! Let them do at least 80 percent of the talking. Wannabe speakers talk too much. World-class speakers listen deeply not only to what the person says but also to what he does not say. You must listen beyond the words and get a real feel for what's not being said and why.

For example, a federal-government agency hired me to speak to their managers. When I started asking my point-of-contact questions, she gave me answers like, "Craig, we just need the managers to commit to all their associates." I asked, "What does that mean?" She answered, "Well, we just need everyone to feel important and equal." Instead of stopping there, I searched for specifics by repeating, "What does that mean? How do you know everyone does not feel important?" I searched and searched for what she was not telling me. Finally, out of relief, she confessed, "Craig, we have managers who only know how to manage people who are just like themselves. If they are Type A managers, they only know how to manage Type A personalities. They need to recognize the importance of managing people who are not like them." Bingo. I had gotten what I needed.

With this new information, I was able to create a pinpoint message for their managers. In fact, during my training program, I actually said those exact words. I said, "You know, some managers can only manage people who are just like them." To my surprise, there was a huge "nodding of the head" factor, along with what I call "agreement grunts." That's when your audience uses hums and uh-huh sounds to share their deep agreement. Later, the regional director (the big boss) approached me and said, "I was against having an outsider do this training. However, you were right on target. Great job. This is going to carry us far!" This success was based on the pre-speech work of finding out location number one: Where are they?

Location Number Two: Where Do They Want to Go?

Just like receiving the location of the H&H Auto Shop, now it's time to find out exactly where your economic buyer wants your audience members to go. Again, it's not about talking; it's about asking questions. Asking questions is the key to being right on target with your message. Here are some of the most useful questions to ask in order to determine their desired destination:

- In the best of all worlds, what results do you want to see from this event?
- What do you want your attendees to think, feel, or do differently as a result of this event?
- What will make this extraordinary for you?
- How will you measure the success of the event?
- What topics should be avoided, if any?
- What specific objectives do you have for my presentation?
- What else is important to know to make this event a smashing success?

Notice that only toward the *end* of my questioning will I even mention my presentation; before then, *it's all about them.* This questioning may take many different forms. It might be one-on-one. You might meet with a group weeks or months before the event. You might call individual attendees and get an understanding, as well as their stories, before the event. Or you might not be able to speak to them, so you simply have them fill out the pre-event questionnaire (more on this later).

For example, I met a regional director, his assistant, and a meeting planner for an insurance company in Pennsylvania. We sat down a full six months before the event, and I let them do at least 80 percent of the talking. For location number two, they explained these themes to me:

"We have too many associates that leave us after we provide them with two to three years of training. We cannot afford to continue losing them after we invest so much in them. We need our managers to find ways to significantly increase the retention of these associates by making them feel involved, important, and appreciated. We also recognize that a change is needed, and we need the managers to embrace the change so their associates will do likewise."

The more and more they talked, the more and more I got excited about the event, because I knew I could provide exactly what they needed. Later, I asked the all-important percentage question by saying, "What percentage do you want as education, and what percentage do you want as motivation?" They responded, "We want 70 percent to be about firing them up to embrace change and 30 percent on tools they can use for inspiring change in others." If you ask and listen, you'll get the exact information you need. So whether it's a group meeting, one-on-one, or even over the telephone, talk less, listen more, and hit the bull's-eye with your message. This is the starting place for setting up your structure.

INTERVIEW AND INTERPRET

This entire process is what I call "the interview-and-interpret method." You interview people related to the event and then interpret what they tell you. You don't look for what they say as much as you look for what they don't. You realize this very important fact: People will not open up to you until they have confidence in you. They gain confidence in you when you show your genuine interest in them. You show your genuine interest in them by asking questions and then hushing up.

Remember the timeless advice of seeking to be interested, not interesting. In the interview-and-interpret method, you need to search for the who, what, where, when, and why of the event. The *why* is the most important. Find out what made them come to the realization that they needed a speaker. Then listen beyond the words.

The Pre-Event Questionnaire: The Secret Tool for Being Rehired

Although the interview-and-interpret method is essential, you should never go into an engagement without offering your pre-event questionnaire for your client to complete. The questionnaire benefits you in the following ways:

- You can create a laser-like message that hits the center of the target
- Your client focuses in on what they actually want to accomplish
- They perceive you as professional and serious about helping them
- You find out wants and needs that might surprise you
- You get rehired time and time again

The questionnaire also provides you with answers to the who, what, where, when, and why of the event. However, to be honest, I used to be shy about asking my clients to complete it. This is because I felt like I was creating more work for them when I should be creating less. Then it happened: I sent my pre-event questionnaire to a client and did not hear back from them for about a month. Needless to say, I was concerned. Then, out of the blue, my point of contact called excitedly and said, "Craig, we are so grateful for you!" Stunned, I asked, "What for? I haven't even spoken yet!" She replied, "We know, but you have forced us to really think and discuss what we wanted to get out of this event. Because of these conversations, we completely redid parts of the program, and the whole thing is going to be much better. We even have a theme now!" Wow. Here I was thinking they were annoyed by the "work" I had given them, when, in reality, they were forced to really focus their objectives. From then on, I have been a huge advocate of always sending the questionnaire. Can you guess what happened after that particular event? That's right: almost immediately, I was rehired. Make no mistake about the following comment: "There is a direct correlation between the pre-speech work you do with your client and the post-rehire that follows. If you do the work on the front end, they will give you more work on the back end."

You will no longer just be a speaker, you will be a partner. Speakers have engagements. Partners have *relationships*. Relationships are the currency to world-class speakers.

See figure 2-1 as an example of a pre-event questionnaire. For your own customizable template of a questionnaire that you can use for your upcoming engagements, visit http://www.wcspeaking.com/templates.

Pre-Program Questionnaire for Craig Valentine's presentation

This pre-program questionnaire is to assist us in helping you make this your greatest event ever! Once completed, return to The Communication Factory at info@craigvalentine.com.

Program Objectives:

Specific objectives for Craig's presentation?_____
_____
_____

How will you measure the success of this event and Craig's participation?
_____
_____

What topics should be avoided?_____
_____

Audience:

Number expected to attend?_____ % male _____ % female _____

Job Positions? _____

Biggest work-related challenges? _____
_____

More Program Information:

Have you used speakers in the past for this program? If so, who? What did you like and dislike about those presentations?
_____
_____

More Audience Information

What makes someone an excellent performer in your in your organization?
_____
_____

We look forward to serving your organization!

Figure 2-1

ONE CAVEAT ABOUT
THE PRE-EVENT QUESTIONNAIRES

Do you think your client will write anything that might be considered questionable on the questionnaire? No. People won't tell you the most confidential—yet critical—needs on a questionnaire, because they don't want to put them in writing. However, what they will not put in writing, they will put in your ears. That's why the interview-and-interpret method is so vital to your success. In order to listen beyond the words, you must have pre-event conversations with your client.

THREE STRATEGIES FROM THREE WORLD-CLASS
SPEAKERS TO ANALYZE YOUR AUDIENCE

If you do the work to analyze your audience, you will connect with them quicker and deeper than most speakers ever will. With these results, you'll be rehired time and time again. There are several methods you can use. Here are three examples of what some speakers have done to analyze their audience in advance:

1. National Speakers Association Hall of Fame Speaker, Patricia Fripp, has actually *traveled with representatives* from her customer's company to get a firsthand experience of what they go through on a daily basis. With this knowledge, she was able to pull stories, examples, and terminology that empowered her to personalize the speech and make an unbreakable connection.

2. Ed Tate, the 2000 World Champion of Public Speaking for Toastmasters International, calls audience members in advance of the

speech. However, he asks the meeting planner to "give me your most *challenging individuals*. Give me contact information for the people who don't necessarily buy into everything. Give me the reluctant ones." Why does Ed want to speak to these people? Ed says, "Because they will tell me the truth." In order words, Ed knows they will not beat around the bush or even watch too carefully what they say. They will put it out there, and Ed will be able to shape it into a message that fits perfectly for them. Once they put it out there, you can put it in there.

The side benefit of this is that, because Ed seeks after these reluctant audience members, he actually turns them from possible adversaries into definite advocates. He can even mention their names and make them the stars of the speech. What better way to connect than that?

3. The 2001 World Champion of Public Speaking, Darren LaCroix, speaks to his audience members in advance of the presentation primarily to *get stories* he can use to make them the stars of the speech. As a result, he easily mixes in a story or two with his regular stories, in order to customize the speech just for that audience. Being a humorist, Darren can uncover more humor in the speech and have certain audience members leave feeling like they are on cloud nine. As Darren always says, "You must first connect in order to persuade."

Directions

Once you know exactly where your audience is and where they want to go, it's time to put together a map complete with directions. This is your message. Are you ready to create it? Let's create a message that not only keeps your audience on the edge of their seats but also helps you get paid when they get up!

IGNITE YOUR AUDIENCE WITH YOUR INTRODUCTION

No matter how strange this seems to you, I want you to read this next paragraph out loud as if you are my introducer and you are introducing me with great enthusiasm. I'm dead serious. Do this out loud. Are you ready? Go ahead and introduce me.

"Our next speaker is the 1999 World Champion of Public Speaking. With more than 175,000 Toastmasters in 68 countries, and over 25,000 contestants, he came home with the first prize trophy and a significant amount of national and international recognition. In addition, our speaker is absolutely oblivious to the fact that we could care less what he has done and that we are much more interested in what we will be able to do after hearing him. Moreover, our speaker seems to have no idea that we are simply hoping for his autobiographical introduction to end so we can start clapping as if we are interested. Finally, he doesn't realize that we are beginning to say to ourselves, 'Wow, since his entire introduction is about him, I bet his entire speech is about him also. Why did I even come here today?' So, with that said, please help me welcome to the stage the person who would have the least effective introduction in history if it weren't for the thousands of other presenters who have introductions just like his. Please help me welcome the 1999 World Champion of Public Speaking, Craig Valentine."

Do you get the point? Have you ever heard an introduction like this one? How similar is your introduction to my old introduction? Is it about you, or is it about the audience? Is it more to build yourself up or to fire your audience up? Of the hundreds of introductions I hear each year, probably 95 percent of them are like these biographies of brilliance that put the speakers in a ditch that they spend the rest of the speech trying to climb out of.

MAKE YOUR INTRODUCTION GIVE YOU A GREAT HEAD START

Everything you do should be about your audience, including your introduction. Most speakers don't spend enough time strategizing to make their audience respond to their introduction by saying, "Wow, I want to hear this! Tell me more." Think about it: your introduction flavors your entire speech. You can use it to get the audience fired up and excited about what they're going to hear, or you can use it to boost yourself up in their eyes. You can use it to whet their appetite with the tools they'll get from your presentation, or you can use it to boost yourself up in their eyes. You can use it to make them lean forward in their seats, or you can use it to boost yourself up in their eyes. Here's one thing I know for sure: once I changed my introduction from me-focused to you-focused, I gained an extreme advantage before I even said one word. You can do likewise.

WHAT SHOULD BE IN A WORLD-CLASS INTRODUCTION?

An effective introduction is the difference between starting off in a hole or on solid ground with a head start. Here are five world-class tools you can use in your introduction to get off to a great start before you even say one word.

Don't go into your next speech without them.

1. **Start it off about them.** Make your very first sentence about them. Instead of starting off with "Our next speaker today is the 1999 World Champion ..." start with something like this:

   "There is a definite process for keeping *your* audiences on the edge of their seats. It is not easy to come by, and it is not easy to use. However, once *you* master it, *you* will find doors opening for *you* that *you* never even knew existed."

   You might have noticed there were five you-focused words in those two sentences. Make it you-focused first. Start with your audience, not with yourself.

2. **Make a promise.** Let them know not only what they're going to get, but also what it will empower them to do and to receive. Hence, they are getting a process that empowers them to keep audiences on the edge of their seats and rewards them with more open doors and speaking opportunities.

3. **Build your credibility, but only with your relevant credentials.** For example, I regularly deliver a teambuilding workshop to Fortune 500 companies and federal and state government agencies. Because it is about teambuilding, I include my collegiate-basketball background in my introduction. I talk about the process we used to win three straight East Coast Conference Championships and play in two NCAA March Madness tournaments. However, do

you think these accomplishments belong in an introduction about presentation skills?

What if you sat in an audience and heard them say, "Our presentation coach today was also a college-basketball player." What would you think? You might ask, "Did he give speeches while dribbling up and down the court? If not, why do I care about his basketball past?" Use only the relevant information, no matter how well-rounded you are. They come for the *process*, not for you.

4. **Use the introduction to set up something in your speech.** For example, I sometimes start my speeches like this:

"Wow, listen to all those credentials. Do you know with all those accolades … people still don't like me? You know why they don't like me? Because I joined Toastmasters in March of 1998. I got my Competent Toastmasters designation in March of 1999. Then I won the World Championship of Public Speaking in August of 1999—on my very first try." Usually the audience begins to clap here. Then I say, "Sure you're clapping but can you feel the haters in the room?" They burst into laughter and applause. Then I go into a story about a speaking failure of mine and promptly give them a process for avoiding that failure in their future. This is all set up by the introduction. Find ways to make your introduction feed seamlessly into your speech.

Another strategy is to have something mentioned in your introduction that you can call back to later in your speech. For example, I have heard the legendary speaker, Charlie "Tremendous" Jones, call back to his introduction in very humorous ways. He said, "You heard in my introduction that my book is in its seventh printing. Well, even that is not the whole truth, but they didn't lie though. The reason the book is in its seventh printing is because the first six … were blurred." This works extremely well because it is self-effacing, takes him off the pedestal, and connects him quickly with his audience. What a wonderful speaker!

5. **Take everything about you and turn it into everything for them.** If you do so, they will be ready and anxious to witness your message. For example, instead of stating "Craig Valentine is the 1999 World Champion of Public Speaking," I could make that actually matter to them by saying, "The *process* you will pick up today helped our speaker become the 1999 World Champion. You can use it to become a speaker in high demand." Get it? Turn everything about you into something for them. Doing this will get them fired up to hear your message. It tickles me now, because when the introducer gets to the end up my introduction, he usually says, "Are you ready for the process?" and people yell out "Yes!" Whoa, that's some great energy to walk into for a speech.

Follow these five guideposts, and watch your audience lean forward in their seats, anxiously awaiting your presentation. While most speakers dig themselves a hole, you'll be on very solid ground and way ahead of the pack.

Tip: I often suggest writing your introduction before you even put your speech together. It's similar to writing the back cover page of your book before actually writing the book. You do this to ensure your message is attractive to begin with. If the introduction does not spark interest, chances are you're creating a message nobody wants to hear. Write your introduction, and test it out on a few people. If they say, "Tell me more," then go ahead and construct your speech around that message. Speaking of constructing your actual message, how do you do that? Use the "Create Your World-Class Speech" Structure Model. Structure is not the sexiest part of speaking, but it's the most significant. Therefore, let's dive into it now.

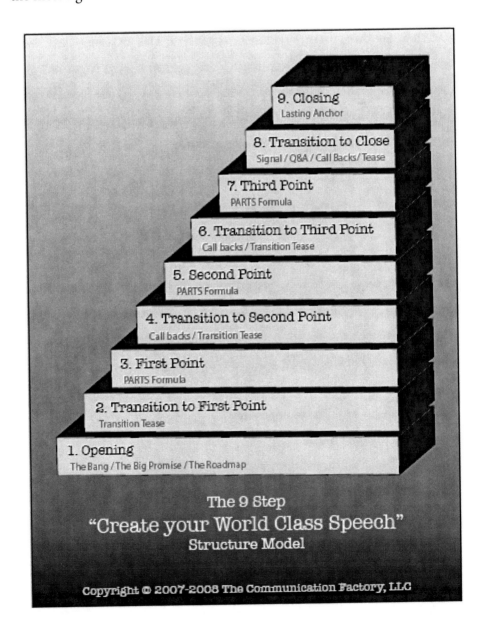

The Nine-Step "Create Your World-Class Speech" Structure Model

You can have the best content in the world and the greatest delivery style; however, if you don't build it on a solid structure, your entire speech will come crumbling down, and your future will be caught in the rubble. As you know, there are three parts to speaking, and all must be mastered. First, there is the *structure* of a speech. Next, there is the *content* that you put into that structure. Finally, there is the *delivery*, which is how you get the speech across. When building a speech, you start with the structure first. Starting in any other way is like building a speech on quicksand.

Great Speeches Start with This Great Structure

If you start with the "Create your World Class Speech" Structure Model (diagram 2-2), you will be light-years ahead of where most speakers begin putting their speeches together. Let's look at it as a whole and then go through it piece by piece. Here is a great sequence for you to follow:

1. Opening
2. Transition to point number one
3. Point number one
4. Call-backs and transition to point number two
5. Point number two
6. Call-backs and transition to point number three
7. Point number three
8. Call-backs and transition to the closing
9. Closing

STEP 1: THE OPENING

Open your speech with a bang! That means throw away what I refer to as the "unpleasant pleasantries." You know the kind of which I speak? Tell me you haven't heard speakers open their speeches in the following normal ways:

"I really want to thank all of you for having me here today. It's great to be in the presence of such wonderful people who are dedicated ..."

"What a great day to be here with you. Thank you, John and Suzy, for making this possible ..."

"Fellow members, guests, and visitors, thank you for the opportunity ..."

Do you know what these three openings have in common? They are weak! They are also normal. That's right, I'm sure you've heard many speakers open their speeches in these ways. But just because it's normal does not mean it's effective. Anything normal is boring. Who cares about these pleasantries? Nobody cares. If you don't use them, believe me, they will not be missed, and you'll begin to stand out as a speaker.

My good friend and 2001 World Champion of Public Speaking, Darren LaCroix, says about these openings, "We don't need a weather report. We were just outside!" The key here is that audiences expect these openings. Therefore, you have a great opportunity to catch their attention immediately by opening in a different way. However, before we go into how to open, let's look at one surefire way to destroy your opening and kill your speech before it even has a chance to breathe.

Don't open your speech with jokes!

If you do, the joke will be on you. The reason for this is threefold.

1. Most of the people in the audience have probably already heard the joke.

2. It sets your audience up to know that what you have is not original. After all, if you begin your speech with an unoriginal joke, it will flavor your entire speech. Your audience will think, "That was not original, so probably everything else he talks about will be copied, too." All of a sudden, in less than a minute or two, you have become an unoriginal speaker in their eyes.

3. It will only take your audience members seven seconds to realize whether they like you. Then it will take them about thirty seconds to realize whether they want to hear more. If you come out either with unpleasant pleasantries or an unwanted joke, you might as well bury the rest of your message, because you snuffed it out with your poor opening.

So how can you open your speech with impact, get the audience's attention, and tease them so they want to hear more?

First, you should understand the entire objective of your opening is to have your audience members say the following: "Tell me more!"

You can accomplish this by using one of the following five original ways:

1. **Go straight into a story** from your first word. I almost always start off by going immediately into a story. It's a bang. It catches my audience off guard, because they're so used to those unpleasant pleasantries. I don't thank anyone up-front, talk about what a pleasure it is to

be there, or discuss the weather. Instead, I jump right into a story that captivates them and gets them thinking, "This is going to be different. I might even stay awake for this one."

2. **Ask a powerful question.** For example, if you are speaking on the topic of change, you might ask, "Have you ever worked with a StatusQuoaholic?" Many people in your audience will get it right away, while others might think, "What's a StatusQuoaholic?" Guess what? If your audience members are asking themselves that question, what does that mean? It means you have their attention, and they want to know more. That's a great sign of a good opening.

3. **Use a startling statement** that jolts your audience from their seats. For example, sometimes, after my introduction, I start off like this: "With all these accolades, people still don't like me. You know why they don't like me?"

   Again, all I am doing with my opening lines is to get the audience to say, "Tell me more." If I have accomplished this, I have a strong opening. In this case, they want to ask, "Why don't they like you?" As long as they are asking that, I have their attention, and they want to hear more.

4. **Say nothing at all.** That's right, just stand there and scan your audience. Ed Tate, the 2000 World Champion of Public Speaking, is a master at this. In fact, we have begun calling this technique the "Ed Tate Scan." Think about it, what do most speakers do immediately after being introduced? Correct, they start talking. Many times their

audience members are still ruffling through their handouts, adjusting to their seats, and getting settled in with a quick hello to the person next to them. Now, imagine this: You come out in the midst of all this ruffling, approach the microphone, and say nothing. What do you think will happen? Everybody's head will pop up, and their eyes will be focused directly on you. This happens because of that old proverb, "He who sleeps in noise awakens in silence."

This takes guts by the speaker, but it's worth it. You will only need a few seconds of silence to pull this off, even though it will seem like an eternity. Again, you'll have your audience members thinking, "This will be different," or asking, "What's he thinking?" Either way, you've got them!

5. **Use an activity.** Normally, I wouldn't suggest this, because, at the beginning, we have not yet earned the right to ask them to do something. However, I have met with success occasionally by opening up with a quick activity. For example, in the past, I have opened my speech in the following way:

"Cross your arms. Now reverse them, and put your other arm on top. How does that feel?" They usually laugh when they notice how uncomfortable it is to put their other arm on top. I continue: "Why do you think that's so uncomfortable?" They usually say, "It's a change. I'm not used to doing it that way," to which I reply, "Are you saying with change comes discomfort?"

As you can see here, an activity can work well if it is coupled with a powerful question, a story, or a startling statement. It does not work well if you use it just for the activity's sake. Everything should have a purpose and a place.

These are just five of the ways to open a speech. However, they are only part of the opening. They should be used to lead you into the hook for the entire speech, which comes next during your opening.

THE BIG PROMISE

The Big Promise is the most important sentence of your entire speech. Read that last sentence again. It's the most important because it sets up the reason your audience members should listen to the rest of your speech. It usually comes after your initial opening story (or startling statement, powerful question, etc.) and leads your audience into the body of the speech. If this sentence does not hook them in, they will mentally tune you out and leave you wondering why. Let's look at an example of a Big Promise that I use with managers:

"In the next forty-five minutes, you will pick up tools to create commitment, not just compliance, from your employees. You'll discover ways to increase employee retention, raise the morale through the roof, relieve your stress, and become the leader others want to follow."

There it is, the entire reason my audience should take this journey with me. The Big Promise tells them exactly what they will walk away with by the end of your presentation. Please notice that I didn't phrase it like many speakers do, which is in the following manner:

"Today, I would like to share with you tools to create commitment …"

Guess what? Nobody cares what you'd like to share with them. What people do care about is what they are going to receive. Therefore, whenever you find yourself saying something like, "I am going to share …" say instead, "You are going to receive …" or "You are going to pick up …" or "You will walk out of here with …." Again, in speaking, the most important word you can use is "you." Take careful pains to make sure you use it often within your Big Promise. Two outstanding ways to phrase the beginning of your Big Promise are the following:

1. "In the next forty-five minutes (or whatever length of speech you have), you will pick up …"

Note: What is the difference between these two phrases "You will pick up tools …" and "You will get the strategies …"? The difference is that "You will pick up tools …" creates more of a picture than "You will get the strategies…." Use words that create pictures. You can picture a tool, but what does a strategy look like?

2. "You will walk out of these doors today with the tools you need to …"

Note: "Walk out of here with tools …" creates a picture in your audience's mind.

Who Cares?

The key to your Big Promise is that it must pass the "Who cares?" test. You will want to test your Big Promise out on some people to make sure it sells. You will need to change it if your audience members ask, "Who cares?" Your goal is to get your audience members to think, "Tell me more." Just as your initial thirty seconds is designed to get your audience to listen to your

Big Promise, your Big Promise is designed to get your audience members to at least stick with you while you transition to your first point.

Create the Big Promise First

One of the very best strategies you can use to create a world-class speech is to create the Big Promise first, and then let everything fall in place around it. In fact, in our "Create Your Keynote" Champ Camp, I usually give attendees an entire hour just to write this one sentence. That's how important it is. The reason it's so important to write this first is because it completely determines what content you leave in your speech and what content you leave out of it. Your Big Promise is the sticky tape to your speech. If you have content that does not support your Big Promise, scrap it. Let's take my Big Promise stated above as an example. If I have a great story that makes a point about the importance of living your dream, guess what? That should be scrapped because it has nothing to do with creating commitment from your employees, retaining employees, relieving your stress, or raising employee morale. Because it does not stick to the Big Promise, I must toss it out, no matter how good and engaging the story might be.

Here is an example of another Big Promise I use with the market of up-and-coming speakers:

"You will walk out of these doors today with the tools you can use to breathe life into your speeches, bring your audience to you by keeping them engaged, and build a speech that sticks so that you get brought back time and time again."

Now it's your turn. Take your time working on your Big Promise, and fill in the blanks when you're ready:

In the next _____ *minutes, you will pick up the tools you can use to*

_____, _____, *and* _____.

THE ROADMAP

While the first part of your opening lays down the tracks and gets your audience excited about what they will pick up along the way, you now need to give them a roadmap to follow along easily and clearly. This is simpler than what it seems. In fact, it usually takes one to three sentences at most. For example, take another look at the Big Promise I use for managers, and pay close attention to the emboldened sentence at the end.

"In the next forty-five minutes, you will pick up tools to create commitment, not just compliance, from your employees. You'll discover ways to increase employee retention, raise the morale through the roof, relieve your stress, and become the leader others want to follow. **This process comes to you in the form of the four Rs to Remarkable Results.**"

That's simple, isn't it? All I did was add on the stops along the journey so that my audience knows what to expect and how to follow along. Now what do you think my audience asks themselves? Hopefully, they ask, "What are the four Rs?" They now know I will go from one R to the next R to the next R and then to the final R. Many times, this only requires adding one sentence to your opening that might begin with something like this: "These tools come to you in the form of ..." That is the roadmap. Likewise, your roadmap should accomplish the following two objectives:

1. Get your audience to ask themselves a question such as "What are the four Rs?" or "What are the three steps?"

2. Clarify how they should expect to follow along (i.e., moving from the first R through to the fourth).

I have used "the three Gs to Greatness" and "the four Rs to Remarkable Results through Change" for different speeches. However, your roadmap does not have to be four Rs or three Gs. It just needs to be clear where you are going. For example, Mark Brown, the 1995 World Champion of Public Speaking, gives more than two hundred youth-related speeches each year. Occasionally, Mark uses the acronym SCREAM, in which each letter stands for one of his major points. Once the students know he is going to follow those letters throughout his speech, they have essentially gained the roadmap they need to follow along. Be as creative as you want with your roadmap, but just make sure you do it quickly. It should not take more than one to three sentences. In addition to the acronym and the three letters, here are three other ways you can introduce the roadmap:

1. **Number the steps**. This is where you simply state something like the following: "In order to get these results (i.e., the results you've promised in the Big Promise, such as raising morale), you will want to follow three specific steps." Hopefully, your audience will ask, "What are the three steps?" Or they might think, "Alright then, take me to the first step."

2. **Give the locations**. For example, I used to use a location-based roadmap by stating, "Our first stop today will be in the 'Land of the Elements,' so you can see what goes into masterful storytelling. Next, we'll head into the 'Land of Delivery' and get the skills necessary for energizing your audience. Finally, we'll end up in 'You-Ville,' and that is where it's all about *you*." Through this roadmap, my audiences knew exactly where we were going.

3. **State all the points.** At times, it might be beneficial to actually state all three of your points up front, especially if it's a sequential process. For example, I once heard the amazing motivational speaker, Willie Jolley, create a roadmap by saying, "You must *dream, decide,* and *do.*" His audience members immediately knew where he was going and that the first stop was at "dream." Once he set it up, we knew he was going to illustrate each point in his own fantastic way.

Regardless of what method you use, you should make sure your audience knows where you are going, and, thanks to coupling your roadmap with your Big Promise, they should also know specifically why they should join you. If you do this well, you will be far beyond what most speakers do, and you'll be able to look out on expectant faces filled with excitement and wonder. You will have accomplished coming out with a bang! Now that we've finished with the opening, let's head over to step two in the "Create Your World-Class Speech" Structure Model.

STEP 2: THE TRANSITION TO POINT NUMBER 1

So there I was, exhausted and trying to sleep in a hotel in Orlando, Florida, as I prepared for a boot camp I was to lead the next morning on creating a keynote speech. I was excited to introduce my keynote model to the group, but I still had reservations about one section: the transitions. I needed a more visual way to explain it to them. Eventually, I thought, *Craig, get some sleep. You can always get up early and think about it.* At that point, I decided to go to sleep. However, ESPN was on and was showing highlights of the college-basketball games from earlier that evening. I figured, *I'll wait until the next commercial break to turn off the TV and go to sleep.*

Just as ESPN was heading to the commercial break, I grabbed the remote control in order to turn off the TV, but something stopped me. It was a voice. It came from the TV. In fact, I heard one of the sportscasters say, "You won't believe what happened in the NCAA basketball game tonight! You won't believe your eyes! See for yourself on the other side of this commercial break." Can you guess what I did with the remote control? That's right—I put it down. Can you guess what I thought? I believe my exact thoughts were, *Well, I'll just watch the next segment and* then *go to sleep. After all, it can't be more than another ten minutes.*

At the end of the next segment, just before the commercial break, I reached again for the remote control with all intentions of turning it off—that is, until the sportscaster said, "The game of the night is coming next. This was a real barnburner, and if you missed it once, you definitely don't want to miss the highlights again. These highlights are coming up right after the break." Can you guess again what I did with the remote? Again, I thought, *I'll just stick around for one more segment. It couldn't hurt.*

I must have gone through this process at least four times and stayed up an extra hour in order to watch segment after segment. Why did I do this? It's simple. That night, ESPN used transitions to die for. They teased me into what was coming next and not only did they keep me awake, they also kept me hungry for more! When I awoke the next morning, I had to laugh because I knew exactly how to explain transitions in speaking.

THE TRANSITION TEASE

Now that you have already given your Big Promise, which lets your audience know what they will get out of the entire speech, it's time to let them know exactly what they will get out of your very first point. You can use what I call the "Transition Tease" to do this. Just as ESPN teased me for what was coming up after the commercial break, you need to tease your audience for what they will get out of your first point. For example, I might transition into my first point in the following manner:

> "So let's get started. If, as a manager, if you want to go from feeling overwhelmed to feeling overjoyed, even while you miraculously get more work done in one day than most managers get done in one week, you'll need to integrate this first tool ..."

Through my experience speaking to managers, I know this Transition Tease passes the "Who cares?" test. Immediately after this transitional phrase, I go into my first anchor, which makes my first point. That is one way of transitioning into your point.

Another way to use the Transition Tease is by asking questions. For example, I might ask the following as a way to tease my audience into the next point:

> "Do you work with StatusQuoaholics? You know...these are the people who are addicted to the status quo. They say things like, 'This is just the way we've always done things around here. Why change?' Do you work with people like that? What do they do to your team? What if you could bring them back from the dark side and have them be a positive force for your team? Well, the good news is that you *can*—but only if you utilize this next tool."

Build Up the Pain during the Tease

The reason this way of teasing works so well is because the questions allow you to build up the *pain* in your audience. Then, you suggest that your next point will not only ease their pain but also make them much better off than they ever were. Keep in mind that many people will not move until it feels too uncomfortable to stand still. These questions build the discomfort, and your tease builds the anticipation for your audience to think, "I've gotta hear this!"

Those are the two major ways to Transition Tease into your next point. One way is to simply state the benefits, and the other way is to ask questions that build the pain and then state that you have the solution. Transition Teases are the sliding board to your speech, and once you get your audience on the slide, they will easily head to your next point. Whatever you do, when it comes to your Transition Tease, don't go into your next point without it. Speaking of next points, let's go to the next step in the "Create Your World-Class Speech" Structure Model.

STEP 3: YOUR FIRST POINT

What's loose is lost. This means that any points you make that are not tied to something (a story, activity, analogy, etc.) will be forgotten. You absolutely must give your audience something onto which they can hang your point. The tool to use here is called an "anchor." Within an anchor, there are five elements that I put into the PARTS formula, which stands for the following:

Point

Anchor

Reflection

Technique

Sale

In a nutshell, this means that when you make your point, you should illustrate it with an anchor, get the audience to reflect upon it, give them a tangible tool to apply it if possible, and sell them on using it. In this chapter, it is simply important to know that your first point, and every point you make, should be tied to an anchor. However, chapter three, on content, will cover the PARTS formula in detail. If you want to make your audience feel like they've had an experience and not just a speech, the PARTS formula is the way.

STEP 4: TRANSITION INTO YOUR SECOND POINT

You might think that transitioning into your second point is the same as transitioning into your first. Well, it is, but with one huge exception. If you want to make a speech stick with your audience so that you get more opportunities to speak in the future, you will need to master this next tool. It is called the "call back." The call back means, before you actually get into making your next point, you should remind us again about the first point you just made. For example, let's say I am giving my Four Rs to Remarkable Results speech. As I transition from my first point (i.e., "reality") into my second point (i.e., "relinquish"), I will first call back to my first point in the following manner:

"So when you *face reality*, how you respond to that reality is critical. Are you hanging around the crabs in the barrel, or will you fly above them with a disciplined mind? Remember, your actions speak louder than your words. Now what comes after you face reality? Well, let me ask you this: do you work with any StatusQuoaholics? You know, these are the people who are addicted to the status quo. They say things like, 'This is just the way we've always done things around here. Why change?' Do you work with people like that? What do they do to your team? What if you could bring them back from the dark side and have them be a positive force for your team? Well, the good news is that you *can*—but only if you utilize this next tool. The key here is to *relinquish* what is in the way. How do you do this? You should have been with me in East Baltimore ....."

Do you see how I called back to the first point of reality and then Transition Teased into the next point of relinquishing what's in the way? Most presenters never call back to their previous points. Another important tool you can use is to not only call back to the points, but also call back to the characters in your story, the activities, the analogies, or whatever you used to help make those points. As you can see in the above example, I called back to the crabs in a barrel, which was an analogy I used during my first point. After my second point (i.e., "relinquish"), I might call back to a character by stating the following:

"… and just like Jermaine Williams Jr. paid the ultimate price by not being willing to let go of his old ways, old friends, and old stomping grounds, we, too, will pay the price by hanging onto our old methods and not embracing change. Remember, you're either on the way or *in* the way. Which one will it be?"

Calling back in this manner allows you to use another wonderful tool called the "catchphrase." Use a catchphrase several times during a speech, and watch as the audience catches on. Several times during my Four Rs to Remarkable

Results program, I say "You're either on the way or *in* the way. Which one will it be?" These catchphrases, coupled with your call backs, will make you a master at leaving a serious imprint on the minds of your audience members. Call backs reinforce the point for your audience members, so that months from now, they will still know your message. The key to this process is twofold.

1. Call back to the previous point

2. Transition Tease into the next point

This is how you get your audience members to slide into your next point. Every point you give from then on will follow the same process of transitioning with the *call back* and *tease* and then presenting your point with the *PARTS formula*. Nothing changes structurally until you're about to close your speech. Therefore, we can skip past those steps (numbers five through seven) in the outline at the front of this chapter and go directly to step eight, which is "Call Backs and Transition to the Close."

STEP 8: CALL BACKS AND TRANSITION TO THE CLOSE

If your audience is still leaning forward with their eyes glued to you at this point in the speech, you've done a masterful job. However, if you don't close the speech effectively, all is lost. It would be like driving all the way down the football field just to fumble the ball on the opponent's one-yard line. In order to close correctly, you must first transition into that close. Here are the elements of this final transition:

A. Signal that you are closing

B. Have a question-and-answer period if necessary

C. Call back to all points

D. Leave them on a high!

E. Transition Tease to the end

A.   Signal that You are Closing

Always tell your audience that you are closing, so they will listen again. Seriously, your audience is trained to see the end coming and think, "Okay, I better listen to this and catch the gist of the message." Be creative in how you do it. Don't just say, "In closing ..." How boring! Instead, use everyday language such as, "Okay, as we wrap it up today, you'll recall that ..." Or state, "Here we are at the end of the road. Just remember that ..." Whatever you do, make sure you send a clear signal that you are closing.

B.   Have a Question-and-Answer Period if Necessary

Never end your speech with the question-and-answer period. Why? It's simply because people remember best what they hear first and what they hear last. Your message should be the final words they hear. Plus, some people can ask crazy questions, right?

For example, I once gave a wonderful two-day management workshop in Missouri. We came to the end of the second day and all was going well, until I got to the end and asked the wrong question, which was, "Are there any questions?" This petite lady in the front stood up and excitedly said, "Thank you so much for these ideas about reinforcing behaviors with my employees. I was just wondering: will these same ideas work for my horses?" I was stunned and silent. Finally I turned to her and, with my best horse impression, said, "Neigh!"

I could already see the dialogue between my attendees when they returned to the office:

Boss: "So, what did the trainer talk about?"

Manager (attendee): "He talked about horses!"

You want your audience members to leave with your well-planned message. Don't leave it up for grabs by ending your speech in confusion and spontaneity. You should get the last word. Therefore, have a question-and-answer period if necessary, but do it before you close in your own powerful and memorable way.

When you begin your question-and-answer period, don't ask, "Are there any questions?" It's much better to ask, "What questions do you have?" Assume they have questions, and they will respond in kind. If, for some reason, nobody speaks up, be prepared with a comeback. For example, if I ask a question and nobody responds, I might say, "This is an English-speaking audience, isn't it?" They laugh, which loosens them up to respond. That's planned spontaneity.

C. Call Back to all Points

Just as you have called back to the previous points while transitioning to the next point, you should call back to all points once they have been given. For example, after I finish all my points and get ready to close, I summarize the points in the following way:

"So, once you face *reality*, how you respond to that reality is critical. Are you hanging around the crabs in a barrel, or are you flying above them with a disciplined mind? Remember, actions speak louder than words, and what gets measured gets improved. Face reality.

"After you face reality, you now know the life-or-death importance of *relinquishing* what's in the way. Are you hanging onto old ways like Jermaine Williams Jr. or embracing change like Jermaine Williams Sr.? Remember that you are either on the way or *in* the way. Which one will it be? Use the SSIP formula to encourage your employees to change.

"Once you relinquish, you know the importance of *relying* on the process of change and the people involved. Are you creating a picture that keeps them fired up, instead of fed up, in the forest?

"Finally, when you rely on the process of change, you can then *reform* to a better way. Do you reform all at once? Absolutely not; you know instead to change small and change often. Changing all at once is a quick fix, but changing small and often is a lifestyle change. This way changes your entire environment and raises the morale for good."

Believe it or not, these call backs take only about forty-five seconds at most. Hopefully you've been calling back after each point you made during the meat of the speech. Once these call backs are made, it's time to transition into the end of the entire speech.

D.   Leave Them on a High

Now that all the teasing is over and the points have been made, what's next? In my opinion, next comes hope. That's right, your job is to leave them on a high so they walk away thinking, "I can do this. I can use these tools to get the results that were promised. These tools will work for me!" So what is the best way to leave them on a high? Finish with a story that demonstrates they can do it. This might be a story about you, one of your customers, or simply a story about someone you know. Either way, the key is to have a story about an ordinary person who used these extra-special tools (the process) to get extraordinary results. However, before closing with the story, you'll need to set it up with the transition.

E.   Transition to the End

This last transition should answer any questions or doubts you think your audience members might still have in their minds. For example, here's how I transition into my closing story with the Four Rs.

"You might be thinking, 'Well, Craig, of course these four R's will work for you, because, when it comes to leadership and speaking, you are a natural—and you're good looking.' Believe me, there is nothing natural about me. In fact, the only reason I stand before you today is because of these tools. You see, I am the least likely person to have won the World Championship of Public Speaking. I am the least likely person to be a professional speaker. I am the least likely person to have met with success in management. In fact, when I was ten years old, something very disturbing happened to me."

At that point, I go into my closing story. The key to this transition is to get across the point that the tools are the stars of the show. The process is king, and anyone can be crowned. The Four Rs will make all the difference, regardless of who uses them. In other words, give the audience hope as you transition into your final story.

STEP 9: CLOSING

If you have signaled you are closing, handled the questions and answers, called back to your major points (and stories, characters, etc.) then 80 percent of the closing is already complete. The only piece left is the actual anchor you leave with them. Again, I suggest using a story that leaves your audience on a high and fills them with hope. I tell a story about being ten years old and having a lisp that was so bad that a father of one of my friends said to me, "Craigy, don't talk any more. Every time you open your mouth, you remind me of Daffy Duck." Then I demonstrate how I used the Four Rs (even though I didn't know what they were at the time) and, as a result, went from Daffy Duck to the World Champion of Public Speaking. When my audience realizes where I started and what got me here, they feel willing to go out there and give the Four Rs a shot.

Types of Closings

Having said that the best way to close your speech is with a story, there are other effective ways to close as well. Consider the following:

Circular—This is when your ending ties into a part of either the opening or body (anchors and points) of your speech.

Quotation—Finish your speech with a quotation that the audience will not forget. Make sure the quote is relevant to the rest of your speech. As with any quotation, make sure you have read at least one book (or significant material) on the person you are citing. People will approach you afterwards and say, "Oh, I just love Will Rogers. Let's talk about him!" It will be an embarrassing moment if you know nothing about him. Plus, you will lose serious credibility.

Poem—Use a powerful piece of poetry to drive home your overall message and leave the audience with their hearts open. Kweisi Mfume (former leader of the NAACP) is a master at this type of closing, and I have seen him integrate soap-opera titles with his poem for a humorous effect.

Call for action—Now that you have laid the points and benefits out, give your audience a charge to do something. Challenge them to take a step within the next three days. If they wait any longer, they probably won't ever get around to doing anything with your message.

Question—Finish with a powerful and thought-provoking question. These types of questions seem to stay with a person like a song you cannot shake from your brain.

Let them speak—Let the audience have the last word. Toastmasters International's 2000 World Champion of Public Speaking, Ed Tate, had the audience finish his World Championship speech for him. He anchored us earlier and at the end of his speech he said, "I guess that was just ..." and the audience finished it by saying, "... one of those days."

Whatever kind of closing you use, have the audience leave on a high note. If you have delivered your speech effectively, depending on the type of speech, then the audience should have gone on a roller-coaster ride of emotions. They may have been happy, angry, upset, shedding tears of joy, and even feeling triumphant. But with most speeches, when you finish, your audience should be on a high. When you close your speech with impact, you will open doors of opportunity.

Use the Rule of Three

Structure your speech around the Rule of Three. What is the Rule of Three? It has many different meanings in public speaking, but for now, I am only referring to the number of major points you use. You'll find out more about this in chapter four, on delivering your speech. However, just make sure you understand that three points beats out six points because people remember best in threes. If you take your six points and separate them into three sections (two points per section), that will work better than simply listing all six. Having three sections helps your audience organize their thoughts. If you have nine points overall, perhaps you can put three of those points in each of the three sections. Not only will it help your audience, but you'll find yourself being better able to internalize your message, too. Why? You also remember best in threes.

DATA DUMPS BELONG IN THE GARBAGE

You can tell a story, make a point, drive home your point with brilliant benefits, pause at all the right times, use vocal variety, look people in the eyes, master the staging, and have the sweetest, most refreshing insights in the world but guess what? If you don't adhere to the following advice, your entire speech will come crumbling down. Everything you put into it will go to waste.

I take my audience members through an activity that drives them crazy. I say, "Okay, I want you to change twelve things about your appearance." Without fail, some start changing twelve things, others look around to see if anyone is doing it, and a few verbally express their displeasure at my instructions. Then, a few seconds later, I say, "Okay … okay … wait a minute. Just change *two* things about your appearance." At that point you can hear an audible sigh as they say, "That's better."

A KEY TO MAKING YOUR PRESENTATION STICK

What's the point of the exercise? It's simple. The same way my audience looked at me when I asked them to change twelve things is the same way your audience will view you if you ask them to do too much. Here is the statement you should write down and keep in front of you at all times:

> Too many speakers try to get across too much information
> in too little time.

There is an old speaker's proverb that states, "When you squeeze your information in, you squeeze your audience out." Less is more when it comes to making your speech stick. Have you ever seen a speaker give the "top fifteen ways to do this" or the "seventeen critical laws for that?" Chances are that that presenter failed miserably. The reason you see it happening is because the speaker has tons of information on the topic, and he wants to get it all across. That's fine, but not for one speech. Let the audience get the rest of your points by either purchasing your products or bringing you back again. You're not being stingy, you're being *sticky*; you're making sure your speech sticks.

Now that you have the structure for your speech, let's dive into creating killer content!

Chapter 3

How to Develop Content that Keeps Them Thirsting for More

Be Original

Ionce read in John L. Mason's fantastic book, *An Enemy Called Average*, the following life-changing quotation: "Most people are born originals but die as copies." Isn't *that* the truth? Unfortunately, it is most evident in public speaking. Wannabe speakers tell hand-me-down stories and jokes from the Internet in order to seem clever and in-depth. World-class speakers use their own fresh material born from their own lives, experiences, and observations of the world.

Et Tu, First Lady?

I heard the story that a former first lady of the United States of America was called upon to speak at a conference years ago, and she did the unthinkable. You would think that, with all the experiences she had had that most of us cannot even fathom, she would have remarkable stories to tell. So what did she do? She told stories from *Chicken Soup for the Soul.* Now, granted, the *Chicken Soup* series is brilliant, thought-provoking, and heartwarming, but this is the first lady we're talking about. Anyone can tell the *Chicken Soup* stories. We want to hear what the first lady has to say about her own life!

THE PROBLEM WITH BEING UNORIGINAL

As soon as you open your mouth to use someone else's material, someone in your audience will know. As soon as your audience members uncover this, they will think the following: "Wow, that story is not his. I bet the rest of his speech is borrowed, too." You might as well take your credibility to the nearest trash can, because you've ruined it. Your audience will mentally check out and never return. You're done. Don't let this happen to you.

WHAT IS A KEY TO CAPTIVATING CONTENT?

Be you. Be original. Be real. When I first started speaking, an older gentleman approached me after a speech and asked, "Valentine, what else do you speak about?" I said with enthusiasm, "I speak on changing your life by changing your mind." Immediately, he said, "You can't speak on life. You have to speak on something more important!" I couldn't believe my ears. What could be more important than life?

As a speaker, you must be careful who you listen to and what you act upon, because many people will attempt to pluck the originality from you. You must *remain original* in your content and your delivery. By far the very best way to do this is with *your own stories*. This chapter contains some of the most important, fundamental truths you will ever uncover about becoming a world-class speaker. However, you won't make a dent as a speaker unless you commit to being the real you. Be you. Be original. Be real. Now let's dive into this chapter and look at how to create content that keeps your audience thirsting for more.

Use the **PARTS** Formula for Driving Home Your Point

There is a definite process for developing captivating content, and you'll get that process here. You already found out, by reading the "Create your World-Class Speech" Structure section, that what's loose is lost. Again, this means you must create anchors for each of the points you plan to make in your speech. Otherwise, your audience will quickly forget them, and you will walk away having wasted their time and yours. When you put together each major point in your speeches, you will want to run it by the following questions to ensure its effectiveness:

- Is it tied to an anchor?
- Can your audience reflect?
- Can your audience act on it?
- Does it sell?

Being *tied* to an anchor means there is something (story, activity, acronym, analogy, etc.) that helps your audience members remember your point.

Having them *reflect* means that your audience members go from being passive spectators to being active participants by thinking about how to apply your message to their own lives. Having them *act* means your audience members have a way to take action on your message. Finally, having it *sell* means your audience knows the benefits of taking action on your message. This may seem like a daunting task, but it is simplified when you use the PARTS formula for driving your point home.

THE **PARTS** FORMULA

- Point
- Anchor
- Reflection
- Technique
- Sale

POINT

Why is it that many speakers don't get their points across to their audience members? You might have plenty of answers. However, here is the real reason: they don't know what their main point is!

The very first step in getting each point together is to begin with a *foundational phrase*. This is the phrase you use when making your point. For example, one of my foundational phrases is "What got you here won't get you there." Another foundational phrase for a different point is "If you don't forgive, it only hurts you." For another point, it might be "You're either on the way or *in* the way." When you start with a firm grasp of what your foundational phrase is, you automatically tighten your speech. Why? It's because anything that's not relevant to that foundational phrase gets thrown out. Only keep what sticks to the foundational phrase. When in doubt, leave it out.

What Goes into a Solid Foundational Phrase?

The foundational phrase is the main reason you used the anchor in the first place. Because it is the main reason we told the story (or used a different anchor), there's only one hard and fast requirement for it. What is the sole requirement? It absolutely must be memorable. If it is, then your audience will carry it away with them. If it's not, then the entire story is a waste. To make it memorable, keep the following three ideas in mind when constructing your foundational phrase:

1. **Make it brief.** Keep your foundational phrase fewer than ten words. Why? If your message is not clear to you, it doesn't stand a chance to be clear to your audience. Some speech coaches say, "If you can write your message on the back of a business card, that means it is short and clear enough." My response to that is, "They obviously have no idea how small I can write." However, by keeping it fewer than ten words, you force yourself to be crystal clear with your message. Look at some of the foundational phrases I have used in the past:
    *   Your dream is not for sale (six words)
    *   Average leaders place blame; exceptional leaders take it (eight words)

- If you can view it, you can do it (nine words)

These phrases are crystal clear. Whatever fits with each phrase will stay, and whatever doesn't will be tossed away.

2. **Make it "you" focused.** The foundational phrase needs to be "you" focused. The line usually makes a greater impact when it puts the focus on the audience members by using the word "you". The word "you" is the most powerful word in any presentation you give. The more you use it, the more they will lean forward and pay close attention. Wannabe speakers focus on "I," while world-class speakers focus on "you."

3. **Make it repeatable.** The line should be easy to say, easy to receive, and easy for people to repeat. If you want the vast benefits that come from having people spread your message like a good virus, you need your foundational phrases to easily flow off their tongues. That's the way you invoke word-of-mouth marketing as one of your biggest assets. It's also important because after a speech, non-attendees will ask the audience members, "Well, what did the speaker speak about?" Their answer should be at the tips of their tongues, ready to be repeated.

When you first develop your foundational phrase, ask a few of your friends to repeat the line after you. Just say the line once, and see if they can repeat it. If they can, test it on a real audience. If they can't easily repeat it, take it to the nearest trash can and either toss it out or recycle it with a clearer message.

I personally use "The Daughter Test" to see if my foundational phrases are simple enough. I ask my five-year-old daughter to repeat my phrase. For example, I say, "Tori, please repeat this: if I can view it, I can do it." I know if she can say it on the first try, it's a go. If she struggles with it, I change the line by making it shorter. I might change it to "See it. Be it." It's also a good idea here to make the line somewhat musical. For example, "What got you here won't get you there." If you can sing it easily, chances are it is repeatable. Have you ever heard a song that you had not heard in a long time, yet all the words came back to you immediately? Music has that power. If your foundational phrases are somewhat musical, believe me, they will be remembered and repeated with ease. It is a magical feeling to have someone you never met approach you and say one of your phrases to you. One day, a man who had heard one of my audio CDs called me in tears and said, "Craig, you convinced me that my dream is not for sale." He is now on his way to reclaiming his dream. That's magical!

ANCHOR

How would you like a surefire way to remember your own speech—no matter how long it is—have your message stick with your audience members for years to come, and keep your audience's energy high throughout your entire speech? If you said yes, then I have good news for you. This surefire way does exist and it's a tool you have at your disposal. It is called an anchor.

Is Your Speech Loose?

Over the past few years of reviewing speeches, I have come to the conclusion that by far the most prevalent problem with the majority of them is that the content is way too loose. What does "too loose" mean? It means the content is not tied to anything. When this happens, the content just floats in midair and hangs on to nothing. It becomes forgettable and a waste of effort. And here's the kicker: some of the points have been absolutely brilliant and life changing! However, they will never shine or change lives when they are so easily forgotten. Here is something you should always remember about the art of speaking: what is loose is lost.

How Can You Tighten Your Speech?

Every single point you make in your speech should be tied to an anchor. Read the previous sentence again. An anchor is anything that helps your audience remember your points. You're about to pick up the top four anchors that I've found to work extremely well. In fact, I work all four of these anchors into almost every keynote speech and training program I give. These are not the only anchors that exist, but they certainly make for a memorable speech.

Some speakers will tell you that, for longer speeches, you should simply keep telling stories and making points. I disagree. A story is the most important anchor, but it's not the only anchor you should use. If you can mix in some of these other anchors, not only will your speech be much more memorable, but it will keep the audience's energy high. There can come a point in a speech when the audience says, "Oh no—here comes another story." But when you place the stories into a mix with these other anchors, everything becomes that much more refreshing. Here are the four anchors you can use to accomplish this:

The Four As of Anchors

1. **Anecdote** – As in a story. When you tell your story and make your point, people will remember the point because of the story. An easy example of this is "The Boy Who Cried Wolf." What's the message

in that story? Whenever you think of the story, you'll remember that telling lies will keep people from ever taking you seriously.

2. **Analogy** – People will remember your point when they can easily compare it with something else. For example, I point out how crabs in a barrel pull each other down every time one tries to get out of the barrel. Then I compare these crabs to negative people who try to bring you and your good ideas back down into their barrel. When people remember the crabs, they remember the point about negativity. Analogies work extremely well when you present them visually and verbally. There is more on giving visual analogies in chapter four, on delivery. The following old saying about these comparisons sums their effect up very well: If a picture is worth a thousand words, a metaphor is worth a thousand pictures.

3. **Acronym** – When you use an acronym such as TALL (Think, Act, Laugh, and Learn), people can hang the points onto the letters in that acronym and walk away from your speech with it burned in their brains. This also helps the structure of a speech because your audience knows you will go from one letter to the next, and they can easily follow.

4. **Activity** – When people reflect on the activity, they recall the point as well. For example, I do a quick activity in which I ask my audience members to stand and touch their chins with one of their index fingers. However, when I instruct them to do so, I physically put my index finger on my cheek instead of my chin. Watching me as their model, most of my audience members put their index fingers on their cheeks as well, even though I told them "put it on your chin." I then reiterate that actions speak louder than words. When they remember

the activity, they remember the point. In fact, by simply using the visual of putting my finger back on my cheek, I can make the point over and over again without having to say one word. You learned about call backs in the structure chapter, and putting my finger on my cheek is a visual call back. No words are needed.

The key to using these anchors is how you transition in and out of them. Use the Transition Tease to give us incentive to join you on your anchor, and then quickly transition from it into your point or points.

Your World Class Speaking Takeaway

Wannabe speakers give loose speeches that are easily forgettable. Their message floats in the ether and quickly gets lost. World-class speakers give tight speeches by tying each point to an anchor. Have you ever heard anyone say that you just need to tighten up your message? This is what they meant. Have the anchor do the work, and follow it with a nice foundational phrase people can remember. Always remember that what's loose is lost, and what's tight stays in sight.

REFLECTION

What's the most important idea I learned about speaking in the last few years? It's that wisdom comes from reflection. Those four words will transform you into the kind of speaker who makes a much deeper impact than most speakers can even dream of making. Do you know what it means? It means we must constantly get our audience members to reflect on their own lives. I have since come up with the following statement that is all too true:

You can't affect if they don't reflect.

In order for people to make a change in their lives, they must first become aware of where they are. They have to become conscious of their current situation in order to change it. The best speakers don't get you simply to memorize what they say. Instead, they get you to realize what you think. I once heard Charlie "Tremendous" Jones say in a speech, "Do not listen and memorize, but think and realize." You want your audience members to think about how they will apply your message. The best way to do this is by asking questions. For example, I might ask the following question toward the end of a story that has the foundational phrase of "your dream is not for sale":

"So your dream is not for sale. Are you letting the good get in the way of the best? Are you too comfortable in your good life to ever reach greatness?"

Or, better yet, I might ask the following questions toward the end of a different story about imagination that has the foundational phrase of "If you can view it, you can do it":

"I stepped on that World Championship stage one thousand times mentally. By the time I physically got there, I felt like I was at home. That's why I won! My question to you is, 'What is your stage? What stage are you stepping on mentally at least one thousand times?'"

These questions are better than the first set, because they require more than a yes or no for an answer. You want to make people dig down deep to think critically and emotionally about their lives. When they come back up from the big dig, they will be ready to make a change. Find ways throughout your speech to ask questions that force your audience members to reflect on where they are with your topics and tools in their own lives. Again, you can affect when they reflect.

TECHNIQUE

Depending on the type of speech it is and how much time I am given, I may or may not give an actual technique to apply my message. Usually I do, because I believe that people will stay motivated if they have tangible takeaways when they leave your speech and return to their lives. You can have a longer-lasting effect on the audience if you provide strategies and techniques to go along with your theories. We should go from the theoretical to the practical and from the general to the specific. For example, after going through the story about imagination, I may say something like the following:

"One way to sharpen your imagination is to *write down your perfect day*. Write it out in as much detail as possible. I did this several years ago, and everything I wrote down is coming to pass. I said I wanted to be a full-time professional speaker, and I am a full-time professional speaker. I said I wanted to own my own business, and I own my own business. I said I wanted a white Mercedes-Benz convertible, and I have a white … Honda Accord! I'm getting there!"

This helps sell the technique of writing down your perfect day, and it gives them something to do long after you have left the speaking platform. How is this different from a simple call to action? Calls to action charge the audience members on what they should do. Tangible techniques and takeaways give them the actual vehicle to do it. For example, many speakers will say, "So go out there, and start envisioning your future." However, the technique of writing down your perfect day shows them exactly how they can envision their future. It gives them the method. It becomes the vehicle they need to complete the call to action.

SALE

Whenever I present to speakers, I regularly tell them, "Raise your hands if you agree with this statement: 'When you are in speaking, you are in sales.'" Guess what happens? All hands go up. Guess what the reality is, though? Common sense is not common practice. Everybody in the audience knows they are supposed to sell something in their speech, but rarely do they do it. Instead, you have people say, "I'm just not the salesperson type" or "I just want to give good information." I say, "I have news for you. Whether you feel like you are in sales or not, speaking is selling. If you do not know how to sell, then you do not know how to speak."

Every Speech Is Selling Something

Some speeches sell ideas, while others sell products and services. Some speeches sell people on the achievements of themselves and others. Some speeches sell people on the need for change. No matter how you look at it, all speeches sell people on something.

Speakers sometimes say to me, "Well, what about me? I do only informational speeches." Again, I ask them, "Do you want your audience to listen?" They say, "Sure." "Then you have to sell them on *why* they should listen, right?" Believe me, being in the industry has afforded me the opportunity to see thousands of speeches, and I have never seen a speech that did not have to sell something.

Even funerals have to sell us on the worthy life of the individual who has left us. Some are easier to sell than others. The key is that *selling is a fact of speaking.* You can either embrace selling and thrive or resist selling and throw away your future as a profitable speaker. Choose to sell.

Welcome to Sales

I am your host, Craig Valentine. The reason all speakers are in sales is because if you cannot sell your message, your audience will not take action, and you will not make any kind of difference in their lives. Knowing this, it is amazing to me how many speakers never study the art of sales. You will profit immensely from what you are about to read. By the end of this section, you will find specific tools on selling that will put you ahead of 99 percent of the people who ever tried to sell anything—be it a message, a product, or a service.

Tools for Selling Anything

Somewhere in this section, you will find a list of three books that, if you read them, will change your fortune. They have meant the world to my development as a profitable speaker, even though they are not books on speaking. In addition, you are about to pick up specific tools, as well as a special formula, that will separate you from the pack of speakers who simply cannot or will not sell. Wait a minute; you read a tool in the last sentence. Did you notice it?

Do You Remember the Most Important Word in Speaking?

Here is what you did not see. Most speakers say, "I am here to talk to you about some tools and a formula you can use to sell." Guess what? Nobody cares what you are there to talk about. We care about what we are going to get. So let's revisit the rule you learned earlier in this book: If you ever find yourself saying something like, "I am going to share with you …," stop yourself. Instead, say, "You are going to receive …" Or say, "You are going to pick up tools to help you …"

Imagine that you are giving a presentation to new managers, and you want to plant a selling seed during the beginning of your speech. Here is what you do not want to say: "I am going to give you eight strategies that help managers transition from the front line into management." Instead, realize that the word "you" is *the* most important word in speaking. Use it often. It is not about what I (the speaker) am going to give. It is about what you (the audience member) are going to receive. Therefore, change the statement to the following: "You are going to walk away with eight surefire strategies that you can use to make the often-difficult transition from the front lines to becoming a star in management circles."

The more you use "you," the better you will sell. It is a small change that makes a huge difference. A wonderful whet-the-appetite-type statement is always, "In the next forty-five minutes, you will gain this or that." For example, "In the next forty-five minutes, you will discover the tools that the top managers use to get more work done through others. You will be able to get much more done with much less stress, and you will create commitment, not just compliance, from everyone on your team." Then, of course, you make their current problems itch until they are desperate, yet excited, for some cures. That might sound crass to you, but let's look at this realistically. Read and digest the following statement: most people do not move until it hurts too much to stand still. It is your job to make them face their own disturbed reality, because deep down, they know they can do better.

If You "Get" This Idea, You Will Get Sales

One very important strategy to use in sales is this: do not sell the feature; sell the result.

I once heard the real-estate and information-marketing guru Ron LeGrand say, "People don't buy paint; they buy beautiful walls." The legendary direct-marketing genius Joseph Sugarman said, "Don't sell the drill, sell the hole." In speaking, you can adapt this to "Do not sell the process, sell the result." People buy results. Far too often, speakers sell the process. They sell the CDs or the DVD, or they sell the paint instead of the beautiful walls. This came into play years ago when I bought my first car. Here is how I explain it in my speeches:

"I was on a lot looking at Eagle Talons when a salesperson approached me and said, 'This car is fantastic. It has antilock brakes, automatic windows, and easy steering.' In other words, he was selling me on the features of the car. I did not know why at the time, but I just didn't feel persuaded. As a result, I left that dealership without purchasing.

"Later that day, I visited another lot and looked at a similar Eagle Talon. The salesperson must have assessed me (being young, hip, and good-looking) before he approached me and asked, 'So, you're looking at that car?' I said yes. He smiled. 'You're going to look great in it. You'll be whizzing down the road, pumping your music, and the girls will be all over you!' I said, 'Where do I sign?' He succeeded because he sold me the results. I already felt myself driving down the highway with several raving female fans. By the way—he lied!"

He did everything correct except for the lie. Do not lie to sell anything. However, do sell the results of using your process.

How Do You Easily Transition from Your Content into Selling Your Message?

When selling your message to your audience, a great strategy is to move from an "I"-focused story to a "you"-focused message. The I-focused story is the story that you tell in the first person (chapter seven will teach you more than you need to know about storytelling). However, at the end, it is critical to focus on "you" (the audience). For example, at the end of my story about having to face my own weight problem, I might end my I-focused story and role into the you-focused point like this:

"So that scale was my reality, and it was what prompted me to change. Reality hurts, but the most important thing you must do as a leader is to get your people to face it. If you don't, they will never change. If you do, you're already halfway to your new vision. They'll follow you willingly."

The scale story was "I" focused but the point was all about "you"; it was "you" focused. You absolutely have to bring it back around to what the audience will get. In this case, what is the result I sell? It is the influence they will have as leaders of their people.

Use This EDGE Sales Formula™ to Get Remarkable Results in Selling Anything

One of the most important ideas to understand, in order to motivate people, is that results fall into four places. They fall somewhere within the EDGE acronym. If you offer results from each one of these places during your speech, you will motivate the vast majority of your audience. If someone is left unmotivated, look at him closely, because he might be dead. The four major places are the following:

Esteem more

Do more

Gain more

Enjoy more

All of the results that fall into these four places answer the question WIIFT (What's In It For Them)?

- **Esteem more** – A result that helps you esteem more is prestigious. You let them know that taking this advice will make people see you in a different light. They will view you as a leader (or recognized expert, world-class speaker, etc.)

- **Do more** – A result that helps you do more is empowering. You let the audience know *"You'll* get much more done in less time by using this process."

- **Gain more** – A result that helps you gain more is profitable. You let them know *"You'll* cut years off your learning curve by taking this advice," *"You* will be able to stop throwing money down the drain by owning instead of renting," or *"You'll* get wealthy."

- **Enjoy more** – A result that helps you enjoy more is fun. Let them know that by taking this advice, *"You* will hop out of bed in the morning with a new zest for life. *You* will not be able to wait to get the day started!" Or you might go against their present condition by stating, "Using this process will immediately lift that heavy weight off *your* shoulders and sweep *your* stress away."

In the "you" focus of my World Championship speech, I made the following promises about the process of spending five minutes alone in complete silence each day:

"Taking five minutes of silence each day will give you confidence exuding from every pore of your being. Five minutes of silence will grant you the peacefulness, tranquility, and serenity that you never even knew existed. And five minutes of silence will sooner or later lead you to feel fulfilled."

Now take a look at the breakdown.
- Confidence = Esteem more
- Peacefulness, tranquility, serenity, and fulfillment = Enjoy more

You can see that I used two of the four places. However, that was in 1999. Today, I regularly sell my messages by using all four places (EDGE) to make sure everyone in my audience is motivated. Use results across the board when you can. Not everyone is motivated by gaining profit. Not everybody is motivated by doing more. Not everybody is motivated by having fun. Not everybody is motivated by garnering more recognition. However, everybody is motivated by at least one of the above. If you use them all, you will light a spark in your audience.

Three Books that Will Change Your Fortune

Did you skip down to this section? Have you been waiting for the list of books? Were you at least curious as to what they were? That is because you were subjected to another sales tool you should regularly use. A very powerful sales tool is to promise to reveal something later on in your presentation, because people will stay alert to find it. Think back to your formative years of education, when the teacher advised you to "read the test questions before you read the paragraph." Remember that? After you read the test questions, you read the paragraph looking for specific information. This sales tool works the same way. The main benefit to you is that, as long as your audience is looking for it, you have their attention. Getting and keeping their attention is always necessary for you to succeed in selling them. Always remember this: Promise something at the beginning that makes them stay until the end. Then make sure you fulfill the promise. Following my own advice, here are the books that will make a great difference in your life and your prosperity:

- *Triggers* by Joseph Sugarman (genius on advertising copy)
- *The Psychology of Persuasion* by Kevin Hogan (genius on influence)
- *Soft Selling in a Hard World* by Richard Vass (genius on sales)

In my opinion, I saved the best for last. *Soft Selling in a Hard World* is *the* book that is primarily responsible for helping me to sell eight million dollars' worth of textbooks in one year through my presentations, to be named the three-time salesperson of the year, and even to win the World Championship of Public Speaking. Selling is speaking. Speaking is selling. Embrace it, and the world will embrace you. If you'd like a hug, learn to sell.

What's Possible for You?

If you utilize the strategies in this section and you read and practice the tools you find in the three recommended books, this is what is possible for you. You will do the following:

1. Stand above the masses of speakers, because they might have great information, but what good is a diamond nobody can see? What good is great information that is sold so poorly nobody buys into it? Most people waste great information.

2. Get more opportunities to speak, because your audience members will buy into your advice and want more of you. Plus, you will be better able to sell yourself into engagements by selling the meeting planner and economic buyer on the results they will get from hiring you.

3. Make much more money by selling the products and services that you make available.

4. Start having more fun and less fear when it comes to selling your messages, products, and services.

These are the results that can begin to flow your way when you follow the advice in this section and read the three recommended books. Okay, I am sure you have caught on by now, right? Those four results went in the order of the EDGE formula. Go back immediately and write the word "Esteem" next to number one, "Do" next to number two, "Gain" next to number three, and "Enjoy" next to number four. Your success depends on how quickly you can make using the EDGE sales formula a habit for you.

Follow This Suggestion to Your Goldmine

Begin watching commercials and immediately determine which of the EDGE results they are selling. This will build awareness. Awareness will eventually lead to internalization and habit. Then begin building your speeches around the EDGE results. You will get a template for doing so later in this chapter. You can also visit http://www.wcspeaker.com/templates for blank "EDGE Speech Results" templates that you can use forever to motivate the vast majority of people in every future audience.

PARTS FORMULA REVISITED

So there you have it, in a nutshell. State your **P**oint, **A**nchor it in some way, get your audience members to **R**eflect, provide them with a **T**echnique, and **S**ell them on why they should put your tools to work. When these PARTS come together, they will make a whole speech that leaves your audience extremely satisfied, yet yearning for more! You just make sure you're there when they call you back. Now that you have the all-important PARTS formula, let's look at some additional strategies for creating excellent content.

WHAT SHOULD WE ALWAYS PLACE ON A PEDESTAL?

Do you remember taking the SAT? If you are not in the United States, the SAT is a test that high-school students take to help them get into the college of their choice. On many speaking occasions, I ask my audience the following.

"Do you remember taking the SAT? Do you know any students who were geniuses and scored close to an 800 on the Math portion of the SAT, or close to an 800 on the reading-comprehension portion? Well, I got a 730 … on the entire SAT!"

This line prompts a hearty laugh, and I then transition into the research conducted by the Yale University professor, Howard Gardner, regarding the various types of intelligences we have. Why do you think I share my dismal SAT score with my audience members? Is it because I want to come off looking unintelligent? Is it simply for me to get a laugh? Do I enjoy the painful reminder? Absolutely not. I do it for one of the most important rules in public speaking, which is: Put the *process*, not the person, on a pedestal. What does this mean? Think about it. If we regularly speak about our successes and how well we have done in life, what will our audience members start to think? First, they will probably say, "Wow, this person is quite full of himself." However, that is not the worst part. Even worse then having them think we are arrogant is having them think we are "special." That's right: having them perceive us as special is worse than having them see us as arrogant. Why?

WHY IS BEING CONSIDERED "SPECIAL" WORSE THAN BEING CONSIDERED "ARROGANT"?

When we bring up success after success, the audience members think, "Wow, he's special. I might was well cast off everything he says, because it won't work for me. The only reason it works for him is because he's special." The last thing you want your audience to ever think about you is that you're special. This is the opposite of what you want them to think. Sure, it might be good for your ego, but it is terrible for your income. On the other hand, when you talk about your failures, such as a poor SAT score, your audience thinks, "Wow, he is just like me. If the process he used worked for him, it has to work for me. After all, I even scored higher than he did on the SAT." When your audience thinks in this way, you have them exactly where you want them. They will act on your message.

Put the process, not the person, on a pedestal. When they take you off the pedestal, they immediately replace you with whatever process you use. Remember, you are always selling the *results of a process*, but you can't shine a light on that process if you're standing in the way. So how do you shine a light on the valuable process? That's easy. Share your failures, flaws, and frustrations.

1. FAILURES

Come on and admit it, you have some failures. Nothing brings an audience to you faster than sharing one or several of your failures. This works because it is the opposite of what the audience expects. Most speakers brag mostly about their successes, and the result is destructive to their goal. Always remember this: when you lift yourself up, you let your audience down

2. Flaws

When you share quirks and things about yourself that are less than stellar, your audience members begin to like you more. Why? First of all, they start feeling better about themselves. Second, you give them permission to openly admit their own flaws. Finally, you prove to them that they can still succeed while carrying these flaws; the flaws won't hold them back. The story that has had the most emotional impact for me is the one in which Mr. H tells me my lisp is so bad that I sound like Daffy Duck. My past lisp was a serious flaw, but it has now become the foundation for my success as a speaker. More importantly, it gives people hope.

3. Frustrations

Frustration is an emotion we all feel, and sharing yours will help bring your audience members' frustrations to the surface. Then, when you offer the cure for their frustration, consider your message as sold.

The Fourth F

There is a fourth "F." While co-teaching the Secrets to Storytelling Champ Camp with my fellow World Champion, Darren LaCroix, he turned to our audience and said, "Craig, do you mind if I add a fourth F?" Knowing Darren, I said, "Be careful." After he laughed, he offered a very important F that he uses extremely well to build a connection. He said, "Share your firsts."

4. FIRSTS

When you did something for the first time, you probably were not at your best. Darren, who has sold tons of products and services in his day, has the good fortune and wisdom to be able to actually show (via his laptop and projector) his very first time on stage as a comedian. If that does not take him off a pedestal, I do not know what will. In fact, the first time I saw the footage, I felt sorry for him. However, look at where he is today! He is a very successful entrepreneur who speaks to thousands upon thousands of business people in several countries. They buy into his message, because he puts the process, not the person, on a pedestal. Oftentimes, audience members see where we are, but sharing your firsts lets them see where we *were*. This gives them hope.

Remember, the process has the power! If you make yourself *similar* to your audience, you will become a very special speaker. You will also get very special results. Find out ways to make yourself similar to them. Put the process, not the person, on a pedestal. Do not let the person get in the way.

DO NOT ADD HUMOR TO YOUR SPEECH

Aspiring speakers regularly ask me, "Craig, how can I add humor to my speech?" I say, "Don't add it." They ask, "What do you mean, don't add humor? I thought speeches need to have humor in them?" That's when I usually give the following statement you should write down and keep in a visible place: "Don't add humor; uncover it."

The humor is already there, and you simply need to dig it out. There's a huge difference between adding humor and uncovering humor in your speech. You can always tell when a speaker adds the humor. How can you tell? Look at the following ways:

- There is a detour that takes you away from the main idea.
- The humor is not organic, meaning it really does not belong.
- The audience knows you're "reaching" with an obvious and often-embarrassing attempt at being funny.

How do I know so much about this? I was the main culprit! Even though I got laughs with my humor, it took my audience on a meaningless detour for me to get those laughs. Deep down inside, I knew that *they* knew that I was reaching too far, just to be funnier.

Why Is Adding Humor Costly?

In the middle of my speeches, I used to force in certain content in order to add humor. For example, here's an excerpt of a speech I gave years ago on presentation skills:

"Has anyone here ever put their kids in time-out? What is time-out? There was a lady who once said to me, 'Time-out is a new concept for dealing with kids.' I said, 'Time-out is not new. My parents used time-out on me when I was a child. It was a little different, though. You see, my mother would spank me until she got tired, then she'd take a time-out and let my father finish the rest!'"

Guess what this humor had to do with my speech? Nothing! It just got me laughs, but at what expense? The detour costs me, because it's an obvious, inorganic stretch and an artificial adding of humor where it does not belong. It's artificial, like a fake pair of biceps, and it causes problems. The audience automatically thinks, "Wow, this guy is trying too hard." The point is that I had to go away from the story just to pick up a laugh, and that's a bad move. This kind of humor is not natural. You don't want to come off like this. I remember in the middle of one of my old speeches, a guy yelled out, "What are you—a comedian? I came to see a speaker!" That's what happens when you try to add humor unnaturally and artificially.

So How Do You Avoid This and Still Have Humor?

Uncover the humor. The humor is already there, and now you simply have to uncover it.

How can you uncover your humor? What's the best way to seamlessly integrate the humor and not have to take detours to "Artificiallville" just to get some laughs? Go to the very best place to find humor. Where is that? It's in your stories. More specifically, it is in your characters' dialogue. Concentrate on what the characters say to each other, because the funny lines will appear. People say funny things every day. Here is an example of how I used to tell part of a story before uncovering the humor in the dialogue:

"I went to my friends and said, 'I'm so excited! I'm going to write a book on public speaking. Who better than the World Champion of Public Speaking to write a book on the art of public speaking! I can't wait.' My friends looked at me and said, 'Don't you know the odds of getting it published? Don't you know it probably won't work? Don't you know even if you self-publish it, you still have to market it? Not that many people know you? Who do you even think you are? Why do you think so highly of yourself? Why don't you just come back down here in this barrel? Join us.'"

Now, that's not bad. There was no humor in the story at that time, but always remember this: no humor is better than forced humor. Forced humor automatically causes resistance from the audience. A few weeks later, I tacked on the following dialogue to the end of the story.

"I was so upset about this, so I called my friend Steve and said, 'Steve, you're a positive person. Tell me something. Please, tell me *anything.*' Steve said, 'Craig, know that when you write that book, I will be the first one in line to purchase it.' I said, 'Steve, [pause] that is $15.95.'"

There are no detours needed here, because the humor is within the story. All I needed to do was extend the story to include my friend Steve and have the dialogue between us. That's totally organic, it fits, it is detour-less, humorous, and—most of all—true. All it took was to uncover one line of dialogue. Most importantly, it does not interrupt the flow of the message the audience needs to hear.

Remember those old Oregano commercials where they'd say, *"It's in there"*? Well, believe me when I tell you about the humor in your speeches: it's in there! When you focus on the characters and their lines of dialogue, you bring forth that humor and add (not subtract) value to your speech and to your listeners. That's no joke.

DO NOT DROP STATS OFF; DRIVE THEM HOME

Many times, you'll see speaker go into a list of statistics in order to prove his or her point. Statistics are certainly desirable in speaking, but only if you use them in an effective way. Simply listing statistics is not enough. You must interpret them so that your audience knows exactly what they should mean to them. For example, I have often used the following statistic when driving home a point about lifelong learning: "Each year, you will spend between five hundred and one thousand hours in an automobile." This statistic might be interesting, but it certainly is not compelling. That's because it hasn't been driven home. Here's how you might drive it home:

"Each year you will spend between five hundred and one thousand hours in an automobile. If you live to be seventy-five years old, you will spend approximately seven to ten years of your life in an automobile. Seven years! Here's my question to you. What are you doing with that time? [pause]. Are you simply passing time or using it? Do you know ten years is enough time for two PhDs? Again, what are you doing with that time? [pause]. I suggest turning your car into a rolling university. You can listen to audio books and quickly become an expert compared to the rest of the country. Oh, but there is one caveat. Please don't use any meditation tapes in the car!"

This is how you can drive a point home by showing your audience exactly how that statistic *affects them* and what they can do about it. Don't just drop off the statistic, but drive it home.

USE STATISTICS WITHIN A STORY

One of the best ways to drive home statistics is by using them inside of your stories. For example, I tell a story about a homeless woman who began teaching me the power of using my imagination to create my future. In the middle of the story, I state the following:

"She struck a chord in me, and anytime someone strikes a chord in me, I go to my Rule of Three. By the way, if you use this rule, you will be light-years ahead of most people in any endeavor you choose. What is it? It's simple: I read three books on that topic. Why? Unfortunately, the average American reads less than one book per year. And 58 percent of Americans—that's almost six out of every ten Americans—never read another nonfiction book after they finish with their formal education. I have to tell you that the world is wide open for people who are willing to read! So I read something somewhere that said if you read three books on any one topic, then you are an expert on that topic compared to the rest of the country. [pause] Don't get excited; you're expert by default, because nobody else reads! Nevertheless, you're ahead of the game. So I read three books on imagination: one was *Creative Visualization* by ..."

If I had stopped at the fact that the average American reads one book per year, then I would have simply dropped off the statistic instead of driving it home. I drove it home by letting my audience know how it *affects them* and how they can *use it* to their advantage. In other words, they can get light years ahead of any competition by reading three books on a single topic. After this statistic, I continue my story about the homeless woman and how the three books on imagination lead to me winning the 1999 World Championship of Public Speaking. Because I cited the statistic within the story, my audience was able to see first-hand how using the statistic to my advantage really paid off. Therefore, they were sold on the benefits and primed to take action (i.e., read three books).

STATISTIC VS. STORY

The problem with simply listing statistics is that they are relatively impersonal and unemotional. Of course we think "Oh, that's terrible" when we hear about millions of people with AIDS or thousands upon thousands of people living in poverty. However, those statistics won't bring us to tears like the story of *one person* will. A story will outdo statistics every time. Please remember that your audience makes decisions based on emotion backed up by logic. The story is the emotion, while the statistic is the logic. Stating that a thousand people were mugged this year won't touch us like the one story about little Jenny being mugged will. Little Jenny will outdo big statistics every time. Use statistics to back up and give depth to little Jenny's story.

LITERALLY POINT US TO THE SOURCE

Whether you cite statistics or a sentence from someone's work, please attribute them. In addition, there is an advanced way to have your audience members leave your speech thinking, "Wow, I really got more out of that than what I expected!" What you can do is not only mention the source where you got your statistic or your statement, but point them directly to it. This gives them the opportunity to further their research it if they want. For example, in my speech, I say:

> "If you pick up Michael Port's book called *Book Yourself Solid*, thumb through to page thirty-six, and look down at the very last sentence in the second paragraph, you will come across the following powerful statement: 'Most business problems are personal problems in disguise.'"

Now isn't that much more visual than simply saying, "Michael Port once said …"? It's better, because it builds credibility for you. Your audience knows you read it firsthand. Plus, it gives your audience a page to turn to in that book and a reason to purchase it. Remember, if they leave your speech and purchase a book you referred, then you are still touching their lives long after you left the speaking platform. That's the kind of impact you want as a speaker. Point them directly to the source.

Use Statistics for Involvement

Finally, you can also use statistics to get your audience involved and to strengthen the kinesthetic connection you have with them. For example, I once heard a fantastic motivational speaker say this at a conference of aspiring speakers:

"Look around you. Look to the person on your left. Now look to the person on your right. Next year at this time, only half you will still be in this organization. Statistics show that half of you will give up. Half of you will not renew your membership. You will give up and quit. Those of you who stay will be winners."

That was very powerful to us newbie speakers, because nobody wanted to be in that bottom half of quitters that would be absent next year. When I have my own tough speeches today, I still think back to what that speaker said. As a result, I keep thinking, "I'll keep coming back, no matter what." His long-lasting effect is what you want as a speaker, and proper use of statistics will help you make it.

Use the Most Important Word in Speaking

What is the most important word in speaking? I'm certain you already know by now. It is the word "you." Unfortunately, it is not used nearly enough. By now, you know the necessity in mastering storytelling so that you can tell a story and sell a point. Wannabe speakers stop here, but world-class speakers take their connection to a deeper level. How? While wannabe speakers wait until the end of their stories to address their audience, world-class speakers connect throughout the *entire story* without skipping a beat with the message.

No matter where you are in your story, you need to find ways to pull the audience in by focusing on and addressing them. Anytime you use the word "you," your audience's ears will perk up, and they will pay closer attention. The problem today is that wannabe speakers tell stories like this: "I did this, and I did that, and I accomplished this." Then, with the last twenty seconds, they simply say, "And you should do it, too." In other words, they ignore the audience throughout their story and try unsuccessfully to tack a you-focused point onto the end of it. This is transparent and is nothing more than a vague attempt and excuse to tell their life story. It's a useless autobiography. World-class speakers take a more interwoven approach to connecting.

A WANNABE SPEAKER'S HUGE MISTAKE

When I was a wannabe speaker, I used to make the huge mistake of thinking you should simply tell a personalized (I-focused) story and then, at the end of that story, make a you-focused point. While that is better than what many speakers do, it's still not enough. We need to find ways to focus on our audience before getting into our story, during the story, and after the story, as we sell our point. If we don't, the audience will most likely lose interest and eventually ask, "So what? Why am I here? What's in this for me?" Pretend you are in my audience, hearing the story you are about to read. This is exactly how I tell this story in my speeches, and I want you to see how it focuses on "you" before, during, and after the story. Here it goes:

"Raise your hand if you feel that sometimes reality hurts? [pause]. Be honest, have you ever stepped on a scale [pause for laughter] and been forced to face reality? I know what you're thinking: You're looking at me, saying, 'Come on, Craig—what do *you* know about stepping on a scale? Look at you—you're built like a Greek statue! [pause for laughter].' Thanks. I appreciate the compliment. But if you had been with me a few years ago, you would have seen a whole lot more of me.

"In fact, you should have been with my wife and me four and a half years ago as we took my six-month-old daughter, Tori, to her doctor's appointment. If you have kids, you know the doctor is always going to measure their length and weight. So the doc walks in with his white coat and glasses, he takes Tori's length, and then he looks at my wife and me and says, "Since Tori can't stand yet, and she can't seem to sit still, we're going to need another method to take her weight. How about this? Why doesn't one of you step out into the hallway and stand on the scale with Tori, then stand on the scale *without* Tori, and we'll take the difference as her weight.

"Now I don't know if you've ever been around someone who just recently gave birth, but my wife was looking at us as if to say, 'That's a wonderful idea—' Then her face drops. '... for Craig to do.' I said, 'No problem, I know what I weigh.' I jumped up on that scale, held my daughter in my arms, and was feeling good. I looked down [long pause] ... I looked at that scale! [confused and astonished look on my face] I looked at my wife and then back at that scale and said, [holding my daughter in my arms] 'Good grief. This is one fat baby!'

"Isn't it interesting how when things don't go our way ... when we don't seem to measure up ... it's almost in our DNA to place the blame on someone else? Isn't it interesting that I blamed my daughter for carrying too much weight? But how often do we blame others for not carrying *enough* weight? How often does sales blame marketing, marketing blame production, production blame engineering—and when engineers learn to speak, I'm sure they'll blame someone!"

KEEP THEIR ATTENTION WITH THE TAP AND TRANSPORT TECHNIQUE™

How were you brought into the story at the beginning? With a you-focused request and a you-focused question. Lots of speakers simply say, "One day I was …" and they get into their stories and just expect that the audience will come along. A great way to get the audience into the story is with a question. I asked them to raise their hands if they felt like reality hurts. This got them involved. Then I asked them, "Have you ever stepped on a scale …?" which also got them thinking about themselves. Therein is the key. Get them thinking about themselves before you bring them into your story.

I call it the "Tap and Transport Technique," because you tap into their world with a question and then transport them into your world with a story. This helps them know that the message is all about them. Do you currently make a habit of tapping into your audience's world with a question, or do you simply move right into your world with your story? World-class speakers tap first then transport later.

DEEPEN THE CONNECTION BY SEARCHING FOR THE SIMILARITIES

After you were brought into the story with the question, how were you (the audience) addressed within the story? What I did is what I strongly suggest you do, which is to *search for the similarities* with your audience members. Always ask yourself, "What do I have in common with the people in this audience?" Sometimes it's a stretch to figure it out, but there are always commonalities. For example, with this particular audience, I knew that many of them probably had kids. Therefore, while in the midst of my story, I turned to them and said, "And if *you* have kids, you know the doctor is always going to measure their length and weight." Whenever I say this, I always see heads nodding to the point of whiplash. That's because they are remembering their own experiences with their own kids. This keeps them engaged. Search for the similarities and make a you-focused statement while in your story. The key is to sprinkle these you-focused statements throughout the story. World-class speakers find the similarities and stress them.

Was there another example of searching for the similarities in this story? Yes. I knew that many of the audience members had probably been around a person who had given birth. As a result, again in the midst of my story, I turned to the audience and said, "I don't know if you've been around a person who has just given birth, but my wife was looking at us ..." Again, this is a you-focused statement that gets their heads nodding as if to say, "I know what you mean. I've been there, and I remember that." You always want them to think, "He's a lot like me." That keeps them engaged and gives them hope.

DON'T EXPECT—INVITE!

Here is another point that wannabe speakers overlook. They simply start their story and expect the audience to come along for the ride. However, the way you transition into your story can and should be you-focused. For example, in this story, I didn't say, "One day my wife and I were taking my six-month-old daughter Tori to her doctor appointment." Instead, I invited the audience by saying, "You should have been with my wife and me, four years ago, when we were taking my ..." Get the point? The word "you" can be used anywhere. I call this "inviting them into the scene." It's slight, but powerful. In another of my stories, I say, "If you had been sitting beside my wife and me on our black leather sofa, with the chocolate-chip cookies baking in the background, you would have heard her say something that can change your life." Where are my audience members? They're sitting next to us on the couch. That statement is an invitation and a great way to put your audience members in the middle of your scene, which is right where you want them. Most speakers simply retell their stories, which leaves the audience on the outside looking in. World-class speakers relive their stories and find ways to invite their audience into their re-living room. This is spellbinding to your audience! Invite your audience into *your* re-living room.

These pointers will keep you from having to look out on an audience with their eyes glossed over and their heads involuntarily nodding. Instead, you'll go far in terms of keeping them engaged, excited, and on the edges of their seats, which is exactly where you want them. Use the most important word in speaking: "you."

What is the One Thing Audiences Will Not Forgive?

Imagine sitting with two hundred sales representatives, waiting for the president and CEO of the Fortune 100 parent company to address you with his speech. This was the man we had seen plenty of times on television interviews, read about on company bulletins, and looked to as the leader of all leaders in our company. Heck, due to it being passed down a couple of generations, the company was still in his family's name! Needless to say, we were excited.

He took the stage to a rousing standing ovation. Imagine that: we stood and clapped before he even said one word. Well, it's a good thing we did, because we certainly did not stand at the end. Why didn't we stand at the end? Because we couldn't stand his speech. Why couldn't we stand his speech? He did the unforgivable as a speaker. He bored us.

The reason this CEO bored us is because he simply gave us abstract thoughts that had no structure and no anchors. This is what most wannabe speakers think is good speaking. An anchorless speech is a boring speech. An anchorless speech is one that will be forgotten—even before it is finished. An anchorless speech made this prestigious CEO shrink right before our very eyes. Each minute he spoke made him smaller and smaller, until we simply couldn't wait for him to go. This man came into the most enthusiastic speaking environment, filled with admirers, and left with a deflated audience, filled with embarrassment. Anchors could have saved him.

World-class speakers put the time in to make sure their audiences are anything but bored. That's why it is critical to master storytelling and integrate an appropriate mix of questions, activities, analogies, surprises, and anything else that will keep them interested and attentive. You'll learn to master storytelling in chapter six. Until then, internalize the PARTS formula and realize that stories will be your most valuable "bread and butter" anchor.

Now that you understand how to create killer content, let's dive into how to deliver your speech in a spellbinding way!

Chapter 4

How to Deliver a Speech that Keeps Your Audiences Enthralled

Captivate Your Audience with Ten Critical Delivery Tools

You might have heard of the old UCLA study that concluded that 93 percent of what we actually communicate is nonverbal. As with most studies, this one has been debated ever since, and there are people who feel it is unbelievable that only 7 percent of what we communicate comes from the words we use. You don't need to care too much about the percentages, just understand the problem most speakers face. Most speakers spend most of their time working on the content and very little time working on the nonverbal cues that will connect them with their audience. I would go so far as to say they spend 93 percent of their time working on the content, which dangerously disconnects them if 93 percent of what actually gets communicated is nonverbal.

Regardless of the actual percentages, just know that you will connect deeper and longer with your audience when you form the right habits with your nonverbal communication. Here are ten delivery skills you can use to build trust with your audience, keep them engaged, and drive your message home. The first five have to do with your nonverbal cues, and the next five have to do more with your tone as you speak.

Five Nonverbal Cues that Build Trust, Confidence, and Engagement

1. Smile

The absolute quickest way to connect with your audience is with a warm smile. Why? When do you think most speakers are the most nervous? If you said "at the beginning of the presentation," you are correct. Now, when do you think the audience members are most skeptical about the speaker? If you said "at the beginning of the presentation," you are correct again. As the 2000 World Champion of Public Speaking, Ed Tate, points out, "That is not a good combination." Ed is correct. When a skeptical audience meets a nervous speaker, a sinkhole can develop, and the speaker, not the audience, will fall into it. So what can you do to show your confidence so that your audience members can gain confidence in you? The very first tool you can use is your smile. Smile before you even say one word.

I know it sounds simple, but how many speakers do you actually see use it? Most speakers are so concerned with their content and how they are going to deliver it that the first thing to leave them is their smile. When you meet someone for the first time, don't you usually introduce yourself with a smile? It's the same here. When you are introduced to your audience, greet them with a smile. Then remember to smile throughout your presentation—at the natural and appropriate times. Of course you should only smile when it's appropriate! You don't want to smile when delivering a line such as, "… and that's when the dog fell off the cliff." The smile will bridge your connection, relax your audience members, and build their confidence in you.

2. Be Open

Have you ever seen a person who had a closed posture? How does it manifest? Are they crossing their arms? Leaning back in an uninterested manner? Turning away from you? Believe it or not, speakers do the same thing. If you stand behind a lectern or table, you are blocking your audience from connecting with you. Anything that physically gets between you and your audience (i.e., table, lectern, projector stand, etc.) will keep you from connecting as deeply as you should.

But What about History?

I can already hear your mind asking, "But Craig, what about some of the best speeches in history? What about Dr. King's 'I have a Dream' speech? What about Lincoln's Gettysburg Address?" I agree that those were the best speeches in history. However, do you notice anything those speeches have in common? They're in history! Historically, it was completely appropriate, and the norm, to speak behind a lectern. Therefore, it did not come off as being a blockage to the audience. Today, people are used to a different kind of speaker. They're used to a different kind of closeness. For example, even if you watch a minister such as Joel Osteen, a former president of the United States such as Bill Clinton, or a talk-show host such as Jay Leno, you'll notice they usually are out in the open rather than standing behind a lectern. Often, they are surrounded by their audience. In today's context, this is the norm. Anything that stands between you and your audience blocks the connection. If you want to connect and stay connected, be wide open.

3. Equalize the Territory

You should have seen me in 1999, speaking in an auditorium in northern Virginia. If you were sitting on the left side of the audience, you would have loved me. If you were sitting on the right side, you would have loathed me. Why did it matter where they were sitting? Unintentionally and unbeknownst to me, I paid much more attention to the left side of the audience than I did to the right. I turned more to the left side. I walked out into the audience on the left side. I even gave a prize to someone on the left side. In fact, after my speech, a person from the right side of the audience approached me and actually said, "Do you have a problem with us?" I said, "What do you mean?" He said, "Do you have a problem with our side of the audience? You made us feel like outcasts." Wow, I had no idea.

For many speakers, having no idea what we do nonverbally is quite normal. However, in this case, ignorance is not bliss. We must become aware of what we do and fix it. Today, I am much more conscious of adhering to the following suggestion: what you do to one side, do to the other.

If you walk up one side of the audience, make sure you walk up the other side. If you tell one story on the left, tell a different story on the right. If you give a prize to one side, give another prize to the other side. Also, make sure you pay attention to the people in the back, in the balcony, and in the corners. Every single person needs to feel you are speaking directly to him or her. Understand the territory and be the great equalizer. This is the reason you should sit in the four corners before your audience arrives, because you will be able to strategize how you will be open, accessible, and equal, even to the people with the worst vantage points.

Remember back in elementary school, when someone from the opposite sex wanted to get your attention? What would they do? They'd hit you. That was their way, and sometimes it hurt. Well, believe me, if you don't pay attention to a section of your audience, then being hit (on evaluations and feedback forms) will hurt even more. It will hurt your pockets and your pride!

4. Scan and Stop

Scanning and stopping refers to your use of eye contact. Despite being told to establish eye contact with your audience members, don't stare a hole in someone's head while you speak. Spread the love. Scan your audience while you speak. Look people directly in the eyes for a moment and then move on to other people. Make sure you look to each side of the audience, the front, and the back. In a small audience (approximately fifty people or fewer) you should be able to actually make eye contact with everyone in the room. However, with a larger audience, you might be looking more into sections or areas of your audience without actually catching each person's eyes. The key is to use your eyes so that each audience member feels you are speaking directly to him or her.

What Does Eye Contact Show?

You might say that it shows interest and attention, and that is true. However, what does it show that's even more important than those? It shows *truth*. Surely you've ever heard someone say, "Look me in the eyes and tell me that." What are they searching for? The truth. You might be the most truthful person in the world, but guess what? Perception is reality. If you can't look your audience members directly in the eyes, they will never believe you. They will never trust you. They will never gain confidence in you, and your entire effort will be a waste.

Stop

Scanning keeps everyone engaged, involved, and trusting. However, you should not scan the entire time. Sometimes it is important to stop and look directly at one person for an entire thought or phrase. Many times, this is the main foundational phrase of your story or anchor. For example, for my story about the vice president who keeps offering me raises to stay with the company, I scan my entire audience over and over again throughout that anchor. However, when I get to my foundational phrase, I fix one person in my eyes and say, "Your dream is not for sale." I hold their gaze for that phrase and then go back to scanning the rest of the audience again. This is important, because you want very little movement when you drive home your foundational phrase. That way, everyone in your audience focuses on the words, and they feel like the world has stopped so they can hear your life-changing message. Because you have been scanning most of the time, it makes your "stop" more meaningful, and your audience members lean forward to see what's coming next.

5.   Nodding

One of the greatest strategies you can use to get and stay connected with your audience members is the nod. Go ahead and nod your head right now. I'm serious. Go ahead and nod your head. How do you feel? Don't you feel something affirmative about nodding your head? Doesn't it trigger something? World-class speakers use the nod to acknowledge their audience members. For example, let's say I ask the following question to my audience: "Have you ever stepped on a scale and been scared to face reality?" As soon as they start making grunting sounds, laughing, and reacting to the rhetorical question, I look at them and nod as if to say, "Me too." The nod *acknowledges their answer*, even if their answer isn't verbalized. We must remember that speaking is a dialogue and not a monologue. The nod breathes life into the dialogue and makes your audience members feel heard.

On the contrary, wannabe speakers ask questions and just keep talking through the answers. For example, they will ask my same question in the following way: "Have you ever stepped on a scale and been scared to face reality? I was with my six-month-old daughter ..." You might ask, "What's wrong with that?" The problem is that they do this without pausing after the question. If there is no pause, there is no nod. If there is no nod, there is no acknowledgment of the audience. If there is no acknowledgment, your audience does not feel heard. If they don't feel heard, they don't engage with the rest of the speech. Always remember that your audience wants to be heard, too. Believe it or not, a small nod goes a very long way in deepening your connection with them.

FIVE MORE ESSENTIAL DELIVERY TOOLS (TONE-RELATED)

The first five delivery strategies in this section will help you use nonverbal cues to connect deeply with your audience. The following five tools will help you deliver your lines in ways that keep the audience excited about what's coming next. There is a true art to *how* world-class speakers say what they say. The tool is called "vocal variety," but it is often misunderstood. Let's dig in.

Have you ever seen a speaker who started with a booming voice and kept booming his voice for the entire speech? Have you ever heard someone speak so fast, you couldn't catch up? Have you ever heard someone speak so slowly, you wanted to yell, "Spit it out already!"? These speakers lacked vocal variety. There are many parts to vocal variety, but let's emphasize the five most important tools you can use for the greatest impact—and the one secret behind all of them.

1. Emphasis

Let's put our ego aside for a second. Don't worry, I'm talking to me, too. Here is the truth: no matter how excellent you are as a speaker, people's minds will still wander while you speak. That's okay, especially if they're thinking about how they will act on your message. However, when you get to your most important points and phrases, it's critical to emphasize them. You can do this by putting a stress on those words and phrases that matter most.

How can you stress your words and phrases? The best strategy is to make sure you *place them in the right spots* in your sentences. Strategic placement of your most important words and phrases is crucial. Many speakers kill their would-be best phrases by putting the critical words in the wrong spot. For example, I tell a story about my movie days (I was a production assistant) and how I ended up coming face-to-face with a certain celebrity. Take a look at how I phrase part of it:

"I said, 'I loved your last movie. It's one of my favorites.' [I look out at the audience, and, with a somber voice and physical expression, I say these next lines] I have no idea what he said to me, but I'll never forget how he made me feel … [pause and slowly raise my energy] like a million bucks!"

Here is a quiz for you: what is the word or phrase that deserves the punch? Of course, it's "like a million bucks." Most of the important phrases will go toward the end of a sentence, rather than the beginning. It would have been much less dramatic if I had simply said it in the following way: "I have no idea what he said to me, but I felt like a million bucks when I left him."

Can you feel the difference? "When I left him" is not the important part of the sentence. The "like a million bucks" is what needs to be emphasized, and that's why I always put it at the end of the sentence. Always ask yourself, "What is my most important phrase? Is it in the most important spot in my sentence?" If not, rearrange it until it is. Having the punch phrase in the wrong place has the same effect as giving an incorrect punchline in a joke. Both are doomed for failure. Take a look at these two corrected examples, and then see if you can rearrange the third one for greater impact.

A. **Less impact:** "Friday is the last day you have to get this done."

   Greater impact: "The last day you have to get this done is Friday." Friday is the word that should be emphasized, because that's what needs to stick in their minds.

B. **Less impact:** "Craig, we're going to pay you three thousand and five hundred dollars for a forty-five-minute speech."

   Greater impact: "Craig, for your forty-five-minute speech, we're going to pay you three thousand and five hundred dollars." The fee of three thousand and five hundred dollars needs to be emphasized because, later in the speech, I compare that figure with the dollar value I felt I delivered. By having the three thousand and five hundred dollars fresh in my audience's mind, the contrasting dollar value I felt I delivered becomes more meaningful.

You try one.

C. Less impact: "It is the truth that you cannot handle."

Greater impact: "_____

_____."

Here are some other ways to emphasize certain words or phrases. If you have been speaking fast, slow down and drag the important phrase out slowly. If you've been speaking quietly, punch the important phrase up with your volume. If you've been moving around in your story, stop, pause, and then deliver the phrase. The visual of you stopping your movement will prompt your audience to think, "Something important is coming. I'd better hear this." There are many ways to stress a phrase. Pick what's most important for your audience to understand, and deliberately practice emphasizing it. Otherwise, nothing will stand out, and nothing will sink in.

2. Rate

In a normal conversation, do you ever find yourself getting so excited that you start talking faster than normal? On the contrary, have you ever felt somewhat subdued, and you slowed down your rate of speech? The point is that we do this in our regular conversations, so we should do them in our speeches, as well. Speeches are enlarged conversations.

What determines what your rate of speech should be? First, understand it should be different at various parts of your speech. If you are inside one of your stories, you are taking on certain characters and delivering their lines of dialogue. Some of these characters speak slower than others, and some speak faster. Once you know your characters, you discover how to deliver their lines. Then, of course, you make your point, and that is usually a good time to slow down, especially when stating your foundational phrase. For example, even though my six-figure story has its ups and downs and is very fast-paced at times, when I deliver the foundational phrase, I slow down and say, "Your dream is not for sale." With your foundational phrase, you want every word to be heard and felt. Slowing down your speech, stopping your movement, fixing a person in your gaze, and deliberately delivering your line is the best way to make that happen.

There is also another very important reason to vary your rate of speech. We have audience members who receive information in three different ways, and this affects their rate of listening.

- **Visual learners** speak rapidly and also listen at a fast pace. If you speak slowly the entire time, they will become frustrated, and their minds will wander quickly.

- **Auditory learners** speak at an average pace. If you speak too fast or too slow, you can lose them.

- **Kinesthetic learners** speak slower than average, and they are the types of people who come up to you afterwards and say, "Can you repeat parts of your message for me? You went over three points, and I only got the first one." When this happens, you know you spoke too fast for too long. If you have a tendency to speak fast, you at least have to have periods of pausing to let people catch up. You probably want to consider slowing down as well, especially if you are in a foreign country where your first language is not their first language. Ask me how I know this!

If you change your rate of speech from slow to fast to normal during your presentation and take generous pauses, you will reach all learners, and they will feel fulfilled.

3. Pitch

When you're speaking to someone one-on-one, do you ever raise your voice in excitement? Please, no details. Well, this should not stop just because you are up in front of an audience. Let your pitch go up naturally when speaking about something interesting. For example, in my six-figure story, when the vice president keeps offering me an increase in salary, I raise my pitch and say, "This is not a financial decision. This is dream decision!" I raise it to demonstrate the desperation I felt and to help the audience feel it, too. If the story calls for it, raise your pitch. At times, your point might call for it, too. Don't be afraid to show how animated your really are. Be loose.

Just as important as raising your pitch is to lower it at other times. There will be times when you calm your audience down and get them thinking deeply about something. Perhaps you start with the great hypnotic word "Imagine..." Bringing your voice down to a lower pitch provides a calming effect and helps your audience slide into a contemplative mood. It's great for the reflection piece of the PARTS formula. For example, I might lower my pitch at the end of one of my stories and say the following:

> "Are you too good to be great? Are you too comfortable with your good life to ever have a great one? In what ways, if any, are you letting the good get in the way of the best?"

4. Volume

How loud or low do you get during your speeches? I suggest going from extreme to extreme in many presentation scenarios. Move from a loud, enthusiastic voice to a voice just over a whisper. Both will help keep the attention of your audience. I have seen some speakers literally have the audience on the edges of their seats while they spoke very softly. Then they built their volume, dropped it, and built it again. This contrast kept the audience hooked. Again, the stories give you complete freedom to get as loud as you want. Then, when making your point, it's critical to come back down to a conversational level. Nobody wants to be preached to, and they will certainly feel like you're preaching if you shout your message at them. Don't shout—share.

5. Silence

If you were to ask, "Craig, what is the most important delivery tool of all?" I would say, "Hush up." No, I don't mean *you* hush up. I mean that the most important tool in delivering a speech is being willing to hush up. Pause and be silent often. When should you use these power pauses and periods of silence? Below is a list of appropriate times.

- Pause after you are introduced and before you say your first words
- Pause before and after you make an important point
- Pause when you transition from your story (or other anchor) to your point
- Pause after you ask a rhetorical question
- Pause after you ask a question to which you actually want a verbal response
- Pause when one character physically reacts to what another character says or does
- Pause when you get a laugh
- Pause when you strike a chord that makes your audience think

- Pause during the transitions outlined in the "Create Your World-Class Speech" formula
- Pause before you respond to a question from an audience member
- Pause after you finish delivering lines at a fast rate
- Pause after you make your audience reflect

Do you know why wannabe speakers don't pause enough? It's not because their audience minds; it's because *they* mind. Like Darren LaCroix says, "The speaker is uncomfortable with the silence." The audience loves it! The speaker abhors it. Therefore, if the whole reason we are speaking is to affect the lives of our audience members, shouldn't we do what they need, even if we're uncomfortable with it? World-class speakers use pauses as strategically as they use words. Pausing definitely lets the audience members taste, savor, and digest what you say before you go onto your next point. Not pausing enough is like force-feeding people who are already full. Give them a break first. Let them digest what they learned.

What you don't say and when you don't say it is often more powerful than what you do say when you do say it!

My Surprise

Have you ever been to Burlington, Vermont? It's a wonderful place, but I absolutely cannot avoid talking about them. Why? Well, if you had been in my seminar in Burlington many years ago, you would have heard me say over and over again, "Pause before and after you say something important." This is timeless advice I learned from Dale Carnegie's books. I repeated this time and time again. However, I didn't find out until later that the entire time I was saying "pause," they thought I was saying "pose."

Can you imagine what their presentations looked like? For the first person, I honestly thought she was just vain. But then the second person took the stage and did the same thing. Every time he was about to make an important point, he struck a pose! Finally I stopped them and said, "What the heck are you all doing?" That's when they said, "Craig, you told us to *pose* before and after we say something important." I have to admit, it was one of the funniest experiences I have had with public speaking.

Here's what I invite you to write down and place somewhere in a high traffic area so you can see it every day: "If you pause, it will show poise."

Do you remember how important your audience's confidence in you is to your future? Whether they invite you back, buy your products, sign up for your newsletter, or join you on future teleclasses is all determined by their level of confidence in you. There is no quicker way to have your audience build confidence in you then to show poise through your willingness to be silent. If you are comfortable enough to allow moments of silence in your speech, your audience will be very comfortable with you. That helps to establish an unbreakable connection. Work on hushing up as much as you work on speaking up.

What Is the One Secret to Using These Five Tone-Related Tools?

The key is *contrast.* Do not speak the same way the entire time. Emphasize only the important words and phrases. Speak from fast to slow. Take your pitch from high to low. Raise your volume, and then bring it down to a whisper. Speak, and then go silent. Mix it up, and you'll keep your audience up and ready for more.

How Can You Become a More Dynamic Speaker?

If you practice using contrast in the dark, it will become second nature to you in the light. What do I mean? I suggest you take a paragraph and read it aloud. Be sure to emphasize the most important words and phrases of each sentence. Then change your rate, pitch, and volume. Finally, find areas where silence works well. The key is to really overdo it. Stretch yourself so it feels unnatural. If you do this every night for no more than ten minutes, you will start to automatically use this contrast in your everyday conversations. This will extend into your speeches. Do it immediately before bedtime, because your subconscious mind will continue to work on it while you are asleep. This really works!

People ask, "Craig, have you always been a dynamic speaker? Are you naturally dynamic?" The answer is no. It is *second nature* that made me dynamic. Everything about becoming a speaker can be learned. I believe speaking is 10 percent talent and 90 percent tools. If you have the right tools and you practice using them, your second nature will kick in and grow you into a world-class speaker. Now that you have these ten essential delivery tools, let's look at some of the overlooked delivery strategies that separate world-class speakers from everybody else.

CREATE A PICTURE BY MOVING WITH A PURPOSE

Have you ever seen a speaker pacing back and forth for no reason? Why do you think the speaker does that? Chances are that the speaker is either nervous or trying to engage all sides of the audience. However, what the speaker is really doing is making the speech unclear. Speaking is about *clarity*, and moving without a purpose destroys that. In order to add clarity to your speech and impact to your message, it's critical to move with a purpose.

How Can You Use Movement and Staging to Add Emotion and Impact to Your Speech?

Most speakers I have seen seem to give very little thought to how they use the stage. They concentrate so much on their content and their vocal variety, but they either forget or neglect to use the stage to their benefit. They need to understand what my speech coach, Patricia Fripp, told me. She said that "people won't remember what you say as much as they'll remember what they see when you say it." In other words, it's absolutely critical to make your speech visual. Create pictures (not with slides), and draw the audience into them. There are three major purposes for moving on stage. They are:

1. Action
2. Timeline
3. Structuring the stage

Action

First, the action in your story prompts the movement in your speech. For example, if the character in my story walks to the front of a boat, I demonstrate that by walking to wherever the front of the boat is represented on the stage. It's important for me to create the scene of the boat and then stick to it. Therefore, I should know exactly where the front of the boat is, where my wife is standing next to me, where another major character is, and, most importantly, where the boat ends. Once I create that scene, I must commit to it. This means I have to remember where I placed everyone and everything on the stage. Otherwise, the audience will get confused.

A Grave Example

For example, at one of my speaking boot camps, a camper gave a speech in which his uncle died. He correctly made a place on the stage for the casket and walked over to say his last words to that uncle. However, later on in the story, he brought us into a scene where he was having lunch. The problem was that he must have forgotten where he had placed everything. Finally, I had to stop him and say, "Do you realize you just had lunch on top of your uncle?"

My friend Darren LaCroix says we need to set up "holograms" and remember where we place them on the stage. The key to these holograms is that you can easily call back to them visually and verbally. For example, the gentleman who spoke about his uncle could have called back later in the story by saying, "Just like when my uncle passed away," and then pointed, with an open hand, to that specific spot on the stage. This adds clarity and impact. His audience will remember the touching scene and, believe it or not, begin to imagine his uncle on that part of the stage.

When I am on the swamp tour (the boat), I tell my audience, "I walked to the front of the boat to get sodas." I walk across the stage to demonstrate. Then I gesture as if I'm reaching down into a cooler. Because I have set up the scene, I never have to tell them what I'm doing. I never have to mention a cooler. Why? It's because they see it and it's clear to them. Then I walk back to where I was, and my audience still knows my wife is to my left and another important character (who looks like a surfer dude) is to my right. Once the scene is set, the action prompts your movement. That's one purpose for moving. If you're telling a story about standing in line, chances are you shouldn't be doing much moving.

Timeline

Another purpose for moving is to create a timeline out of the floor. For example, if you give a speech that's sequential, make the first part of the speech happen at the beginning of your timeline. Remember that everything you do has to be backwards, so that it can be accurate from your audience's point of view. For example, they read a timeline from the left to the right. Therefore, you must move to your right (their left) to be at the start of the timeline. Then you can tell a story and sell a point in that spot. Afterwards, you want to make a transition statement while also physically transitioning. For example, you might say, "Fast-forward with me seven years." While you say that, you can physically walk a few steps to your left (your audience's right). That way, you have moved verbally and visually up the timeline.

In that new spot, you might tell another story and sell another point. Once finished, you can use another transitional phrase, such as "… and over the next two decades, I …" Of course, as you do this, you will also physically walk a few more steps up the timeline. Again, you transition visually and verbally.

Finally, as you get to that third spot, you use another story and sell your third point. This is where it gets interesting. If you've been counting, how many points do you have? How many spots on the floor do you have? That's right, there are three for both. This is where you can use one of the most powerful emotional-trigger-producing techniques, called the "call back." As you know, the call back helps your audience remember your message. However, if you call back both visually and verbally to the various stories, characters, and points along the timeline, your audience can fill up with emotional as well.

For example, at the conclusion of my speech, I might call back by saying, "And just like when I was ten years old and realized that life is not fair …" I visually gesture over to the spot where the ten-year-old story happened. Then I'd say, "And like when I was a teenager and came to understand that life won't give you more until you do something with what you already have …" I point to that spot, as well, as I give that line. Finally, I might say, "And just like I understand today, life ..." and I stand in the spot and conclude my speech. If you use call backs visually and verbally like this, by calling back to spots on the timeline, that will become a speech I will pay to see. More importantly, that will become a speech you will get paid to give. Using the floor as a timeline is another purpose for moving onstage.

Structuring the Stage

Using the stage to help set your structure will make your ideas very clear to your audience. For example, if you have three points to your speech, you might give a big promise like this:

In the next forty-five minutes, you will pick up tools to keep your very next audience on the edge of their seats. First, you'll find tools to breathe life into your speech and captivate your audience. Next, you'll uncover methods to bring your audience to you and keep them engaged. Finally, you'll walk away with the tools to build a message that sticks, so that you get called back over and over again.

Do you see the three major benefits there? Well, with each benefit (section) comes a spot on the stage. When I go to the first point about breathing life into your speech, I say that from the audience's left. When I say, "Next, you'll uncover ..." I walk to the middle of the stage and deliver that line. Then, when I say, "Finally, you'll walk away with ..." I move again to the audience's right and deliver that line. Now they not only hear a message with three benefits, they see it too. Always think, "How can I use the stage floor to help create a picture out of my content?" The floor becomes a kind of mental, graphic organizer that your audience can use to better retain your message. Using the floor to set up the structure for your speech will do wonders for the clarity. Plus, you'll have great call-back opportunities as you move along with the speech.

IF EVERYTHING IS MOVING, NOTHING IS MOVING

If you highlighted every sentence on this page, nothing would stand out, right? That's what happens when you constantly move while you speak. Nothing stands out. When you move with a purpose, your movements start to mean something. You can use them to add emphasis, impact, emotion, and clarity, and they won't get lost in a sea of constant motion. If you master your staging, you will have a great chance to really own the stage and spellbind your audience. Move with a purpose.

MAKE THEM FEEL YOU ARE SPEAKING DIRECTLY TO THEM

Imagine speaking in front of an audience of two hundred people in a packed hotel ballroom, and you're about to say your first words. With your first question, you want to get a feel for the number of people who have ever been to Baltimore in their lives. Do me a favor and write down the question, exactly how you would phrase it to this group of two hundred people:

Question: _____

_____?

Before we move on, you need to understand that the tool you are about to pick up is what's called a "slight-edge principle." That means it is a slight change in the way you do something that makes a significant difference in the impact you have on your audience. I can't emphasize its importance enough. However, I feel complete conviction in saying that if you carry this tool throughout your entire speech, you'll feel a connection deeper than you ever felt before. Are you ready?

When your audience members leave your speech, hopefully at the end, which one of the following thoughts do you want them to have?

A. "Wow, I really felt like I was part of a group."

B. "Wow, it really felt like she was speaking directly to me!"

Which one do you want, A or B? Surely you want B. When I bring participants up to demonstrate this in front of my audiences, this is how they usually phrase the Baltimore question: "How many of you have ever been to Baltimore?" Did you phrase it that way, too? When my participants phrase the question that way, how many people are they speaking to? They are speaking to everybody. How many people should they speak to? They should speak to one. Okay, I can hear you asking, "How can you just speak to one when there are two hundred people in the room?" Well, let me answer your question with a question. Can my participants rephrase the Baltimore question to make it sound and feel like they are speaking to one person rather than to two hundred? How can they do it? Write down a couple of ways:

Question: _____

_____?

Question: _____

_____?

Here are the new, rephrased responses I usually receive:

"Have you ever been to Baltimore?"

"Raise your hand if you have ever been to Baltimore?"

Do you notice anything about these two new, rephrased questions? They sound and feel like you are speaking to one person rather than two hundred. Here is the key that you should write down, frame, and place in a high-traffic area: speak to one, but look to all.

Too Many Speakers Speak to Too Many People

Too many speakers are speaking to far too many people. It manifests itself in many ways, so you must be very careful and deliberate about the words you choose. See if any of the following phrases sound somewhat familiar to you:

1. Ladies and gentlemen, you …
2. How many of you have …
3. I want you all to know that …
4. We should leave here today …
5. Everyone in here has a special gift …
6. Have any of you ever been …
7. Those of you who have …
8. All of us here today are …
9. Thank you all for coming …
10. Some of you might think …

These speakers might as well be yelling, "Friends, Romans, countrymen …" It's the same thing. Each audience member should walk away from your speech thinking, "He was speaking to me." That will build their confidence in you quickly. Don't speak to everyone, speak to one and look to all. That means you use your eyes to scan and connect with everyone while you use your words to make it feel you are speaking to each of them as an individual. For example, I ask, "Have you ever been to Baltimore?" As I ask the question, I scan the audience and raise my hand, because I have been to Baltimore. Those who have been to Baltimore automatically raise their hands, too. Each person feels I am speaking directly to him or her.

Let's take another look at the ten statements above and rephrase them so that you can speak to one but look to all. Look back at each of the statements, and then look at the new statement in its place.

1. You ...

   Note: Get rid of the "Ladies and gentlemen." It is not needed. Speak to one.

2. Have you ...

3. I want you to know ...

4. You should leave here today ...

5. You have a special gift ...

6. Have you ever been to ...

7. If you have ... or you might have ...

8. You are here today ...

9. Thank you for coming ...

10. You might think ...

THE HALLWAY TEST

This issue of speaking to too many people manifests in many different ways, so I have come up with a surefire test to ensure you are speaking to one and looking to all. I call it "the Hallway Test." If you can walk up to one person in a hallway, say your line, and have it sound correct, you will pass the test. For example, wouldn't it be strange if I walked up to you in a hallway and asked, "How many of you have ever been to Baltimore?" You might look at me and say, "Hey buddy, I'm only one person. Why are you acting like I am with a group?" That line fails the test.

However, what if I walk up to you in the hallway and ask, "Have you ever been to Baltimore?" That would sound okay, right? That line passes the test. Would it sound correct for me to walk up to you and say, "Ladies and gentlemen?" Based on your level of security, you might even feel offended.

That line fails the test. Therefore, it is not needed. Instead, use the most important word in speaking, which is the word "you." Whatever you do with the delivery of your speech, make sure you refrain making each person feel like only a grain of sand. Instead, make them feel like they are the ocean. Connect to each one individually by speaking to one and looking to all.

MORE DELIVERY HELP

I admit the "speak to one, but look to all" concept is more difficult to explain here than it is to explain in person or on video. Therefore, for a complete visual understanding of how to use this tool to connect deeply with each member of your audience, visit www.wcspeaking.com and review my "Own the Stage DVD Set." This set demonstrates dozens of delivery tools you can use to captivate your audience, own the stage, and keep them wanting more.

BE YOU, BUT ENLARGED

What does it mean to be an enlarged version of yourself? Well, imagine whispering a secret in someone's ear. Will they hear it? Sure. But if you whisper in one person's ear, the rest of your audience probably will not hear it. Therefore, you must exaggerate as if you're whispering in the entire *audience's* ear. Also, take your gestures, for example. If you have a small group, you can use small gestures, and they will still see you. They will even pick up the slightest smirk you make. However, with a larger audience, you will need to use larger gestures and a more definitive smirk in order for them to perceive what you're doing. The larger the audience, the larger you must become with your gestures, your voice, and your facial expressions. Don't mismatch your size with the size of your audience. If you do, you'll suffer from a definite disconnect, even if your message is brilliant.

HOW NOT TO USE GESTURES

I wish you would have been sitting next to me in an audience in 1999, watching a man give a speech on how to use gestures when presenting. You wouldn't have believed your eyes. He said, "You must be very deliberate about the gestures you use. It's very important that you use gestures to help make your point." As soon as he said the word "point," he literally pointed his index finger at the audience. Then he said, "Gestures will help your audience think." As soon as he said "think," his thumb went on his chin with that forefinger extended to his cheek as if he was thinking. He continued, "That is how you will get your audience into the palm of your hand." As soon as he said "hand," he pointed his forefinger of one hand to the palm of his other hand as if we needed a visual of where the palm of our hand is. I thought back to Dale Carnegie's words about being natural, and I had to laugh to myself. This particular speaker was the most unnatural gesturer I had ever seen! Everything was so contrived and so obvious. No wonder he didn't connect that day.

HOW TO USE GESTURES

You know by now to use gestures that are natural for you. I heard a story once about the late Cal Ripken Sr., the former third-base coach for the Baltimore Orioles. A former classmate of mine attended one of Mr. Ripken's speeches and said that his gestures in his speech were similar to the gestures he used as a third-base coach for the Orioles. My response to that was, "Maybe that's his natural way." I asked if those gestures were distracting and the guy said, "No. They actually kept my attention." I would look silly using those kinds of gestures, because they are not natural to me. Mr. Ripken's gestures actually added value to his speech, because those gestures were natural to him.

Although we must be natural with our gestures, there are ten general guidelines to consider when using them:

1. **Don't use the same gesture over and over again.** This is evidence of a habit and most likely distracts from your presentation.

2. **Watch out for your resting position.** This is the position your hands fall to when you're not using a gesture. For example, my hands used to fall together in front of me with my fingers interlocking. It was distracting.

3. **Don't move all the time.** If you are always moving, then no movement will be meaningful. Your audience will never know what's most important. Move with a purpose. When there is no reason to move, don't.

4. **Use your characters' gestures.** Keep in mind that speaking is utilizing captivating stories to make your points. Each story has its own characters, and each character probably has his or her own way of gesturing. When you take on the role and persona of that character, you should use his or her gestures.

5. **Let the emotions drive.** The emotions in your story and in your point will drive your movements. If you are intoxicated with your emotions while telling your story or making your point, the

appropriate gestures will come. It will be effortless. When you're really angry at someone or something, do you have to think about what gestures to use? No, they come automatically. If you build the emotion, the gestures will come.

6. **Use an open hand.** It's better to point to your audience with an open hand rather than an index finger. It's less threatening and more inviting. The open hand is also effective when calling back to spots on the floor as you revisit the points, characters, and stories you previously used.

7. **Gesture 360 Degrees.** Many speakers gesture in front of them and on the side. World-class speakers realize there is an entire area around them, and they utilize it. Feel free to gesture down for the lower dimension. For example, when I speak about a swamp tour my wife and I took, I talk about the alligators that surrounded the boat. At that point, I gesture downward with the open hand. Then I describe the trees that were hanging down as if they were trying to grab onto us. At that point, I gesture upward to the upper dimension, using my hands to emulate how the trees hung and swayed. At times, I point behind me to the back of the stage or in front of me out into the audience. I might point to my right to signify the past and point to my left to signify the future as I use the stage as a timeline. The key is to go up, down, back, forth, and side to side in order to paint a whole (surround-sense) scene for your audience—in order to invite them into it.

8. **Use bigger gestures for bigger audiences.** Don't mismatch the size of your audience with the size of your gestures.

9. **Don't forget about your face.** Your facial expressions are more important than any hand or arm movement you make. The eyes are indeed the windows to the soul. What you do with them can make or break your entire speech.

10. **Smile.**

MEET THEM WHERE THEY ARE

Have you ever witnessed the following scenario? There's a room filled with somewhat-subdued audience members waiting for their next speaker. The energy is low, and the room is quiet. The audience is, at best, laid back. After the speaker is introduced, he grabs the microphone and, with all the energy and enthusiasm he can muster, shouts, "Hey, how are you? Are you ready to get started? Okay—let's go!" Be honest: if you were in that audience, what would you do? Mentally, you would probably look for the nearest exit.

Let's look at Scenario number two. Picture a highly energetic audience awaiting their next speaker. They are pumped up and ready for the speaker. Then the speaker takes the stage and, with a very low, monotone, and unenthusiastic voice, says, "I'm so happy to be here. I just can't wait to get started." Again, they are looking for the nearest exit. Why? They want to leave, because the speaker has mismatched the energy of the audience.

YOU MUST MATCH THE ENERGY OF YOUR AUDIENCE

One of the biggest reasons and quickest ways speakers lose audiences is by neglecting to *match their energy*. You must match the energy of your audience at the very beginning of your speech. If it's a low-key audience, come out more low-key than usual. If it's a highly energetic audience, come out with more energy. The key is to *meet them where they are.* Now, here's the best part: once you match their energy and meet them where they are, you can take them wherever you want them to go. The key is to connect with them at their level first. In NLP (Neuro-Linguistic Programming) this is called "pacing and leading." Match their energy, and then lead them where you want them to go.

For example, when I notice a somewhat-subdued audience, I will usually take the stage, stand completely still, and say, in a low-key way, "When I was in prison ... visiting." This gets a laugh, and I continue on their energy level for a while so that we can connect where they are. If the audience is more pumped up, I will come out with visible energy, stand still and say with lots of excitement "You have to understand ... when I was in prison ... visiting." It can be the same content but with a different level of energy in your delivery. So the next logical question is how do you assess the energy level of your audience? Here are two ways.

Two Ways to Gauge the Energy Level of Your Audience

1. Watch the other speakers before you, and see the responses they get. You might notice that it is not a highly energetic audience. You might also notice that you have to slow down because they don't speak English very well. Take one guess how I know this!

2. Watch your audience during your introduction. Darren LaCroix puts a humorous line in his to see what kind of effect it has on his audience This helps him assess where they are. In fact, one time Darren's introducer gave the line, which always gets a good laugh, yet

this particular time, it was met with complete silence. Darren then turned to the speakers-bureau representative and whispered, "This is going to suck." At least he knew what he was dealing with, and he was able to adjust. He adjusted so well that, after his speech, a long line formed at his product table. He signed book after book after book and wondered, "Are you the same audience I just spoke to?" Find ways to watch your watchers and listen to your listeners. If you match them where they are, you'll find your connection to be nearly unbreakable. You'll connect immediately.

If you don't make the effort to meet them where they are, then you'll basically be speaking to yourself. After all, if you come to pick me up at the airport, and I'm at the train station, we'll never meet. You must meet them where they are first and then take them to your intentional destination.

TAKE ADVANTAGE OF GROUP DYNAMICS

Have you ever walked into a room that felt dead in terms of energy? Unfortunately, this is the case sometimes as a speaker. The worst is when you have a venue that is much too big for the number of people attending. For example, if you have an auditorium or ballroom that holds five hundred people and fifteen people show up, the energy will be strange. In that case, you have some work to do. Here's what I recommend. Gather the attendees together in one spot rather than having them spread around the auditorium. Remember that people act differently alone than they do within a group. If they sit by themselves, they probably will not be as vocal or as eager to laugh. However, when they sit aside others, they will easily lose themselves in the group and let go of their self-consciousness. Gather those folks together and build the energy.

REMOVE THE EMPTY SEATS

Look at it almost as if you're gathering sticks to make a fire. The only way you'll ignite them is by getting them close to each other and delivering a dynamic speech. If possible, remove the surrounding empty seats so the attendees don't say to themselves, "Man, why did I even show up? Obviously, nobody else did. What do they know that I don't?" This is surely not the mindset you want them to have as you begin.

A good way to accomplish gathering them together without demanding is by placing handouts where you want them to sit. Usually, they'll get the hint and sit in those spots. Whatever you do, work hard to gather that energy and ignite that audience. Occasionally, you won't have a choice, and you'll just have to do your best. Once, in Ohio, I did a two-day training session, and one person showed up! This made it difficult to do group work. It felt strange getting to the activities and asking, "Any volunteers?" This is the exception. Most of the time, you'll be able to gather the energy and ignite your audience.

THREE WAYS TO BRING YOUR AUDIENCE BACK FROM THE DEAD

You will lose an audience eventually. Any speaker that says he has never lost an audience just hasn't spoken enough. Whether we know it or not, we do lose audiences. Sometimes it's more obvious than others. For example, when I once spoke at a high school and the students faked snoring out loud, I obviously knew I lost them. So, have you ever lost an audience? What did you do to get them back?

HERE'S THE ISSUE WITH LOSING YOUR AUDIENCE

If you lose your audience, and you simply stay on the same track, you will crash and burn. Do you know what that means? It means you must do something to get them back. Here, you will pick up three world-class-speaking tools you can use to not only get your audience back but to make your connection even stronger.

THE THREE "BRING 'EM BACK" TOOLS

I learned something within the last two years that by not knowing before probably hindered my career as a speaker. I would venture to say that the majority of professional speakers do not know the truth and impact of the following statement: If you are always dynamic, you are no longer dynamic.

That's right; we've been taught to be dynamic speakers who regularly use vocal variety and change our stress, rate, pitch, volume, and pauses, right? Well, guess what? If we stay dynamic the *entire* time, we are no longer dynamic. We have fallen into what I heard Patricia Fripp call "sameness." Our constant "dynamic ways" have become sameness, and the audience tunes out sameness no matter how dynamic it is. Does that make sense? It will when you test it out.

So what do we do about this sameness? First, reflect on this quote by an anonymous author: "He who sleeps in noise awakens in silence."

Sometimes the only way to bring your audience back is to completely remove the spice from your presentation. Take all the mustard off of it and "make it plain." That's right, you're about to read a speaking suggestion that nobody else will dare ask you to do. Here it is: temporarily take all the vocal variety out of your presentation. This means to make it as plain as possible, almost as if you are having a quiet conversation with your spouse while trying not to wake your sleeping baby. Don't do this for long, just long enough to draw them back in. This is needed for your audience at times. It's counterintuitive, because we think, "Oh no, I'm losing them ... I've gotta get more energy and get in their face to get them back." No, many times you need to do just the opposite. Do what I call "drop and draw." Drop your variety and draw them in.

"BRING 'EM BACK" TOOL NUMBER ONE: DROP AND DRAW

When you are in your stories, it's great to be dynamic. However, when you begin transitioning to sell your points, your tone should be much more conversational. I never knew that being dynamic could be a bad thing. In the past, I delivered my points in the same exact manner as my stories: with lots of energy and vocal variety. Now I understand that if noise is constant, people pay attention to silence. People will always pay attention to *change* and *contrast*. When you take off all the spice, you are definitely showing a contrast.

Three Ps to Go with Your First Tool

So here's what you can do bring them back with the drop-and-draw method. When you come out of your anchor (story, activity, anecdote, analogy, or whatever you use) and have conversations with your audience, use the following three Ps:

1. **Pause** to get their attention.

2. **Plain talk**. Bring your vocal variety down to a baseline level, take off all the spice, and make it plain.

3. **Pitch**. Speak with a slightly lower pitch if possible. I've been reading a new book, entitled *NeuroMarketing*, by Patrick Renvoise and Christophe Morin. If you turn to page 158, halfway down the page, you will read the following: "Research has proven that a voice with a lower pitch is more persuasive." I've always believed this, but now there is research to back it up. So when you get to these profound parts of your speech, lower your pitch.

Think of this almost like a *secret* you're telling your audience and you don't want the rest of the world to hear. Draw them in with your pause, your plain talk, and your pitch. This breaks up the sameness, and you'll be astonished to see everybody quickly locked back into your speech with their eyes and ears. You'll immediately feel the connection strengthening.

What Can Be Your Main Use for This?

I use it mostly during the Transition Tease you learned about in chapter two. For example, in my transition I say, "If you implement this next tool, you will find yourself walking toward your dreams and goals even while you sleep. The serendipity, grace, and providence will show up, and the wind will be at your back, pushing you almost effortlessly toward the life you desire." I say this plain as if I'm simply stating a matter of fact. I use it to build up the benefits to draw them into the next section.

Think of the *Rocky* movies. Although the fights and training scenes are legendary and certainly dynamic, the movies do not stay at that level of "sameness." Instead, they take all the punch out of the next scene and bring the tone way down. They go to a scene in which Rocky speaks quietly to his wife. These scenes draw us in as much as the fight scenes, because being plain contrasts with the dynamics of the rest of the speech. Audiences pay attention to contrast.

This baseline level is good for profound thoughts, anyway. It keeps all our attention on your words. Like Dale Carnegie once said, "A good speaker should be like a good window. He should not draw attention to himself, just let the light through." Of course, the light is the message, and it will shine through effectively when you are out of your own way. Make the shift from your anchor to delivering parts of your message in a plain, spiceless way.

"BRING 'EM BACK" TOOL NUMBER TWO: FLEXIBILITY

The second tool you can use to bring them back is flexibility. At times, an American-football quarterback will call a play and then bring his team up to the line of scrimmage to run that play. Then, he analyzes the defensive formation and decides to change the play right there on the spot. This is what's known as "calling an audible." It takes flexibility and courage, but the results are often tremendous.

At times, you will have a game plan, look out over your audience, and realize they are drifting away from you. Guess what? It's time to call an audible. It's time to change the play right there on the spot. It takes courage, but your results can also be tremendous. You must be flexible enough to change your game plan in mid-speech, and you can do this best by re-sequencing your anchors. As you recall, anchors are the tools you attach to your points so that people will remember them. Again, the four main types of anchors you can use regularly are the four A's:

1. Anecdotes (stories)
2. Analogies
3. Activities
4. Acronyms

When you listen to your listeners and watch your watchers, you definitely notice when they start to drift off and disconnect. If I see this in my audience, I might have a story that's supposed to come up next, but I immediately switch to an activity instead. Why? It's because I need the audience members to get their physical-energy level back up before I go into that story. In another instance, I might have an analogy that's supposed to come up next, but I replace it with my story instead. This is because the audience needs an emotional tug. Hence, the concrete story comes first, followed by the more abstract analogy.

You must be confident enough to be flexible with your anchors. Wannabe speakers stick to the script regardless of what's happening with their audience. World-class speakers *analyze and adjust* on the spot. That's why it pays handsomely to use the PARTS formula for every single point you make and to be flexible with the sequence of those anchors. Using this modular approach effectively helps you get your audiences back quickly and deepens your connection with them. Analyze and adjust. The key is to manage your programs by the *energy level*. Constantly analyze where the audience is in terms of energy, and then adjust to bring them back where they should be. Don't be afraid to call an audible. You just might score big!

"BRING 'EM BACK" TOOL NUMBER THREE: SHARE YOUR FAILURES

You've already learned this tool, but now you will gain an understanding of the most important time to use it. One surefire way you can get your audience back, without fail, is to share your failures. Believe me, this *always* pulls your audience back in. They absolutely love to take delight in your failures. Wannabe speakers share success after success. World-class speakers share failures and successes and, most importantly, the lessons learned in between. Your key is to plan points in your speech where you share these failures. If you lose your audience before you get to those points in your speech, consider moving the stories up, because they will bring your audience back quickly. Sprinkle these failures throughout your speech. You will connect deeper than you ever knew you could, until you feel the bond is unbreakable.

HERE ARE THE "BRING 'EM BACK" TOOLS FOR YOUR TOOL-BELT:

- Take all the spice off
- Be flexible with your anchors
- Share your failures

If you use these three tools, you will have much less chance of losing your audience. However, if you happen to lose them, you will have a much greater chance at getting them back quickly. Speaking is about connection. Nothing happens if you don't connect. Use these tools to connect and to inspire. And remember: he who sleeps in noise awakens in silence.

USE HANDOUTS THAT MAKE THEM THINK, NOT MEMORIZE

World-class speakers use handouts that add value to their audience members. Wannabe speakers use the kinds of handouts we received in the fourth grade. Surely you have received fill-in-the-blanks handouts. Let me ask you a question about those types of handouts. Do they force you to listen or invite you to *reflect?*

ARE THEY LISTENING OR REFLECTING?

This is the question you need to ask yourself as you put your handouts together. The most effective handouts don't make people listen for a word and fill in a blank. That's elementary. The most effective handouts invite people to think about what was said and realize how they can *apply* it to improve their own condition. That's world-class.

When your audience members go back home, how often do you think they'll read over a document that has nothing but fill-in-the-blanks on it? The reason people don't usually review those kinds of notes is because the notes are useless. Plus, the audience members were not really involved in creating them. On the contrary, if they have *their own* notes, ideas, and strategies written on your handout, how often do you think they will review them? Chances are that instead of memorizing your fill-in-the-blanks, they will internalize their findings and act on them. That's effective. You want to make your audiences TALL (Think, Act, Laugh, and Learn), and this type of handout will lead to them taking action.

Sure-fire Speaking Success

*"Of the modes of persuasion furnished by the spoken word there are three kinds. The first kind depends on the personal **character** of the speaker; the second on putting the audience into a certain **frame of mind**; the third on the **proof**, or apparent proof, provided by the words of the speech itself."*
Aristotle (384 B.C. – 322 B.C.)

Tool 1:   Commit to the S_____

Tool 2:   Give your characters a chance

     ...to be s_____
     ...to be k_____
     ...to be h_____

Great d_____ = Great story

Tool 3:   Let the river run through it

Tool 4:   Be specific!

Tool 5:   What keeps our message from sticking with them?

Bonus Tool: Access the 37-second window

Get the tools to make your next audience T.A.L.L. (Think, Act, Laugh, and Learn)! Get two **FREE**
15-minute audio lessons (sent to you IMMEDIATELY via e-mail) by signing up for my **FREE** bi-monthly
e-newsletter at...

www.craigvalentine.com

Figure 4-1

How to Keep Your Audiences on the Edge of Their Seats!

"I learned more from you in one hour than I have in years of giving speeches. You are a master of your game. Thank you for inspiring me to find my own voice and greatness as a speaker!! Thank you!"

Pele Raymond Ugboajah; Author, Speaker, Business Coach
DreamBanc, L.L.C

A. Breathe Life into your Speech

1. _____
2. _____
3. _____

B. Bring your Audience to You

1. _____
2. _____
3. _____

C. Build a Message that Sticks

1. _____
2. _____
3. _____

"I gave the speech last Monday and everyone raved about it. Thank you so much for your help. I went in very confident, knowing it was a very good speech... In fact, they hope to get me back again and several said they want to find out where else I'm speaking so they can come hear me again."

Christine Duvivier
Managing Director, Impact Partners

Figure 4-2

Wrong vs. Right

Take a look at figure 4-1 and let's discuss what is wrong with it. Then, let's compare it to figure 4-2 and see why this kind of handout works better. I have used both of these and, since I've been using figure 4-2, everything from the impact I have on my audiences to the income I generate from them has grown substantially. Let's dive into the differences, starting with the Rule of Three.

The Rule of Three

Looking at figure 4-1, you can see I have outlined six tools my audience will pick up from my speech. Even in a fifty-minute speech, six major points can seem like a squeeze. Plus, what happens if, to make up time, they cut my speech to thirty minutes? Do I take a pair of scissors and cut the handouts in half? If I have six points on there, my audience expects me to cover all six, no matter how little a bit of time I have.

The solution is to go with the Rule of Three. As you know, people remember best in threes. You can see from figure 4-2 that I have three main sections that each have three lines for my audience members to jot down their notes. Hopefully, they will not jot down what I said; rather, they will jot down what they *think* about how to *apply* it. Separating them into groups of three helps my audience sort through and apply them easier. As with everything in public speaking, we must search for clarity. The Rule of Three makes your structure very clear.

The Title

Can you tell me the main difference between the title on figure 4-1 and the title on figure 4-2? Okay, let's ask it this way. With the title "From Lackluster to Blockbuster Storytelling," what is missing? Let's review. What is the most important word in speaking? Shouldn't it be somewhere in the title? "How to Keep Your Audiences on the Edge of Their Seats" has a form of "you" in it, and that makes a difference. From the very beginning, let the audience know your presentation is about them.

Testimonials

You must realize that your handouts are supposed to be marketing pieces. Sure, they help your audience organize your message. Sure, they help your audience make realizations that can help them improve their condition. Sure, they give your audience valuable takeaway techniques. However, these handouts should also start building confidence in them and *selling them on your processes* before you even take the stage. That's right: your handouts should start selling them before you even say one word. You can accomplish this by using testimonials on your handouts.

The kinds of testimonials you use will make or break the confidence your audiences have in you. The wrong kinds to use are those that say how great you are, but don't say anything about the results they've been able to achieve by using your tools. The right kinds to use are those that are results-based and come from those who are *similar* to the people in your audience. If Bill Cosby gave me a testimonial, that would do wonders for my prestige and credibility. However, it wouldn't do much to give my audience members hope. Why? Bill Cosby is not similar to them. Admittedly, I would paste that one everywhere! Rules can be broken. It's best, though, to have testimonials that show the results of working with you and using your special processes.

Don't Listen, Think!

There I was, riding in my car, listening to a speaker named Charlie "Tremendous" Jones. As his CD played, I had no idea I was about to hear one of the most precious and important lessons I ever picked up in all my years of learning. He advised us not to listen and memorize, but to *think and realize.* In other words, we shouldn't simply listen and write down what the speaker says. Instead, we should write down what we *think* when the speaker says it. We should take notes on how the ideas the speaker gives us can apply to our lives. When we do this, we can take home meaningful ideas and follow up on them. Ever since hearing Charlie, I have used this advice with every book I have read and every speaker I have heard.

As a speaker, are you prompting your audience members to listen and write down what you say, or are you inviting them to think and realize what will make a difference for them? The fill-in-the-blanks handout you see in figure 4-1 does not require thought as much as it requires listening. Using that form only distracts my audience by giving them a certain word for which to listen, which effectively shuts them off from realizing anything else that can benefit them. Yes, I know it's a form of active listening, but, ironically, it leads to inactivity once they leave.

On the other hand, figure 4-2 still gives a structured outline but also provides my audience members with the freedom to write whatever they feel is most important in each section. They are not distracted by listening for one certain word or phrase. Instead, they take down the meaningful notes that lead to them acting on my message. They will do the same with yours if you give them this critical freedom.

Easy Tweaking

Of course the side benefit for you is that you can easily tweak your presentation from sixty to thirty minutes, without skipping a beat, if necessary.

Nobody will approach you and say, "What about tool number five?" Instead, they will get what they get from your three sections and will not feel like they have missed something. Give your audience credit for being intelligent enough to hear your message and determine what they should take out of it. After all, you're there for them, and only they know what they need. People buy into what they help create. Make them part of the process, and watch as they buy into a message they can use in their life.

Build Your Handouts on Benefits!

Finally, the most important difference between figure 4-1 and figure 4-2 is that the latter is built on benefits. Let's begin with the title: "How to Keep Your Audiences on the Edge of Their Seats" is a benefit-driven title. The title alone lets the audience know what's in it for them to attend. Then, each of the three major sections is broken into its own specific benefit. First, you (my audience) will pick up tools to *breathe life into your speech*. Then, you'll uncover strategies to *bring your audience to you*. Finally, you'll grasp ways to *build a speech that sticks*. With the title and the three benefit-driven sections, my audience is somewhat hooked before I even begin speaking. If you plan to fire up the interest in your audience before, during, and after you speak, use a benefit-driven handout of your own.

One Last Critical Thought on Handouts

Do not have people pass out your handouts during your presentation, especially if it is a keynote speech or a speech under one hour. If it's a one- or two-day seminar, you can hand them out during the breaks. However, passing them out during the presentation takes your audience members' focus off your presentation and onto the unwanted distraction. Either have the handouts waiting for them on their chairs or tables as they sit down, or don't hand them out until the entire presentation is finished. It might seem strange to hand them out afterwards, but that's okay if it's less of a note-taking page and more of a summary of your presentation. Therefore, they don't need it during the presentation, but they can simply take it home and use it to reflect and follow through on your message.

Speaking Is a Dialogue, Not a Monologue

When holding presentation boot camps, one of the biggest problems we see with speakers is that they have a monologue and not a dialogue with their audiences. How do we know? Consider this as an example: A speaker gets up and knows that opening a speech with a question is a very good way to start. So she says the following:

> "Have you ever worked hard on a project that failed? How did it make you feel? Well, in the year 2000, I went to …"

Now, you might ask, "What in the world is wrong with that?" The problem is not in the content; it is in the delivery. Here is how the questions should be delivered:

> "Have you ever worked hard on a project that failed? [Pause, pause, acknowledge, pause] How did it make you feel? [Pause, pause, acknowledge, pause] Well, in the year 2000, I went to …"

So many speakers ask questions and never wait for the audience to respond. You might ask, "Well, aren't those rhetorical questions?" Yes, they are. However, you still must wait for your audience members to respond in their minds. They need to chew on the question and digest it before you continue speeding through to your next thought. When you speed through it, you are having a monologue. Always remember this: Your audience is speaking, too! Your audience wants to be heard, too!

Too many speakers disregard the pause, which is one of the most powerful tools in speaking. You should pause when you get laughter. Let the audience laugh, because that is one way they are speaking to you. Pause when you get hums. Hums come when you say something very powerful and poignant. When they hum, this is another way they are speaking to you. Pause when you change from one point to another, so that you audience can digest the previous point. Pause when you change from one scene to another, so that your audience can adjust with you. Pause, pause, pause, pause, and pause.

WHAT HAPPENS IF YOU DON'T LET THEM SPEAK?

If you do not let your audience speak, they will shut up. After they shut up, they will shut down. After they shut down, your speech is over, even if you keep talking. For example, if you generate laughter but then step on that laughter by speaking before they finish laughing, guess what happens? They will not laugh as long next time. If you do it a few times, they will stop laughing completely. Why? Because you did not let them be heard, too. In a sense, you trained them not to laugh. The same goes for stepping on thoughts. They will stop thinking and tune you out. Let them be heard, and they will listen to you forever.

Here are seven tools you can use to let your audiences be heard, too:

1. Pause after you ask questions, whether rhetorical or not.

2. Pause after you give a powerful statement that makes your audience think deeply.

3. Nod and acknowledge when someone in the audience says something that adds to your presentation.

4. Repeat questions that your audience asks, so that everyone else in your audience can hear them.

5. Watch your audience, and see when they have inquisitive looks.

6. Regularly use the names of audience members to keep them engaged and make them feel special.

7. React to the reactions you get from them. Listen to your listeners. Watch your watchers.

HAVE A CONVERSATION WITH YOUR AUDIENCE

One of the problems presenters have with connecting is getting past their own perception of what a speaker is. For example, many times, I have sat across from someone and had a wonderful conversation that flowed naturally. Then, this person is called upon to speak. As they approach the podium, I can see their demeanor change. They go from this natural conversationalist to a robotic, oratorical JFK wannabe. Then they take the microphone, and in a voice that is emulating JFK or Dr. King, they might as well say, "Four score and seven years ago ..." I look at them and want to say, "Who the heck is that? That is not the same person I was just talking to. What happened?"

What happened is that people do not understand that speaking has changed over the years. Today, speaking is more of a conversation and less of this distant oratory. Today, thanks to the power of television, we audience members feel closer and more intimate with the entertainers and speakers. Jay Leno appears to speak directly to us, not to a large crowd that we happen to be in. He does not shout as if there is a huge crowd that he has to yell above. No, instead he speaks conversationally, as if he is standing in front of you.

Speaking is a *conversation enlarged*. There are times when your stories take you into drama, but you will always come back to having a conversation with your audience once the story or activity is done. Don't preach to them; don't lecture to them; just have a conversation.

AVOID STEPPING ON THE LAUGHTER OR THE THOUGHTS

There are times in your speech where you will uncover humor and the audience will hopefully laugh. Whenever I used to say a funny line that got a laugh, I usually followed it with, "I'm just kidding." Guess what? That's one of the reasons my humor sucked. When you give a funny line and your audience laughs, guess what you should do? Nothing! Don't say anything and don't do anything. Just let them laugh.

DO YOU STEP ON YOUR AUDIENCE?

When they laugh, do you stop and let them finish? If not, guess what happens psychologically to your audience? They say to themselves, "Well shoot—if he keeps cutting me off, I won't laugh next time." Let them laugh, and let them laugh fully. When they get to the end of their laugh, move on to your next thought. For example, I was giving the acronym SSIP to one of my audiences, and I told them the following true story about me:

"I have done lots of management seminars for NASA. These are rocket scientists! One day, I said to them, 'Here's an acronym for praise and encouragement, and it is SSIP.' To my surprise, one rocket scientist practically scolded me by saying, 'Wait a minute; SSIP is not an acronym. Acronyms actually spell out something, and SSIP does not spell anything. Therefore, it is not an acronym.' Thankfully, another rocket scientist jumped up and said, 'Well, flip it upside down, Jim!'"

At this point, my audience erupted into laughter, and I waited it out. Sometimes, you'll need to wait five, ten, fifteen, or even twenty seconds for the laughter to die down. Don't rush! You're in the middle of a great conversation with your audience. They deserve a good time, so let them have it. Someone who later purchased the audio CD of that program called me and said, "Do you know you got an eighteen-second laugh with that SSIP piece?" That's funny, because when I was a wannabe speaker, I would have cut them off at four or five seconds. However, now I let them laugh until it dies down. Do the same for your audience. Give them that respect. Grant them that experience. Wait it out, and then move on.

DON'T STEP ON THEIR THOUGHTS

Many speakers know not to step on the laughter, but we must also avoid stepping on the thoughts of our audience. When you say something very powerful or poignant, you need to stop and let them digest it. So often when I coach speakers, they blaze past lines where they should stop in their tracks to let us see fully. For example, there is a point in my speech where I say, "What you drive is not as important as what drives you." People love that line, and they need a moment to digest it. In the past, I used to just keep talking afterwards, thereby stomping all over their thoughts. Don't do this to them. They don't deserve it. Pace your speech so that *your most powerful lines are followed by your most meaningful pauses*. Let them laugh, and let them think. If you let them digest it, believe me, they will want more.

What about Slides? Stop Lip-Synching Your Presentation with Your Slides

Imagine receiving a phone call like this:

"Hi Craig. This is Brent Joyner, and I run a small business that is seeking funds from venture capitalists. We need help with our presentations to potential investors. Craig, we already have the presentation, we just need to know what we are going to say. Can you help?"

Now, you might think this question is confusing because Brent stated that they already "have the presentation" but he does not know what they are going to say. However, I knew exactly what he was saying, because I have heard of it far too often. Basically, what he meant was that they already have the slides laid out, and now they need something to say in between them.

This is a classic mistake that ruins most business presentations. Brent started developing his presentation by creating slides. You should *never* do this. Instead, start by creating your message, and then determine whether or not you even need slides to say it! This is so important that it needs to be repeated.

Do *not* start by creating slides and then figuring out what to say about them.

Do start by creating your message and then figuring out if slides will help you say it.

Sure enough, when I went to see Brent give his presentation, it was filled with slides. In fact, in a twenty-five-minute presentation, he had twenty-seven slides. That's more than one slide per minute. Contrast this with my presentations. If I do a two-day management seminar, I will use fewer than ten slides. Why? They are not needed. Chances are that most of the slides you use are not needed to tell your message. In fact, they probably distract from your message.

WHY DO MOST SPEAKERS USE THEIR SLIDES?

Let's be real. The real reason most speakers use slides is not to help their audience, it is to help themselves. Just the other day, I saw a prominent literature specialist give a presentation that was filled with PowerPoint slides. He had the kinds of slides that each listed four to five bullet points, and he restated them without much elaboration. What I (and everybody else in the audience) noticed was that he actually looked up on the screen to see what was coming next. It was as if he was as surprised as *we* were with the sequence of his presentation. If we keep it real, we know he was simply using these slides to keep his place, not to enhance our understanding. He is not alone. This is what most presenters do, and it is selfish. Everything you do should be to improve your audience's condition, not yours. Don't use PowerPoint as a crutch. Use it as a tool.

SLIDES ARE SUPPOSED TO BE VISUAL "AIDS"

"Visual aid" means it is supposed to help your presentation, not *be* your presentation. Anytime you use slides to say the same thing you say verbally, you are lip-synching your presentation. By the time I finished one day with Brent, he had trimmed his presentation down to eight meaningful slides that aided in telling his story. As a result, his presentations drew much more interest and potential investors.

ARE YOU COMPETING WITH YOURSELF?

It is important to understand what happens with your audience when you use too many slides. Think about it. Chances are your audience has a handout. They also are watching you. And they are consistently looking up at the screen to see your slides. Can you picture them trying to figure out where to look and when? Their internal dialogue is screaming like this:

"Should I look at the handout? Should I be looking at him? Oh no, I think I just missed what was on the screen. Was I supposed to take notes on that? Oh no, I'm getting behind. I give up."

And there you have the result: they give up. You competed with yourself and lost. Do not put your audience through this. Instead, understand this fundamental fact: *you* are better than your PowerPoint!

You are the person they came to see. If your PowerPoint slides say everything you say, then one of you is not needed. In that case, your audience could have stayed at home and received the presentation via email. Do not destroy the human connection with technology. Use it to aid your speech, not to give it.

WHAT KINDS OF SLIDES SHOULD YOU KEEP?

So am I against using slides in a presentation? Of course not. However, like any tool, it can be used for good or evil. The kinds of slides you should keep are the ones that help clarify your message. For example, charts, graphs, visual images, pictures, timelines, and graphic elements add value to your message because they clarify it. With Brent, he had financial-forecasting charts that he definitely needed to keep in his presentation.

HOW SHOULD YOU USE THE SLIDES?

Picture an airport runway. What do you see? Can you see planes taking off and planes landing? This is exactly how slides should be used. Use these slides as a place where you take off and land. For example, say I had the following chart as a PowerPoint slide:

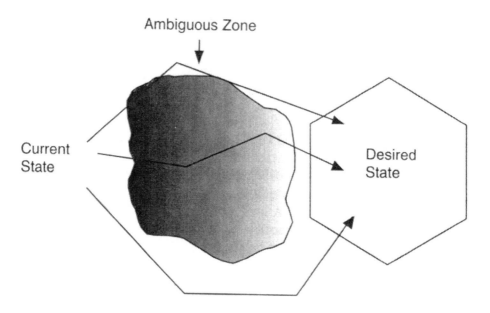

(Note: This chart is from a book, by Dr. Alan Weiss, called *Process Visuals*)

I would "take off" by explaining the slide like this:

"Take a look at this graphic. Do you see the Current State? That is your current reality. Now look over to the other side to see the Desired

State. That is where you are looking to go. What do you see in the middle? That's right: it is the Ambiguous Zone. What do you think happens in the Ambiguous Zone? [wait for a few answers]. Correct. And what many leaders don't understand is that it is normal for their employees to feel uncomfortable and anxious while in the Ambiguous Zone. What are some of the ways this discomfort manifests in your employees? [wait for answers]

"So, what is the job of the leader during this time? [wait for a couple of answers]. That's right, the leader needs to help them see where they are and be confident they are on the right track. Most leaders walk their people through blindly, but the exceptional leaders light the way. They provide milestones to let folks know they are on the right path. Finally, they create the most important piece of all, which is a vision. You should have been with me years ago when I …" [start of a story and sell a point].

That is how you can use a slide to clarify your message by using it as a taking-off point. Then, you should come back to the runway, at the end of your point, to land. For example, using this same graphic, I might end simply by stating the following:

"So that's how you keep the morale high and keep your employees feeling confident while in the Ambiguous Zone. You must have a vision. Be driven by your vision, or you'll be taken for a ride in someone else's. Be driven by your vision."

The foundational phrase is "Be driven by your vision." The PowerPoint slide helps my audience understand my story and my point. If your slide does not aid your audience, toss it out. Here are some guidelines to follow to determine whether or not you need a slide:

1. Does it help clarify your audience's understanding of the concept? If so, keep it.

2. Does it say the same thing you're about to say? If so, toss it out.

3. Do you list bullet points on it? If so, toss it out.

4. Is it there strictly for entertainment purposes (i.e., cutesy stuff flying across the screen with sound effects)? If so, toss it out.

5. Is it there to help you (the speaker) remember what comes next? If so, toss it out.

6. Do you have useless and irrelevant graphics and pictures on it? If so, toss it out.

As you can see, there is only one reason to keep a slide and many reasons to rid yourself of it. If it helps your audience understand the concepts, keep it.

The "B" Button

Here is one final critical lesson about PowerPoint. When giving a presentation that includes PowerPoint, you should not have something on the screen the entire time. First, this prevents you from being able to walk on that side of the room, because the image will shine on you. Second, the audience should be focused on you, not your slides, for the majority of your presentation. My good friend and an outstanding speaker, Darren LaCroix, taught me about the "B" button. It is as simple as this. Hit the "B" button on your laptop or computer while you are making your presentation, and the screen will go blank. Then you can be as mobile as you want. Hit it again to bring the screen back to life. That's it. It is simple, yet effective.

Use PowerPoint if need be, but do not abuse it, because the people that feel the pain are your audience members. Whatever you do, don't lip-synch your presentation.

DON'T STRIVE FOR PERFECTION

I remember leaving one speech in Maryland in the year 2000 and going home ecstatic about how it went. I thought, "Wow! That was a great one. I didn't miss a beat. I'm getting better and better." About a week later, a package arrived in the mail with a VHS tape inside. I took it out, popped it in, and died. Why did I die? Because the VHS tape I saw was of me in that same event. Guess what? I sucked!

I had all the words right, paused in all the right places, and gave a flawless performance. So what was the problem? I told you I sucked. Okay, why did I suck? Because it was perfect and perfection sucks. Write this down:

Perfection sucks.

What Is Better than Perfect?

Anything is better than a perfect speech. Like mine, perfect speeches usually have no connection with the audience, because the speaker is too focused on being perfect. All we should be focused on is *improving our audience's condition*. When we focus on our audience and give up the need to be perfect, we connect. In order to have an effect, you must first connect. Don't strive for perfection; strive for a *connection*.

ONE FINAL THOUGHT ABOUT DELIVERY

Two weeks ago, I traveled to Cincinnati to speak to financial advisors on the topic of mastering change to get remarkable results, even in tough times. I arrived at the hotel late the night before, and I was hungry and tired. So I did what I often do, and that's to order a pizza. The company said, "We'll be there in thirty-five minutes." An hour and a half later, they still hadn't arrived. Finally, I called to make sure they had not forgotten about me, and shortly after that, it arrived. Guess what? The pizza was cold! Why am I telling you this? Because no matter how good the content (pizza) is, it will be directly affected by the delivery. If the delivery fails, the content falters. Your audience is hungry for your message. When you take great care in its delivery, they will walk away feeling more than satisfied. And chances are, they will call on you again!

Now that you have your structure, content, and delivery, let's explore how you can use your presentations to generate profits!

PART II

How to Generate Leads,
Customers, and
Huge Profits from
Your Presentations

Chapter 5

Begin with a Profitable Marketing Mindset

Do Not Leave Money on the Table!

If I told you how much money I have left on the table since I began as a speaker, you probably wouldn't believe me. If I told you how much money you'll leave on the table if you do what most speakers do, it would make you sick to your stomach.

Marketing? Hated It!

I fought against marketing for six years. In case you're counting, that's two years longer than the Civil War! My justification was, "I'm an artist. I'm a speaker. When I perfect my art, business will come." Well, I'll tell you one thing: this type of thinking absolutely works if you are starring in a movie. However, in the real world, your *Field of Dreams* approach of "If you build it, they will come" turns into a forest of nightmares. Oh, you'll be an artist, all right—a starving artist. That is what I became.

Finally, someone asked me, "Craig, what do you think it's costing you not to market your products and services?" Instantly, I remembered a host of opportunities that passed me by, only to be picked up by less effective speakers. I thought back to the audiences that needed to hear my message but never would. I recalled all the frustration I used to feel when I watched other speakers live my dream. In truth, this person's question almost drove me nuts. Before it did, however, it drove me to change.

I changed so much that I quit my PhD program and told my wife, "Honey, you know that I am the world champion of public speaking. Now I'm going to turn myself into the world champion of marketing." She said, "Well, you already read at least one book every week. Why don't you spend an entire year reading all about marketing?" That's what I did. I read sixty-two books on marketing in that first year, invested heavily in some classes, and started on the road to generating leads, customers, and huge profits.

The Jackpot!

Then I hit the jackpot. After reading the book *Success Secrets of the Online Marketing Superstars* by Mitch Meyerson, I enrolled in his Guerrilla Marketing Coach Certification program. It was by far the best business decision I have made in the last ten years, and it brought me income gains that shocked me. As a certified Guerrilla Marketing Coach, I now teach what I used to be afraid to learn. How ironic. I'm a late bloomer to marketing. This means one thing for sure: if I can grasp it, you can too.

Let's get back to Mitch. Mitch Meyerson, my coauthor, is, in my opinion, the greatest marketing coach in the United States. He is the author of *Mastering Online Marketing, Guerrilla Marketing on the Front Lines*, and several other books, and he is the founder of the Guerrilla Marketing Coach Certification program and other online courses (www.mitchmeyerson.com). Fortunately for you, you'll pick up many of the same processes he teaches in his courses in this book. As a result, I'm sure your income will rise significantly, and your new, attractive business opportunities will seem endless. Whether you're a late bloomer to marketing or a seasoned veteran, you'll find in this chapter just what you need to rapidly build your profitable business. We can thank Mitch for that. Let's dive in!

MARKETING HAS CHANGED

There is good news for you: Marketing has changed so much in the last ten to fifteen years that much of the landscape is uncharted. Many marketing veterans are absolutely lost because their old ways no longer work. Remember when people first tried to use their websites simply as online brochures? Remember when they thought that what worked in print could simply be transferred to the web? Remember when that thinking led them to crash and burn? That's what happens when old ways collide with new times. On the other hand, many new professionals are adjusting quickly by starting off with the right tools for today.

The more I studied marketing, the more I couldn't help but apply the principles. As this happened, my bank account swelled. Today, I now have to turn away the same customers I used to beg for, because my cup runneth over.

I have had to rearrange my entire business so these prospects and customers can access public speaking and marketing tools without having to get them directly from me. I owe all of this success to the tools you're going to pick up in these next few chapters, many of which I learned from Mitch. However, none of them will matter if you don't first start with a marketing mind-set. What was I leaving on the table? My future. If you don't adopt a marketing mind-set, you will leave a very lucrative and exciting future on the table. And the worst part about neglecting to embrace marketing, is that someone else will snatch up your opportunities and live your dream. That's called being "dream-jacked."

What Is the Marketing Mind-Set for World Class Speaking?

When marketing becomes like breathing to you, you have the marketing mind-set. Marketing is like breathing. If you stop breathing, you stop living. If you stop marketing, your business dies. It's the same thing. Many people think marketing is about putting on an event or sending out a mailing. That's not marketing; that's event management. So what are some of the traits of the marketing mind-set? Let's take a look at a few.

Marketing Is Not an Event—It's a Process

Marketing is ongoing. I once heard one speaker tell another, "I tried marketing before. I sent out a mailing, and it didn't work." Was that really marketing? No. That was an event. Marketing is about consistency and being in constant contact with your target market. The opposite, "one and done," will kill your business. Consistency of contact will construct it.

Marketing Is All About Having Them Build Confidence in You

A couple years ago, a CFO from a biotechnology company said, "Craig, I want you to work with me and our CEO on the art of public speaking." Because I'm a marketer, I said, "Great. Where did you hear of me?" He said, "I searched the web for speech coaches in Maryland and came across your name along with several others. However, I chose you because I actually saw you speak one time at a meeting in Baltimore County. I appreciate your style, and I know we can learn a lot from you. That's why I chose to call you instead of the others on the search-results list." I began coaching the CFO and CEO every few months. After approximately ten months, the CFO called and said, "Craig, we would like to put you on retainer as a speech coach. That way, we can keep you up to speed with our progress and pick your brain when we need to." I eventually agreed, and we worked out a contract. Today, I have a profitable retainer agreement with them, and I am excited to help them reach their goals. What happened here is a perfect example of what marketing is all about.

As a Guerrilla Marketing coach, I know that the reason people decide to do business with you usually comes down to one thing: confidence. Do they have enough confidence that you will help them achieve their objectives? If so, they will most likely utilize your services. That's why the best tool for marketing yourself as a speaker is to be damned good on the speaking platform. When people see you, you will automatically instill enough confidence to make them say, "We've got to bring him into our organization." The good news is that once you get in and exceed their expectations, they will rehire you time and time again. Why? They have confidence in you.

The biotechnology company's CFO chose me over the others listed in the search results not because of my website or because of my title of world champion, but because he gained confidence in me. How did he get this confidence in me? The same way prospects will gain confidence in you: through *familiarity.* Familiarity is the key. That's why staying in contact with prospects and customers is so very important. This CFO saw me speak at a free event, and that speech, coupled with his search results, made him confident in me. Then, once they brought me in for several months, they gained a new level of confidence and decided to offer me a retainer agreement. I, too, gained confidence in them and decided to take them up on their offer. If prospects and customers have confidence in you, the world is your oyster!

Let's take another situation that I find myself in often. People send me emails all the time that say, "Thank you so much for the extra CD you sent me." What extra CD are they talking about? They are referring to the extra audio CD I send out to first-time purchasers. Why do I send an extra audio CD to them? Because they are promised something (whatever they ordered), but they automatically receive more (the extra CD). Are they expecting it? No. Are they happy to receive it? Yes. What does it cost me to send this extra CD? It costs about a dollar. What does it earn me as a reward? It earns me the confidence of my customers, and that is priceless. What are you doing now to over-deliver on your promise so that you build their confidence in you?

Marketing Is Everything You Do

As stated, everything you do either builds confidence in you or breaks confidence in you, in the eyes of your prospects and customers. Therefore, watch what you do. Here are some examples of how we break confidence without even knowing it:

- Broken links on our website
- Misspellings on our website or on printed materials

- Unfriendly or unprofessional voicemail greeting
- Non-energetic conversations with potential customers
- Cheap-looking packaging
- Long delivery time for getting products to customers
- Sloppy attire and wardrobe
- Unstructured and/or boring speech
- Unattractive and repelling nonverbal signals
- And many, many more

We need to be aware of everything we do, because it all counts. Imagine receiving a very enticing letter that is so well written that it persuades you to call the company to inquire about doing business with them. Now, imagine them picking up the call and, in an unprofessional voice saying, "Who dis? Holla at me. Whatcha want?" Is that call going to build confidence or break it? Do you see what happened? The best marketing letter can be destroyed by an unprofessional tone of voice and lack of grammar skills. Everything goes together and, as a world-class speaker, you must be aware of whether you are building or breaking confidence in your prospects and customers.

You Are Not Only a Speaker, but an Expert Who Speaks

This is a key realization for many people. If you look at yourself as just a speaker, then how many options do you have to generate income? You will most likely see yourself generating income through your speaking engagements. However, if you look at yourself as an expert who happens to speak, how many ways can you generate income? Infinite ways! If you are an expert, then people want your expertise, regardless of whether they get it from you live on the stage, from your book, from your special report, from your online audio lesson, from your CD, from your DVD, from your blog, from your podcast, from your teleseminar, from your webinar, from your e-course, or in any other way. Open up your world by realizing what you are. You are not just a speaker. You are an expert who speaks.

WHAT'S THE MOST IMPORTANT MARKETING TOOL OF ALL?

Once you get this mind-set of being a marketer, you'll have the foundation you need to use the most important marketing tool of all: the marketing plan. Let's dive right in!

CREATE A MARKETING PLAN

Have you ever seen a speaker and wondered, "How did he get that engagement?" Have you ever been frustrated and wondered, "Why can't I get engagements like that?" Have you ever wondered why some entrepreneurs have multiple income streams while others have bank accounts that are leaking? The answer can be summed up in one word: marketing.

Knowing about marketing and acting on marketing are two different animals. By far the most important next step you can take in your business is to put together an effective marketing plan.

You might already have a business plan, a financial plan, and even a production plan. However, if you don't have a marketing plan, you might as well bury the other plans. They will be of no use to you. Marketing is everything in business, and moving forward without a plan is one of the biggest reasons why most small business fail—and fail hard.

How Do You Create Your Marketing Plan?

Every marketing consultant you come across will have his or her own formula for a marketing plan. However, they generally cover the same six or seven areas of focus. If you go through the following six questions and put serious time and effort into answering them, you will accomplish much more than most business owners and entrepreneurs (in terms of focusing your business). You will come away with a laser-like focus for your business, which will make it very difficult for you not to meet with great success. Here are the six questions to develop your marketing plan.

Marketing-Plan Question #1: What Is the Reason for Your Marketing?

What exactly do you want your marketing to do for you? Do you want to build your list of prospects? Do you want to sell your products via the web? Do you want to get people to purchase your services as a speaker or coach? What exactly do you want your marketing to do for you?

The best way to answer this is to find out what your business goals currently are. For example, one of my goals this year is to increase my prospect list by ten thousand. Therefore, the reason for my marketing is to build my list. More specifically, the reason for my marketing is to drive prospects to my website and have them immediately sign up for my e-newsletter or mini-course. As a result, most of my marketing communications are not designed to have people call me or immediately purchase my products. Instead, these marketing strategies are strictly focused on driving people to one place so they can do one thing (sign up for the e-newsletter or mini-course).

The question to ask is, "What is the exact *next step* I want people to take after receiving or viewing my marketing messages?" As a speaker, you might want them to call you, download your electronic one-sheet, or view your demo video online. Be very clear on the specific next step you want them to take.

Then the next question you need to ask yourself is, "What kind of *bait* am I using to get them to take that next step?" For example, let's revisit my goal of getting ten thousand more prospects this year. I want to drive people to my website (www.wcspeaking.com or www.craigvalentine.com) and get them to sign up for my e-newsletter or mini-course. Well, guess what? Everybody has a newsletter! Why in the world would someone want to sign up for mine? I realized a long time ago that nobody wakes up in the morning and says, "I can't wait to be on another newsletter list today!" However, people do wake up in the morning and say, "I wish I could become a better speaker today" or "I really wish I could get this job" or "I wish I had a strategy to get more clients."

What Is Your Bait?

In order to get people to sign up for my newsletter, I need to offer free bait that 1) shows them what's in it for them to sign up, and 2) helps them build their confidence in me. For me, if you visit www.wcspeaking.com, you'll see that I offer an entire seven-part e-course called The World Class Speaking Toolkit. It's valued at ninety-seven dollars, but I offer it for free for the purpose of converting visitors into prospects. That's a heck of a bait! It no longer costs me anything, and the entire course is delivered through auto-responders that link to audio lessons, but it makes a tremendous difference in whether people will take that next step or not.

Name That Newsletter

If you go the newsletter route to build your list, it helps to brand your newsletter by embedding a benefit with its name. "World Class Speaking Toolkit" implies that you can use it to become a world-class speaker. Far too many speakers and other entrepreneurs are simply stating "Sign up for my newsletter" without giving a reason why or offering any kind of bait. If you are a financial-services consultant focusing on debt reduction, you can call it the "Get Out of Debt Now FREE e-newsletter." That will definitely hit the spot with some people. If you are an Internet-marketing consultant, perhaps you can have a "Conversion Kit bi-monthly FREE e-newsletter." Whatever you decide, make sure you offer bait that shows them specifically what's in it for them to take the desired next step. Remember, you are an expert who speaks, so make sure you offer your expertise freely as bait.

Know the Exact Next Step

If you visit www.craigvalentine.com, you'll notice a video I use that is designed to get people to take one specific next step of signing up for my newsletter. I have seen many other videos on other websites that basically tell the visitor all about what's on the site but don't focus them on taking a specific next step. This is usually a waste of good technology, which is the result of the website owner not having a marketing plan. If you know the exact next step you want your suspects, prospects, or customers to take, your marketing communications become less expensive and more effective. So, let's review:

- What is the exact next step you want your suspects, prospects, or customers to take?

- What is the bait you will use to drive them into that next step?
- What's in it for *them* to take that next step?

When you have answered these questions, you will know the first piece to your marketing plan, which is your reason for your marketing. Keep in mind that you might have an exact next step for each target market. For example, my exact next step for my aspiring-speakers market is my World Class Speaking Toolkit e-newsletter. However, my exact next step for my clients (companies that hire me to speak) is to fill in my online contact form and describe their needs. I use free-preview audio and video as a reward for them. Of course, these audios and videos are speeches given by me that have a similar message to what the prospective clients want their event's attendees to hear. The materials build their confidence in me, which again is the number-one reason why they will choose me over someone else.

MARKETING-PLAN QUESTION # 2: WIIFT, SPECIFICALLY?

Right now, before you do anything else, write down the top three benefits your prospects get from hiring you or purchasing your products or services. Seriously, go ahead and write them down. Was that difficult? The number-one mistake that wannabe speakers and wannabe entrepreneurs make is that they talk about what they do, rather than *what their customers get*. The quickest and easiest solution to this is to stop saying "We do ..." and "I am ..." and to start saying "You get ..." and "You will pick up ..."

For example, imagine you and I are in the proverbial elevator, going up to the seventh floor, and I ask you, "So, what do you do?" What is your thirty-second commercial going to be? If you start off like most people, you'll say something like, "Well, I am a marketing consultant ..." and if I had a game-show buzzer, I would set it off. Why? People don't want to hear what you do. They want to hear what they *get* from what you do. Therefore, start with "you," not with "I" or "we."

Prospects don't want to know what you do. They want to know what you do *for them*.

Start with a Focus on the Word "You"

If someone asks me what I do, I will say, "Have you ever seen a speaker give a boring presentation? Have you ever seen another speaker keep his or her audience on the edge of their seats? That's what I help presenters do. By working with me, you pick up tools you can use to keep your audiences leaning on your every word. Then you get a process to use these same powerful presentations to generate more leads and customers in one hour than most small businesses get in one month. How do you currently use presentations to build your business?"

Did you notice a trend here? My thirty-second commercial is filled with questions. This is because you don't want people to simply listen to you; you want them to *think* about themselves. Questions are the best way to make them think, and they should be in your thirty-second commercial. Once you internalize your thirty-second commercial, it will be much easier to put together all of your marketing pieces, because they will be rich with benefits. Start by putting together your commercial and branch out from there. If your thirty-second commercial is weak, the rest of your marketing materials don't stand a chance.

Four Criteria for a Captivating Thirty-Second Commercial

    A. Do you begin by focusing on the word "you?"

    B. Do you state the main benefit?

    C. Do you point out their pain?

    D. Do you finish with a question?

You understand the importance of beginning by focusing on the word "you." You also surely understand the importance of showing them what's in it for *them* to do business with you. However, what about the importance of pointing out their pain?

Point Out Their Pain

The most powerful question you can ask a potential customer is the following:

What is that costing you?

As marketers, we have to understand that people won't move until it feels too uncomfortable for them to sit still. Whether you like it or not, you are responsible for making them feel uncomfortable. That's the only way they'll make a change. For example, with potential clients that want to hire me to speak on the topic of change, I ask them the following question:

"Do you work with any StatusQuoaholics? These are the people who are averse to change. They say things like, 'This is the way we've always done things around here. Why change?' Do you work with any of these folks?"

By that time, my prospect is already feeling the pain, and they say, "Yes, we do have those people here. That's why we need a speaker to address everyone." Instead of jumping into the solution of having me as a speaker, it's much more effective for me to *drive home the pain* by asking, "What is that costing your group? What kind of effect are these people having on them?" Once they dig deep into this pain and assess the cost, guess what? The cost now weighs so heavily, my fee no longer matters!

You might disagree with what you're about to read in this very next sentence, but eventually you will find it to be true: It's important to make them sick and then make them well.

Fifteen years ago, when I started my sales career, this was one of the first sales rules I ever learned, and it is absolutely applicable today. People don't know how bad their pain is until you point it out. Then, and *only* then, will they work to change it. Perhaps that change means hiring you, or perhaps it doesn't. Either way, you have helped them to help themselves.

Why Finish with a Question?

In the list of criteria for the thirty-second commercial, letter D states that you should finish your commercial by asking your prospect a question. Why is that? It's because of the following fact about communications: whoever asks the questions guides the conversation.

You might think you're controlling the conversation because you're doing most of the talking. Nothing can be further from the truth. Whoever is asking the right questions and hushing up to listen for the answers is in control. When most people end their thirty-second commercials, there is an awkward silence between the two parties. Then they split apart, having accomplished nothing. On the contrary, when you ask a question at the end of your commercial, you then put the ball back into their court as they disclose more of their needs. When dealing with prospects, you should spend at least 80 percent of the conversation listening and only 20 percent talking.

Craft Your Language in Results

Whether you are in front of a prospect giving your thirty-second commercial, generating content for your website, or sending out a marketing piece such as a postcard or mailing, you must be very clear on what your prospects and customers get as a *result* of working with you. Let's take a look at what most wannabe speakers say and what world-class speakers do:

Wannabe speakers say: "I will work with you to understand your financial situation."
World-class speakers say: "You will love the feeling of being debt-free."

Wannabe speakers say: "I will show you how to manage your time and priorities."
World-class speakers say: "You'll have much less stress and still get much more done. You'll go from feeling overwhelmed to overjoyed."

Wannabe speakers say: "I'll teach you the skills you need to be a public speaker."
World-class speakers say: "You'll keep your next audience on the edge of their seats."

Do you see the difference? Wannabe speakers talk about themselves and their processes, while world-class speakers talk about the *results* their customers will get. Get used to using the phrase "You get …" Get used to using the phrase "You'll pick up tools to help you …" Get used to using the phrase "You'll walk away with …" These phrases keep the focus where the focus should be, and that's on your prospects and customers.

What Are the Three Greatest Results They Will Get?

Although there are multiple ways you can help your prospects and customers, you will want to focus on their top three needs. These will probably be the ones that are most closely associated with their pain. For example, when dealing with the first-time supervisor market, I outline these results as my top three: "You will pick up tools to …"

1. Create commitment, not just compliance, from your employees
2. Raise the morale through the roof
3. Become the leader others actually want to follow

These are laser-focused results. Now complete these sentences for the three major results your customers will get from working with you …

- You get …
- You'll pick up …
- You'll gain …

Does It Sound like "Anywhere, USA?"

When people receive your marketing communications, you want them to have the following thought: *Wow, this is a perfect fit for me.* In other words, you want them to feel like what you have is dead-on for what they need. It's tailor-made for them. The only way to do this is by offering results (or benefits) that are *specific*. These results cannot sound general. For example, when I ask many speakers and entrepreneurs to sum up the benefits of working with them, here are the typical answers they give:

- "I will help you reach a new level of success in your business."
- "You will learn the processes you need to win at all levels."
- "We help businesses reach peak performance."

What's the problem with each of these benefit statements? They don't speak to anyone specifically. What do they even mean? Nobody who receives this message will think, "Wow, this is a perfect fit for me." This is because of the following truth: when you reach out to everyone, you touch no one.

For each target market you have, you must craft a message that shows the specific results they will get. For a market of new managers, they will pick up tools to "Get the respect of their friends and former co-workers." When a new manager sees that benefit, they get excited because they know it is specifically for them. On the other hand, what if you are marketing to organizations needing to undergo change? You might state, "You will be able to get even the most reluctant employees to buy into your new direction." Again, when the training director sees this benefit, he or she will think, "That's exactly what we need." When marketing to an aspiring speaker, I don't simply talk in generalities about success. Instead, I dive into the specifics of "keeping your next audience on the edge of their seats." A speaker sees this message and thinks, "He is speaking directly to me." That's the thought you want them to have, and it will occur only when you reach out with specific results rather than general fluff.

MARKETING-PLAN QUESTION # 3: WHO IS YOUR PERFECT CUSTOMER?

I must admit that the main reason I fought against marketing for several years is because people kept telling me to narrow my focus and select a target audience. You might echo my thoughts, which were, "I don't want to narrow my focus or pick a target market. I want to speak to everyone! Why do you people keep telling me to narrow down? I want more opportunities, not fewer." Then I even reached a level of suspicion and started thinking, "I know what these folks are trying to do. They're trying to make me stay in my lane, so I won't merge into theirs and take their customers. They're threatened by me." Guess what? I'll be the first to tell you that, in those days, I thought like a loser. Those thoughts I had were not only stupid, but they were very harmful to my development as a speaker and businessperson. Nobody was out to get me; they were out to *help* me. Fortunately, I wised up. Here's the paradox that you must come to appreciate and understand about marketing: when you narrow your focus, you broaden your opportunities.

How to Strike It Rich

Nobody ever struck oil by digging an inch deep. You must narrow your focus and dig deep, because that's where you'll hit pay dirt. That's where the profits are. Everyone who stays on the surface by being all things to all people will forever be frustrated and mystified by the vast success and profitability of those who are wise enough to sharpen their focus and dig deep. Think about it, if you try to reach everyone, to whom will you tailor your message? Again, if people see a general message that doesn't speak directly to their specific needs, they will let it pass by and barely notice it. Many speakers say, "Okay, I need to narrow my focus. I'll talk about these three subjects." That's not the solution. The solution is to not decide on your exact message until you first decide on your exact customer. Start everything with the customer. Who is it? What does he want to avoid? What does she want to attain?

Your Perfect Customer

Perhaps the most meaningful exercise you will do to make sure your message hits your recipient in the heart and in the mind is to visualize one perfect customer sitting in front of you. Instead of seeing them as a mass market, look at one individual as a representation of your entire target market. For example, let's take a look at my aspiring-speakers market. I call my perfect customer "Jesse." Here is who Jesse is. Jesse ...

- wants to master the art of public speaking
- wants to master the business of public speaking
- has experience speaking (possibly in Toastmasters, NSA, or as a presenter/trainer elsewhere)
- is approximately forty-five years old
- has an annual income of more than $65,000
- has more than a decade of successful work experience but also the desire to have a profitable business of his/her own
- is a dedicated lifelong learner
- has at least a high-school diploma and probably a college degree
- knows the difference between investments and expenses
- wants education, not just validation
- is a member of Toastmasters, NSA, or ASTD

That's my Jesse. Do you know your perfect customer as well? If you don't, then you will never be able to create marketing materials and communications that reach his or her heart and mind. However, if you do get to know your perfect customer this well, you will rarely ever miss the mark with your marketing. You'll get more leads, more sales, and much more profit. And the best part about it is that you will accomplish all of this with very little cost. That's the power of knowing your perfect customer.

Keep in mind that this is just *one* of my markets. You can have more than one market, but you must create marketing communications that you tailor and tweak for each. That way, they will receive these pieces and think, "Yep, they are speaking directly to me. This is for me. I should act on this." For my market of new supervisors, I have a completely different Jesse, but I know that Jesse just as well as I do the one who is the aspiring speaker. I suggest that you create a list like mine to describe your perfect customer in detail. Complete the following exercise by filling in the bullet points below.

My perfect customer, _____(name),

is_____,

knows_____,

wants_____,

has_____,

is_____,

knows_____,

wants _____,

and has_____.

How Can These Individual Customers Help Build Your Speaking Business?

You might be thinking, "Craig, this is great for selling products and services to individual customers, but what about getting paid to speak by corporations?" Although we will cover the traditional practices in chapter seven (on how to generate leads), please understand one very important revelation about building a list of individual prospects and customers: these individuals become your best informal salespeople!

This is absolutely true. Many of my corporate speaking engagements are initiated by individuals who receive regular marketing communications from me! It's amazing. It will happen for you, too. Why? When people build up *confidence* in you through becoming *familiar* with your valuable offerings, they will recommend you to their organizations time and time again. Lots of speakers depend on speakers' bureaus to get speaking engagements. This can come back to bite the speaker, because none of those clients belongs to the speaker. However, when your individual prospects and customers refer you, the client is yours. What do these individuals get out of recommending you to speak? When you captivate that audience, they look like a star for bringing you in. Plus, in all honestly, they'll probably ask to spend some time with you, too, while you're "in town." That's time worth spending, because they are the reason you're in business.

Keep Two Files on Your Perfect Customer

Do you know what your customer wants to *avoid* and wants to *attain*? Keep a file for each. Keep a file labeled "Avoid." Every time one of your prospects or customers expresses what they want to stay away from, put it in your file. Also, keep a file labeled "Attain." Any time one of your customers expresses what they want to get in business or in life, put that into your file. These two files will help you do three things:

A. Write much-more persuasive marketing copy

B. Streamline all your efforts

C. Reduce your cost and increase your ROI

One of the Greatest Marketing Secrets of All Time

Let your prospects and customers tell you how to sell to them. Instead of guessing what they want, write marketing copy that reflects what they tell you. If you keep your ear to the ground, your prospects and customers will tell you absolutely everything you need to know about selling to them. I write exactly what they tell me, in exactly the same way. Their thoughts become my marketing copy. You can't get any closer inside the minds of your customers than this! *What comes out of their mouth goes into my marketing.* This helps me strike oil. They tell me what my products and services are doing for them.

For example, let's say I get a testimonial that states, "Craig, you really helped demystify the storytelling process for me." What do you think is going in my next marketing piece about storytelling? I will be sure to put in a bullet point that states the following:

- This program helps you demystify the storytelling process

How do I know this? My customers told me. And they will tell you all you need to know. Are you listening to them? Don't guess what they want; listen to what they need.

Visualize Your Jesse

Whenever you sit down to write your marketing copy, whether it's to be posted on your website, written in a home-study course, or set on a postcard, visualize your own Jesse sitting across from you. Review your "Avoid" and your "Attain" lists. Write as if you are speaking directly to Jesse, showing him or her how to avoid what is unwanted and how to attain what is desired. Chances are very high that you'll hit the mark and have Jesse say, "Wow, this is for me. What's my next step?"

MARKETING-PLAN QUESTION # 4:
WHAT'S YOUR SPECIALTY?

In every industry, there are areas of specialty that I like to call "slices of a subject." For example, in the public-speaking industry, you have speakers who carve out their own niche. You have experts who specialize in teaching you how to get paid to speak, develop presentation skills, create keynotes, coach, train, use technology to get your message out, and many more slices. Even within the art of public speaking there are slices. I am known as a master storytelling coach for aspiring speakers. That's one of my slices of the public-speaking-industry pie.

Keith Harrell is one of the top motivational speakers in the country, so what is his specialty? His specialty can be summed up in one word: attitude. When prospects want to bring in a speaker to talk about attitude, Keith is many times the first person who comes to mind. He essentially owns the word "attitude." In fact, I recently visited his website and saw his headline as "America's Attitude Coach." That's his specialty, and he is reaping the benefits. Of course, it doesn't hurt that he is a brilliant speaker!

What is your industry? How have you positioned yourself within it? The tighter you decide to focus, the better your chance at striking pay dirt. When people need help with their stories (which is the heart of effective public speaking), they turn to me. What is the specialty for which you want to become forever linked?

Let's take the marketing industry as another example. Many marketing consultants carve out their own slice by specializing in a specific aspect of marketing and sometimes even tightening their focus in additional ways. For example, a marketing consultant who specializes in helping dentists' offices in Maryland might position herself as "The Top Marketing Consultant for

Dentists in Maryland." You might think she is narrowing her focus too much, but if you are a dentist in Maryland and you have to choose between her and a generic marketing consultant, who will generate more confidence? By narrowing her focus and going so deep, she will eventually own that niche in the mind of her tight market. When she digs that deep and strikes pay dirt, it will definitely be worth smiling about!

Marketing-Plan Question # 5: What Marketing Tools Will You Use?

As a certified Guerrilla Marketing Coach, I help my customers understand the vast array of marketing tools that are at their disposal. In fact, we regularly review a hundred of these tools, and half of them are free. The problem with most entrepreneurs is that they use only a few tools and get frustrated at their lack of results. The secret is to use many tools but to get them all driving your prospects to the same destination.

For example, below is a list of seven additional marketing tools I decided to use more frequently about one year ago. As soon as I put these additional tools to work, my lead generation soared through the roof. I had high hopes, but even I was surprised at how many new prospects came my way. Remember, lead generation was my main purpose for marketing, so these results were purposeful. Here are the tools I put in place to drive people to sign up for my newsletter:

1. **My 800 number:** I had been using an 800 number for years, but, before my marketing was purposeful, I simply had a voicemail greeting asking people to leave a message. Today, I use the voicemail message to persuade callers to visit the website for the free toolkit

(newsletter). Do you use voicemail? Where is your voicemail driving your callers? Always have a specific next step.

2. **Audio lessons:** I started sending out free audio lessons that have fifteen-minute tutorials. Each one focuses on one public-speaking strategy. For prospects who are considering hiring me to speak, many times I send them audio CDs of my full-length keynotes so that they can gain confidence in me with no risk to them. Can you give a short clip of your presentations for free and tease people into wanting more? If so, you'll want to use audio lessons as well. Visit www.wcspeaking.com to see the system that I use and highly recommend for Internet audio. In addition to the audio lessons, I have also have free downloadable "special reports" on sales, management, and storytelling. These reports are two to three thousand words in length and are designed to have prospects build confidence in me as a speaker.

3. **Postcards:** One of the most important marketing strategies you can use is effective follow-up with prospects and current customers. I signed up with www.sendoutpostcards.com and have regularly sent out postcards to thank customers and encourage prospects. These little letters continue to pay off handsomely, because *buyers are buyers.* Buyers will continue to buy. How do I know this? I'm one of them! I'm an avid shopper for information. Buyers are buyers.

Your buyers already have confidence in you, and that's the main criteria for making their purchasing decisions. I have a speaker friend who took my advice and recently decided to contact five of his past customers. He immediately landed two paid engagements from them. What did this marketing cost him? Nothing. What did it gain him? I'd guess at least fifteen thousand dollars. Don't forget: your best customer is someone you've already served. Give them a second serving. Follow up. Who can you send postcards to? The first time you get that ecstatic call of someone thanking you for thinking of them, you'll be sold on the importance of using these postcards.

4. **Inserts:** I decided that every single product of mine that gets shipped must have an insert that markets additional products (or "Champ Camps") and entices people to revisit my website. What can you cross-sell as people purchase your products? If you don't have a next step for them, you are leaving tons of money on the table.

5. **Tip Sheets:** When you give a presentation, leave your audience members with a well-constructed tip sheet. It might be the tips on the "Top 10 Ways to Get Buy In from your Employees" or the "Top 10 Mistakes People Make in Managing their Time and Priorities." If your tip list is well-done, your recipients will rarely throw them away. As a result, your marketing piece will constantly stare them in the face. I have done this with a time-management tip sheet. One day, approximately two years after one of my speaking engagements, I walked through a customer's office and saw my tip sheet tacked up on the wall of his cubicle. Do you think he remembered me? What top ten tips to do or ten tips to avoid can you provide your audiences as takeaways from your speech?

6. **Articles:** Perhaps the greatest and fastest way to generate interest from your target market is by writing articles and submitting them into online article banks. Once you submit your articles to the banks, people can reuse your articles on their websites, in their newsletters,

and anywhere else they want. They benefit from getting good content, but you benefit from having your resource box with your contact information visible at the bottom of each of your articles. As a result, if the people who read your article are inclined to contact you, they can easily click a link and there you are! This can bring loads of prospects and customers to you. You'll get what Alan Weiss, author of *Million Dollar Consulting*, calls "Marketing Gravity." Instead of having to go out and cold-call clients, you can attract them to you. Perfect example:

A friend of mine is a small-business coach, and she did this a couple of years ago. She went from having just a few hundred Google results with her name to having more than sixteen thousand web pages that have her articles on them. This happened as a result of her writing these articles and submitting them to the article banks. This is a very inexpensive way to getting recognized as an expert in your industry while capturing leads that can turn into tremendous profits. Have you written articles for article banks? Type "article banks" into Google, and get a list of them. Find which ones will reach your target market. Submit a few and watch the explosive results.

7. **Email signature:** With my purposeless marketing, my email signature was simply my name and some links to my products. However, because the purpose of my marketing is to generate leads, I now have sufficient bait in my email signature that entices people to visit my site and get the free toolkit. Where is *your* email signature sending people? Is it purposeful?

These are just seven tools, but the assortment is purposeful and strategic. The tools all work together, as a team, toward the specific goal of building my list of prospects. What is your specific purpose for marketing? Are you using an assortment of marketing tools to serve it? If you're interested in the hundred marketing tools (half of them free), you can visit www.wcspeaking.com/resources and review the Guerrilla Marketing Toolkit.

MARKETING-PLAN QUESTION # 6: WHAT IS YOUR IDENTITY?

Your identity is the *personality* of your organization. It has to do with what your organization *stands for*, more than what it offers. For example, FedEx delivers packages. However, it stands for being fast and reliable. Nordstrom sells merchandise. However, it stands for excellence in customer service. Southwest Airlines provides flight transportation. However, it stands for fun and engaging. What do you stand for?

Discover Your Identity

The best way to discover your identity is to listen to what your customers have been telling you. Most of the time, our identity is right under our nose, but it's so obvious that we overlook it. For example, year after year, my customers and audience members gave me feedback such as "Craig, I really appreciate the specific, practical tools you gave me to develop as a manager." Or they said, "You provided me with the nuts-and-bolts tools I can use to enhance my speeches." Suddenly, it hit me! I am "Mr. Nuts and Bolts." While there is tons of fluff and theory out in the market, I provide people with the actual practical, tangible, nuts-and-bolts tools they can use immediately to improve their condition. That's me. That's my identity. What's yours?

What Do You Do with Your Identity?

Here is where it gets good. After my realization, I began standing for nuts and bolts. That became my identity. As a result, everything I offer has to fit the description of being practical and tangible. In other words, it must provide people with the nuts and bolts. I once had a good friend of mine (and an excellent speaker) ask, "Craig, can I be a guest author on your Nuts and Bolts Newsletter?" I said, "Send me your proposed article, and I'll take a look at it." He sent it, and I noticed it was all theory. There was not one specific strategy in it. Although it was a theory that people needed to understand, I could not include the article in my newsletter. Why? Because it did not meet the criteria of what I stand for. It was not about the nuts and bolts. I have to protect my identity, and so do you.

When you decide what you stand for and what your identity is, it will help drive your decision-making processes. If your identity as a speaker is "Making the Complex Easy," then, with everything you offer, you must refrain from using complicated terms. You must let your identity as "The Simplifier" shine.

Why Is Having an Identity So Important?

McDonald's has an identity of consistency. Wherever you go in the world, you can be assured of what you're going to get from McDonald's. What does that do for you? It builds the all-important confidence that influences you to choose them over another restaurant. FedEx's reliability does what? It builds confidence that your package will arrive at its intended destination, within your necessary timeframe. With Southwest Airlines, you know what to expect, and you settle in for a fun ride. The point is that each one of these companies has an identity that builds your confidence in them. If you don't have an identity and you don't sing it from the rooftops, you cheat yourself out of customers and profits. Even worse, whoever *does* have a clear confidence-building identity will take the customers that should have been yours. That hurts!

How Can You Let Your Identity Shine?

Once you uncover your identity, with the help of your customer feedback and testimonials, you must *sing it from the rooftops*. You accomplish this by making a consistent and coordinated effort with all of your marketing pieces. For example, after I uncovered my identity as Mr. Nuts and Bolts, here are some actions I took:

- I wrote a book entitled *The Nuts and Bolts of Public Speaking*
- I created seminars and workshops entitled "The Nuts and Bolts of Management" and "The Nuts and Bolts of Communication"
- I founded the Communication Factory, which goes with the "nuts and bolts" theme
- Instead of using "steps" on my handouts, I now describe each strategy as a "tool," in order to reinforce the "nuts and bolts" theme
- I had a designer create a logo for the Communication Factory, which resembles a factory wheel with an eye (for communication) in it
- Instead of carrying a briefcase or a regular bag, I began carrying a toolbox to my presentations, in order to reinforce the "nuts and bolts" theme
- I offer a "Toolkit" as my newsletter
- I mention nuts and bolts in conversations, interviews, websites, and on my marketing materials

- I call myself Mr. Nuts and Bolts
- With every audio lesson, I end it by saying, "Here are the 'nuts and bolts' takeaway tools for your toolbelt …"

The key is, once I uncovered my identity, all of these changes became *intentional*. Your marketing must be intentional. It should all work together for good. Once you uncover your identity, you need to be intentional in making a consistent message shine through all of your marketing materials and communications. The ways you dress, put together your handouts, design your logo, and communicate all need to reflect this intentional identity. Everything you do should reinforce your identity.

What Is Your Identity?

Based on the feedback you've regularly received from your customers, what do you perceive your identity to be? Now, how can you sing it from the rooftops? List at least five strategies you can use to make that identity shine over everything you do, so that you build the confidence others will have in you. When you raise your identity, you'll raise your income.

How Can You Implement Your Marketing Plan?

Now that you have the makings of a solid marketing plan, it's time to put it to work for you. You need a timeline to go with your tools. The very best way to hold yourself accountable for your marketing plan is to set marketing goals and put them on a "Monthly Marketing Timeline" (see Figure 6-1) as a sample. For additional blank templates that you can download and customize for your own usage, visit www.wcspeaking.com.

Sample Monthly Marketing Timeline

Month of May

Tools	Cost	Comments	Date	Results
E-Newsletter	0	To entire prospect list	5/1	32% Opened
Speeches (back of room sales)	0	Winnipeg	5/4 and 5/5	14 Packs sold
Speeches (back of room sales)	0	Oakland	5/11 and 5/12	13 Packs sold
Send Audio Postcard	0	To current customers	5/14	71% opened
Speeches (back of room sales)	0	Hong Kong	5/18 and 5/20	53 small packs sold
Print Ad	$250	$1,250 Split cost with partners 5 ways	May	Already 11 new sign-ups for boot-camps
Lunch	0	Hong Kong	5/18	Possible Partnership for offering more products in Mainland China
Free Live Coaching Event	$250	Cost is for the space	5/22	Got 2 new Annual Members
Speeches (back of room sales)	0	Doha	5/25	21 packs sold
Inserts	$40	Send out with orders	Everyday	Cross sales

Figure 5-1

Once you build a Monthly Marketing Timeline, you will benefit in two major ways:

1. You will get a very clear understanding of which marketing tools are working and which are ineffective. With this information, you can cut out the ineffective tools and double your efforts on the tools that bring the best return on investment (ROI). This leads to much higher profits.

2. You will hold yourself accountable and follow the most important law of marketing, which is *consistency*. You must market yourself consistently. Remember: Marketing is like breathing. If you don't continue breathing, you die. If you don't continue marketing, your company dies. It's as simple as that.

Acting consistently on your Monthly Marketing Timeline will put you light-years ahead of where most speakers and entrepreneurs currently stand in their businesses. Plus, you will look up a year from now and find yourself swimming in profits and having more opportunities with high-level people than you ever thought possible.

FINAL THOUGHTS ON YOUR MARKETING PLAN

Take your time and really go point-by-point through the six questions that determine your marketing plan. Once you do this, carefully plan out your Monthly Marketing Timeline. Perhaps you can contact an accountability buddy to hold you to what you state on your timeline. When you put the tools from this chapter to work for you, you will be absolutely unstoppable! If you want more resources and background information on creating your marketing plan, as well as information on the Guerrilla Marketing Coach Certification Program, feel free to visit www.gmarketingcoach.com.

Chapter 6

BECOME A MASTERFUL STORYTELLER AND PROFIT FROM THEIR BUY-IN

KEEP YOUR AUDIENCES SPELLBOUND WITH FIVE ESSENTIAL STORYTELLING ELEMENTS

There are several elements that go into telling a story and selling a point. However, the five you find in this chapter will get you moving quickly in the right direction for mastering the art of storytelling. For an in-depth course that will change your future and fortune as a speaker, I suggest picking up my system entitled, "The Edge of Their Seats Storytelling Home-Study Course for Speakers." You can find it at www.edgeoftheirseats.com. In the meantime, let's find out what makes a world-class story, as we dive into the five key elements. In order to understand this section, it is critical to review the following sample story first. Read it through, because we will refer to it as you move through the chapter.

SAMPLE STORY: "6 FIGURES"

I used to work for an Internet company, and I wanted to go into full-time professional speaking. That was my dream. Raise your hand if you have a dream or goal ... raise your hand if you want to do anything in life. I went to the new vice president ... he was a young guy, had the black, slicked-back hair, and kind of looked like Pat Riley.

I said, "Steve, I'm going to be leaving. I'm going to be leaving the organization, because it's always been my dream to be a full-time professional speaker."

He said, "That's your dream, Craig?"

"Yes, it is."

He said, "Well, that's great. I mean, I really admire you for having one. But you can't leave."

"What do you mean I can't leave?"

He said, "Well, we've been thinking about it, and we're going to raise your salary up to this."

"Steve, this is not a financial decision. I'm flattered, but this is a dream decision."

He said, "I understand. But how about if we raise your salary up to this [higher level]?"

"This is not a financial decision. This is a dream decision." Do you know, he raised it four times? I kid you not, he kept saying, "We're going to raise your salary up to this [higher level]."

I repeated, "This is not a financial decision, this is a dream decision!"

He said, "Okay, Craig, how about if we raise your salary to well above six figures?"

I said, "Dreams are overrated!"

Come on, six figures! That was a lot of money back then. That's a lot of money today. I could fill up my gas tank for a week on that kind of salary.

I said, "Steve, before I say yes, I've got to go home and talk to my wife about this."

So I went home to my wife and said, "Honey, I don't know what to do. What should I do?"

My sweet wife looked up at me with her big, brown eyes and said, "Take the money, fool!"

But if you had been sitting beside my wife and me a few minutes later on our black leather sofa with the chocolate chip cookies baking in the background, you would've heard her say something that can absolutely change your life. I know it changed mine. She said, "Craig, you've wanted this ever since we met. This is all you've ever talked about. I don't care how much money they give you, Craig—your dream is not for sale."

That's deep, isn't it? Your dream is not for sale! Let's look at what happens in most people's lives. Most people think the number-one thing that gets between them and their dreams is some kind of bad obstacle. That's not it. The number-one thing that actually gets between them and their dreams is something good—and they settle for it. That's right, sometimes the enemy of the best is the good. My question to you is: Are you too good to be great? Are you too comfortable in your good routine to ever reach greatness? Don't let the good get in the way of the best.

I looked at my wife and said, "See, girl, that's why I married you." And I went back to work the next day, looked at the VP in his eyes, and I was firm! I looked him directly in his face, and I was bold … and I said, "My wife said my dream is not for sale!" I left, and that very year, I spoke 160 times in 44 states and 5 countries—and I'm happy to say I've been running my mouth ever since.

There is nothing special about me, but my wife gave me a special message. Well guess what? That message is also for you. Your dream is not for sale, either. Again, I ask you: Are you too good to be great? Your dream is not for sale.

Note: To listen to this story live, please visit www.craigvalentine.com/stories and click on "6 Figures." This will give you an idea of the effectiveness of the story. Now that you have read (and hopefully listened to) the story, let's dive into how to make your stories come to life.

WHAT MAKES A WORLD-CLASS STORY?

It is important to know the major difference between a story from a world-class speaker and one from a wannabe speaker. Write this down and keep it in constant view:

"Don't restate your story. Relive it
and invite your audience into your re-living room."

As a storyteller, you must put your audience members somewhere in your scene so that they hear what you heard, see what you saw, and feel what you felt. Wannabe speakers retell their stories as if they happened in the past. World-class speakers relive their stories and invite their audiences to come with them. The five tools below are designed to help you relive your stories, draw your audience into your re-living room, and have them walk away with a message that can change their lives. Let's start with that message.

The Edge-Of-Their-Seats Storytelling Model

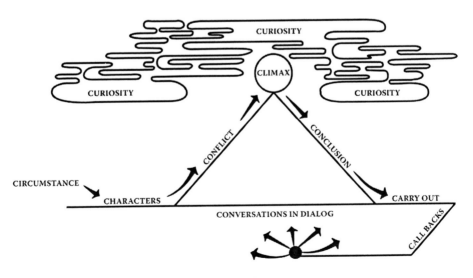

Figure 5-1

Storytelling Tool #1: Carryout Message

Whenever you craft a story, it is critical to start by knowing how you will sell the "carryout message." This is the foundation of your entire story and determines what you keep and what you throw away. *Before* you construct your story, know your message. Even though you don't usually give the message until the end of the story, you still must be clear on what it is before you start developing the story.

The carryout message should come in the form of the *foundational phrase.* Again, this phrase should be fewer than ten words and should pack a powerful punch. For example, one of my foundational phrases is "Your dream is not for sale." Another of my foundational phrases is "What got you here won't get you there." I take each of these phrases and build a story on top of it. Whatever doesn't reinforce the phrase should be tossed out. Whatever does reinforce the phrase should be kept in. Limiting it to fewer than ten words forces you to be crystal clear on your message. If you're not clear on it, your audience doesn't stand a chance of receiving it with clarity.

Once your foundational phrase is clear, you then have to clarify how you intend to sell it. You can do this by writing down two "If ... then" statements for your message. Also, make sure you use the EDGE sales formula. Remember to "push" them into the "pull." The "push" is what your audience wants to avoid. The "pull" is what they want to attain. Use both back-to-back.

Example (push): "If you live on "get set," then you will die on "get set"—taking all your greatness to the grave."

Example (pull): " ... but if you learn to go for it, then you will surprise yourself at what you can do! You'll live the kind of life that leaves people in awe."

When it comes to your foundational phrase, it's not enough to state it. You must also *sell* it. Constantly ask yourself what your audience will get by using your tools. As you learned in chapter three, decide what results you'll claim. Will they

Esteem more?

Do more?

Gain more?

Enjoy more?

Although the carryout message will probably come last in the sequence of the story, it needs to come first in the development of it. Everything gets built on top of this phrase. In terms of your content, when in doubt, toss it out. If it does not fit the foundational phrase, trash it.

OVERVIEW OF THE STORY

Now that we know our foundational message and how to sell it, we need to examine the four most important areas of storytelling. They are the characters, conflict, climax, and conclusion. Let's start with four major questions. As we develop our story, we should have a skeletal approach. This means being able to answer the basic necessities of the story before diving into each section and adding meat to it. Here are the four questions we need to know with absolute certainty.

1. **Who is in this story (main characters)?**

Example: Steve (the vice president), my wife, and me.

2. **What happens to them (conflict)?**

Example: I am forced choose between a higher salary and my dream.

3. **What is their turning point (climax)?**

Example: My wife says, "Your dream is not for sale."

4. **What is the result (conclusion)?**

Example: I say no to the boss, live my dream, and speak 160 times in that first year.

Once we have these four questions answered clearly, we know we have the basis for a real story. If we don't have clarity with this skeletal story, we should stop and get clarity before adding the meat. It does absolutely no good to build on top of a faulty foundation. Now it's time to dive into each of these four elements in detail.

Storytelling Tool #2: Characters

Every good story has interesting characters, and many times, your characters are what give you the strongest connection with your audience members. In fact, at times, your audience members connect more to a certain character in your story than they connect with you. In a way, you connect with them indirectly through some of your characters. For example, I spoke at some senior-citizens' homes when I was about thirty years old. Do you think I connected with them based solely on my experiences? Of course not. Instead, the seniors connected to other characters in my stories and hence connected with me through them. Characters connect you to your audiences, but only if you give your characters the following three *chances*: a chance to be seen, a chance to be known, and a chance to be heard.

A. Give Your Characters a Chance to Be Seen

How can audience members connect with characters that they cannot see? My speech coach, Patricia Fripp, explained to me that the audience members remember what they see in their minds while you speak.

Therefore, I believe it is important for us to make our characters visible. How? Give a brief one- to two-line description of your characters, so that an image will pop into the mind of each audience member. For example, the wonderful motivational speaker Keith Harrell describes an experience that he had in kindergarten, when he sat next to a girl who wore glasses and pigtails. What image pops into your mind? What do you already assume about the girl? Well, when he delivers her lines, she turns out to be exceptionally smart for a five-year-old. I already saw her as intelligent in my mind.

I sat in the audience when famed Ohio sportscaster Jimmy Crum told an unforgettable story of two young siblings. Before he delivered the young girl's line, he described her as having blonde hair, blue eyes, and "innocence written all over her face." I could tell that we all had our own vision of her. It was so powerful that the next day in my seminar, I asked the audience members (same audience) to tell me what she looked like. In unison, they yelled out, "Blonde hair and blue eyes!" Twenty-four hours later, they were still seeing her. In fact, they probably still see her now. I know I do.

Following the Rule of Three, let me give you one more example. Remember the story I gave about the vice president who tried to keep raising my salary so I would stay with the company? Well, this is how I described him: "He was new to the company ... had black, slicked-back hair, which made him look like a young Pat Riley." If you don't know who Pat Riley is, you can still see the VP from the description given. If you do know who Pat Riley is, you can see the VP even more clearly.

Whatever you do, give your characters a chance to be seen, so that we can connect to them.

A Takeaway Task for You

With your upcoming stories, make sure each major character you introduce has at least a brief description. The more important the character, the more specific the description should be. Find creative ways to describe the person. Give your characters a chance to be seen.

B. Give Your Characters a Chance to Be Known

It is not enough to see your characters—we also need to *know* them. If your audience members do not come to know the characters, they will not care about them. If they do not care about them, they will not connect with them. So how do you get your audience to know the characters? Give them an idea from whence those characters came. How? Simply give another line or two about their past. I call this "giving pieces" of the character's personal history. If they don't know where your character came from, they won't care where he is going!

Sometimes, rather than doing it in narration, it might actually be better done in character dialogue. For example, I give a story in which I am speaking (in dialogue) to a character named Jermaine Williams. I describe him and give pieces of his personal history by using the dialogue between characters. Here's how I do it with me speaking to Jermaine:

> "Jermaine, look at you. Eighteen months ago, you walked through these doors as a six-foot-two-inch, hundred-and-twenty-pound, disheveled man. Your beard was all messed up; you had no light in your eyes. And you told me you felt spiritually and emotionally bankrupt ..."

As you can see, this entire description and personal history was given by one character (me) to another (Jermaine). I didn't turn to my audience and say, "Jermaine Williams Jr. was a six-foot-two-inch, hundred-and-twenty-pound African-American man who had a drug problem ..." That's not a story, that's a CNN report! Narration leads to a report. Dialogue leads to a masterful story. Find ways to creatively let us know something about the personal history of your characters. Let's take a character named Bryan. It might be as easy as having the following dialogue: "Wow, Bryan! It's great to see you. When did you get out?"

What do you think? Do you know something about Bryan now? Here's the key to always remember about character development: give your audience members a hint, and let them mentally fill in the blanks.

People buy into what they help create, so let your audience members fill in the blanks of what the character looks like, as well as from whence the character has come. I learned this the hard way. During one of my public-speaking workshops in Ohio, I asked my audience to remind me what one of my characters looked like. Usually, my audience members said things like, "He looked like a surfer dude from Malibu, California." That is actually the correct answer. However, this particular time, a big burly guy in the front row stood up and said, "He had a ponytail." Everyone laughed, and I went over to the guy and said, "He didn't have a ponytail. What makes you think he had a ponytail?" This irritated Mr. Burly, and he stood up with authority and bellowed, "That's how I saw him!" I immediately backed down and said, "Perhaps he *did* have a ponytail."

Let me ask you, should I care exactly how Mr. Burly sees my character? No. What I should care about is that he sees him at all. I gave the hint, and then Mr. Burly filled in the rest of the character's picture. That should have been fine with me. As long as your audience sees your character, you should be fine with that. If Mr. Burly wants to give him a ponytail, so be it. If he sees him by creating his own image, he can connect with him better. Give your characters a chance to be *seen* and a chance to be *known*.

C. Give Your Characters a Chance to Be Heard

Finally, give your characters a chance to be heard. Too often, we give stories where we pass on all the wisdom through our own voice. Look, we did not fall off the encyclopedia truck with all the answers. Your audience wants to know what you know and how you came to know it. Tell stories where another character is the hero or is at least the one who gives the wise statement. *Give your characters the best lines*, and that will keep the audience from perceiving you as a wannabe know-it-all.

In the sample story about the vice president, the lines of wisdom came from my wife. When I was tempted to follow the money and stay with the company, she looked up at me with her shining, brown eyes and said, "Craig … I don't care how much money they offer you, your dream is not for sale." She shared the wisdom, and *she* was heard. She got the best lines. So many audience members approach me afterward and say, "Thank you for that story and for that message." The interesting thing is that they almost always say, "Thank your wife for her message." My wife is the hero, and she is heard.

Dialogue! Dialogue! Dialogue!

By far the biggest mistake most speakers make with their stories is using too much narration and not nearly enough dialogue. Narration puts your audience in the past, as though you are retelling an event. Dialogue puts your audience in the present, as though you and they are reliving the event. Dialogue puts them into your re-living room. If a story is the heart of a speech, dialogue is the heart of a story. It pumps life into the stories. Here's an example of the difference between narration and dialogue:

Narration: My son, who was three years old, turned to me and told me I work all of the time.

Dialogue with narration: My three-year-old son turned to me and said, "Daddy, you work all the time!"

If you heard this during a speech, which one would you *feel* more? The dialogue adds emotion, humor, and real drama to a story. Use it often.

STORYTELLING TOOL #3: CONFLICT

What hooks an audience into a speech? Is it the poignant point? Is it a super story? Is it the delivery? No, it's none of the above. The hook is the *conflict*. Conflict is the hook. Everyone likes a battle. Can you imagine going to a 1980s boxing match and watching "Sugar" Ray Leonard and "Marvelous" Marvin Hagler shaking hands and congratulating each other for twelve rounds? No, because we want to see the fight and understand what strategies are used to win.

Merriam-Webster's definition of "conflict" is: "A clash between hostile or opposing elements, ideas, or forces." In other words, it is a battle. I coach many speakers, and one of the most easily identifiable mistakes they make is not having a story that hooks the audience. Why? No conflict! Conflict helps the audience know where you are going, because they know eventually you will have to face up to that conflict and somehow transcend it. If you build it up and resolve it, they will be interested in the strategies you used and most likely be inspired to use them in similar circumstances.

You may say, "Okay Craig, I get the importance of the hook. So tell me, how can I become a better hooker?" Wait—maybe that should be rephrased as, "What are some best practices for creating an irresistible hook?" If you utilize the following three tools, you'll hook even the toughest of audiences.

A. Identify the Kind of Conflict

First, remember that conflict can be developed in many ways:

Person vs. Person

Person vs. Society

Person vs. Nature

Person vs. His/her environment

Person vs. Himself/herself

Once you know the kind of conflict you have, you can then see how to build on it appropriately. The best conflict is one that eventually comes down to person vs. himself/herself, because it becomes more about *choice* than about chance. When your audience members witness the choice your character makes, perhaps this will influence them to make a similar choice in the future. Remember, we don't speak for what happens that day. We speak for what happens three days, three months, and three *years* down the line in the lives of our audience members. When they get to their next decision point, will they choose their old way or will they remember your story and choose a new way?

B.   Establish the Conflict Early

Once you figure out the kind of conflict you have, it's important to establish that conflict very early in your story. I suggest that you establish the conflict as soon as you have introduced your characters. Throw them into the fire. Put them into a battle. The earlier you do this, the earlier your audience will be hooked. Look at figure 6-1, and notice how quickly the characters get thrown into the conflict. For example, let's go back to my sample story. The conflict started when he said to me, "Craig, you can't leave the company." I established that conflict immediately after introducing him as a character. Do likewise with your story. Sooner is better when it comes to conflict.

C.   Intensify the Conflict

What if the water never rose on the *Titanic*? That movie would have sucked! It's not enough to establish the conflict; now you must intensify it. On the *Titanic*, the water level kept rising and rushing down the halls of the ship until people had to make life-changing decisions. Watching the movie, we were riveted because we wanted to see what strategies people used to get out of that horrible situation. How are you going to raise the water level in your own story? How will you intensify the conflict to such a point where something must give?

In my story, each time the vice president offered me more money, I got more and more frustrated. That was the intensifying of the conflict. Finally, it got to a point in which something had to give. If your conflict never gets to that point, you have not raised its intensity enough. You must find a way to do so. Turn up the heat.

Conflict is the hook to your speech. Therefore, don't go in with stale bait. Go in with these three tools and watch how you catch your audience's attention time and time again.

STORYTELLING TOOL #4: CLIMAX

Too many speakers leave out the most anticipated scene in their story and thereby leave their audiences dissatisfied. In reality, they are cheating their audiences. Think about it: if you bothered to intensify the conflict to the highest peak, then your audience will feel like something needs to give. This is the scene we've been waiting for. Skipping this climactic scene would be like waiting for months for the Muhammad Ali and Joe Frazier fight. We see each boxer going after each other and talking trash in the press conferences, and you can feel the tension rising. Finally, you get to a point where they both stand in the ring, face-to-face, waiting for the bell to start the fight. At that point, we are dying to see what's going to happen. Then, for some odd reason, the TV cuts straight to a post-fight interview with Ali, who is recapping how he won. Wouldn't you feel cheated? This is what speakers do to their audiences all the time. They jump to the conclusion without showing us the actual turning point.

As an audience member, you say, "What? Wait a minute! I need to see the fight. I need to see the strategies and tactics Ali used. I need to see what he avoided and what he employed. I want to see the fight!" If it was pay-per-view, you would certainly ask for your money back. Well, it's the same with stories. If your stories don't have this crucial, climactic scene, not only will your audience members want their money back, but they'll want their wasted time back, too. Think about it: when you waste someone's time, you actually waste part of his *life*. Have you thought about that? Give them what they've been waiting for. Give them the climactic scene! Surely you remember the movie *Jerry Maguire*, in which Cuba Gooding Jr.'s character kept yelling, "Show me the money!" Well, I feel like yelling, "Show me the fight!" Show your audience members the fight and not just the resolution.

Let's get back to my sample story. If you look at figure 6-1, when the conflict rises (due to the numerous raises in salary), it reaches the climax. During the climax, I am completely at my wit's end, and I go to my wife for advice. That scene is the fight. In other words, it's the inner battle I have until my wife comes in and gives her life-changing advice. She says, "Craig, your dream is not for sale." What she gives me in the climactic scene is a cure. This cure makes all the difference for me and becomes the tool I use to choose my outcome. When you raise your conflict to the climactic scene, who or what comes along and gives you your cure? What is that cure? These are the questions that need to be answered in the climactic scene.

The Steve Story

In another one of my stories, I share how my friends discouraged me from writing my first book. They said things like, "Don't you know the odds of getting it published? Don't you know it probably won't work out? Don't you know that even if you self-publish it, you still have to market it, and not that many people know you?"

Okay, based on what you know about this story, what is the conflict? Of course, it is me trying to battle through the negative opinions of my friends. How is it escalated? With each negative comment, I feel worse and worse until I'm about to burst. Finally, we get to the climactic scene, which I affectionately refer to as "The Battle at Bursting Point." In this scene, I called my friend Steve and asked for his help. Steve said, "Craig, you go ahead and write that book, and know that I will be the first one in line to purchase it." Relieved, I said to him, "Steve … that is $15.95."

Let's go back to the two questions that must be addressed in the climactic scene.

A. Who or what came along and gave me the cure? The answer is Steve.

B. What was the cure? The answer is the positive, affirming statement from Steve that refocused me and pushed me through all the negativity.

Steve was the hero. Are you sensing a trend here? The key is to make someone or something else the hero. Are you doing that with your stories?

Simply put, you need a scene in which the obstacle (the conflict) is transcended. That scene is called the *climax*. Look again at figure 6-1, and think of the climax just as it sounds: like you have "climbed" to the "max." It is the maximum point of the mountain. This scene is where everything comes to a head, and we finally get to see what strategies are employed and what results they bring. After the climax, at least some of the characters will never again be the same. The characters will have changed as a result of what they learned in the journey so far. Many times this is a *revelation* scene, because the characters gain an insight they didn't previously have. It's the *breakthrough* scene. Always ask yourself, "What is the revelation?" If *you* don't know it, *we* won't know it.

What Else Should the Climactic Scene Include?

The climax scene should include a *significant emotional event* in which a realization or revelation occurs within the mind of a character. My scene was emotional because I went from being so upset about my so-called friends' negativity to being relieved by Steve's encouraging words.

In addition to having a significant emotional event, this climactic scene should also include a passing of wisdom, lessons, or strategies. I call these "new ways." This new way might be a new way to look, think, or act about something. It might be a new strategy, tool, or solution. In this Steve story, I learned a new way to look at my situation (I received hope) and obviously decided to write that first book.

Finally, in addition to the significant emotional event and the passing on of the new ways, the best climactic scenes also involve someone or something providing you with this new way. I call this someone or something "the guru." This person or thing is where you get the new way. In other words, the guru provides you with the cure you've been dying for as the intensity of your conflict increased.

In my story about the VP increasing my salary, who was the guru? That's right: my wife was the guru, by sharing with me that my "dream is not for sale." In this story about me wanting to write a book, my friend Steve was the guru, by giving me a positive outlook.

So always ask yourself: "Am I cheating my audience by not showing them the fight? What was my revelation? What was the significant emotional event that made the difference during the climax? What was the new way I, or one of my specific characters, learned? Who was the guru?" If you can answer these questions, chances are you'll give your audience more than what they expected. That's a very good thing!

STORYTELLING TOOL #5: CONCLUSION

By "conclusion," I mean the conclusion of your story, not of your entire speech. Let's revisit the fourth question we asked at the top of this section: what is the result (conclusion)? In other words, once you get the cure or new way, what does it do to the characters? Let's go back to my sample story. Once I get the cure from my wife (i.e., "Your dream is not for sale"), do I *change*? Yes, I change as a character. With this change, I go back to the VP and let him know I am not selling out my dream for a higher salary. As a result, I end up speaking 160 times that very year. I did not let the good get in the way of the best for me.

The conclusion is such a key because it *sells people* on your message before you even get to your carryout message. The story does most of the selling, because the audience sees my results, and its members figure they can get similar results with whatever they want to achieve. Their inner dialogue goes something like this: "So if I don't let the good get in the way of my best, I can live my dreams, too. I'm going to take that class (or make whatever change)."

Here are the two questions you must answer during the conclusion of your story (not your speech):

A. How have your characters changed as a result of the climax?

In my story about wanting to write the book, my friend Steve gave me the new way of thinking, through his positive affirmation. What was the conclusion? The result was that, despite my friends' negative opinions, I wrote the book, and it became quite popular. *The Nuts and Bolts of Public Speaking* still sells many copies today. That is the result that came from Steve's wisdom.

B. Have you answered all the questions in the mind of your audience members?

For years, I had been telling a story about my wife and me on a swamp tour of the Louisiana bayou. I shared how we got the chance to hold a live alligator. However, we ran out of film, and we wanted proof. Then I explained how this gentleman next to us said, "I'll take a picture of you with my camera, and then I'll send it to you." I always went on with the story, not thinking twice about what I was doing to my audiences with that scene. Finally, one courageous young lady approached me after one of my speeches and said, "There is something that has been bugging me for most of your speech." I asked, "What's that?" She said, "I just need to know: did you ever get the picture from that guy?" I answered, "Yes, I did. In fact, I have the picture on my computer."

Do you see what happened here? *She was stuck in the swamp!* She still had a question in her mind that I had left unanswered. Far too often, speakers leave their audience members still pondering something about their story. The time to wrap up all questions is during the conclusion. This is your final catch-all period, and nothing should be left unanswered. With this lady, even though I had gone on in my speech, she was still stuck in the swamp. Unanswered questions are invitations for your audience members' minds to go off on tangents. When this happens, *you* don't happen. Your message gets lost, because your audience is no longer mentally there to receive it. The solution to this is to check and recheck to make sure all questions are answered during the conclusion. We must know how the characters have *changed* as a result of the story.

FINAL THOUGHTS ON STORYTELLING

Again, wannabe speakers restate their stories. World-class speakers *relive* their stories and invite their audience members into their re-living room. You'll find specific ways to do this in my "Edge of Their Seats Storytelling Home-Study Course for Speakers." To master speaking, you must master storytelling. This only happens as a result of studying and practicing with the right tools. You'll learn how to invite your audience into your scene, captivate them when they are there, and leave them feeling extremely grateful for the experience.

If you send an email to craig@edgeoftheirseats.com, you will immediately receive a code that gives you 20 percent off the purchase price of the home-study course. The story is the heart of any speech. When you master storytelling, you bring your speech to life!

Chapter 7

How to Systematically Generate Leads with Your Presentations

Most small businesses and entrepreneurs would be absolutely shocked if they knew just how much money they are leaving on the table by either not using or misusing the art of public speaking to market their business. After this chapter, you will have an unfair advantage in using presentations to quickly generate leads, customers, and huge profits. You will learn how to accomplish more with a one-hour speech than most will accomplish with a full month of frustrating marketing efforts. If you want to rapidly raise immediate and long-term profits, this chapter is one of your most essential tools. Come with me to uncover its power. In the next few pages, you will learn how to use your presentations to generate more qualified leads in one hour than most entrepreneurs get in one month.

GENERATE MORE LEADS IN AN HOUR
THAN MOST ENTREPRENEURS GET IN A MONTH

A few years back, my business partner, Darren La Croix (founder of The Humor Institute), kept telling me, "Craig, you have to start collecting names when you speak. You need to begin building your list." I always replied, "List shmist—who needs it? I am doing fine with my product sales at my events." Little did I know how much money and recurring income I was leaving on the table each time I spoke. Then, one day, it happened. Darren called and said, "Craig, I just sent out a marketing sales letter to my list, promoting my new course, and guess how much I sold?" Not really paying much attention, I said, "Okay, Darren, how much?" He answered, "A little over twenty-three thousand dollars. *Today.*" Stunned, I perked up and asked, "Okay, Darren, what was that you've been saying about a list?"

Suddenly, I was sold on building my list. Building a qualified list of prospects and customers will propel you far beyond most entrepreneurs who attempt to turn their presentations into profits. Using the storytelling formula from chapter six to sell your products will be profitable. What you learn in the upcoming chapter eight about back-of-the-room sales will also bring you loads of revenues. However, you will still be leaving tons on the table if you do not follow up with those who have not purchased from you.

Here is a phrase that Darren and I came up with that you should burn into your memory: "Speak TALL and carry a big list." (Of course, TALL stands for "Think, Act, Laugh, and Learn.") Making your audience TALL, while consistently generating your list, will lead to a remarkable connection with them and passive recurring revenues for you. That means that you'll eventually make as much money while you're asleep as you do while you're awake.

You Must Follow Up

The key to Darren's profits, and now to mine as well, is the list, because it allows us to do follow-up marketing to qualified prospects and actual customers. The question is, how do you build this list from the speaking platform? There are several methods we use, but none will work if you are not making them TALL (Think, Act, Laugh, and Learn) during your presentations. That's why it's critical to master chapters two through four for structure, content, and delivery. After all, speaking is the perfect opportunity to quickly build confidence and familiarity with your audience. As a certified Guerrilla Marketing Coach, I understand that confidence and familiarity will determine from whom your prospects will buy. Let's look into four of these list-building strategies:

1. **Use clipboards.** Toward the end of your presentation, you can have volunteers pass around several clipboards to your audience members. Each clipboard should have sheets with about twenty-five spots for names and email addresses. The key is to make sure you have built up one of your *processes* (i.e., "4 Steps to Walk out of Debt") so that your audience is excited about the results they can get from it. They desperately want access to it. Then you offer part of that process *for free* when they place their name and email address on the clipboard. Part of the process might be your free four-part "Walk out of Debt Toolkit." Whatever your process is, your audience must see the clear and compelling results of signing up.

2. **Name that newsletter.** As we covered in chapter five, but which is worth repeating, nobody wakes up in the morning saying, "I just can't wait to get on someone else's newsletter today!" However, people do wake up thinking, "I really would like to know how to become a better speaker" or "I would love to have some tools to build my business" or "I have got to get my finances together; I wonder if anyone can help me." That's why it always floors me to see presenters say things like, "Sign up for my newsletter today. It's *free!*" So what? I can sign up for a million newsletters for free. The question is, what will I get out of it? What's in it for me? I used to have a hard time getting people to sign up on the spot for mine, until I changed the name from "Craig Valentine's Free e-Newsletter" to "FREE Public-Speaking Mastery Toolkit!" Since then, I have put together the "World Class Speaking Toolkit" as well, and the benefit (i.e., "Become a world-class speaker!") is implied. Now that the results of signing up are embedded in the name of the newsletter, people line up to sign up in droves. Name your newsletter with a promised "result," and you will start seeing lines of people anxiously waiting to become your next prospects.

3. **Offer a drawing to collect business cards at your event.** The key here is to offer one of your products for free and promote the results of using it by selling it with a story while you do the drawing. This kills two birds with one stone, because now you are building *a lust for your product and a list for your profits.* Later, you can use online tools and relevant content to entice them to

opt into your newsletter. There are some people who cannot stand when the speaker sells from the platform. The great thing about using a drawing is that nobody gets offended when you talk about a product that you are about to give away. People love freebies, so they get wrapped up in wanting your product, and they yearn to hear all about it!

Build a lust for your products and a list for your profits.

4. **Place signage on your resource table.** As you now know, everything you do should be intentional in getting your prospects and customers to take the next logical step in your process. Once you get audience members to visit your resource table, you can easily motivate them to become a subscriber to your newsletter, blog, or membership site by making your offer visible and clear via signs. For example, here are three examples of what your sign can say:

    - FREE Get Out of Debt Toolkit! Sign in here
    - FREE World Class Speaking 7-Part e-MiniCourse! Sign in here
    - 5 FREE Special Reports for Motivating Your Employees! Sign in here

Of course, these signs can also say "Today Only!" in order to create the sense of urgency. With these signs, it will be difficult for visitors to leave your resources table without signing up. Make sure your sign up forms are clear enough and provide enough space for them to put their names and email addresses. See figure 7-1 as an example of a clear and simple sign-up form.

The "Edge-of-Their-Seats" Storytelling Home-Study Course for Speakers

The price is low compared to the high cost of standing still...

SIX SPECIAL BONUSES	Special Speaking Pack!
Home-Study Course!	**Free Bonus!** **FREE Bonus!**

6CDs + 65 pg Workbook!   **5 Online Training Audios**   **Model Keynote Speech**
$297.00   + $50.00   + $30.00

Total Retail Price = $377.00 – Special Conference Discount = $197

Total price for everything (with discount) is...

Only
$197

Yes, credit cards are accepted!

Name: _____

Card #: _____

Card type: Visa ☐   MC ☐   AMEX ☐

Expiration date _____ / _____   **Discount Price = $197**

Address: _____

City/State: _____ Zip _____

Email: _____ @ _____

Phone: _____

Signature: _____

Fax your order to **410-381-8417** or visit www.EdgeOfTheirSeats.com
Copyright © 2007-2008 The Communication Factory, LLC.

Figure 7-1

As you can see from figure 7-1, you can put check boxes for various interests. Look at each one of these boxes as a *separate prospect list.* For example, if they check off the "Edge" box, I'll put them in a prospect list to receive information and offers from the World Champions' Edge Company. If they check off "Cruise," I'll put them in a prospect list to receive information about the next speakers' cruise. Give them the choices, and let them get on as many lists as they want.

These are only four ways to build your list while you speak. Again, none of these ways will work unless you make your audience TALL (Think, Act, Laugh, and Learn), because that's how you build their confidence in you. You will find that the deeper you connect with them, the faster your list will grow.

Build Your List and Watch Your Number of Corporate Engagements Soar!

You'll also find that many of the individuals who sign up for your lists will begin to recommend you to their various organizations for speaking opportunities. Don't think that just because you're dealing with individual prospects, you're not building your corporate business, too. It's quite the contrary. The majority of my corporate prospects come from individual subscribers to my newsletters and blogs who have built up confidence in me over months and years. The same will happen with you. Speak TALL and carry a big list!

ONE LAST THOUGHT ON BUILDING YOUR LIST

What you do with a little, you do with a lot. What does this mean? It means you must get into the habit of building your list, no matter how small the numbers are in your audience. If you speak to ten people, build your list. If you speak to a hundred people, build your list. What you do with the ten forms the habit for what you do with the hundred. I used to think, "Oh, well, there are only ten people here. There's no need to take out my clipboard and build my list." This thought process set me back years, because of three major pieces of understanding I didn't have back then.

1. What you do with ten, you do with a hundred and five hundred and a thousand. I didn't correctly form the habit of building my list.

2. It takes only one qualified person to bring you hundreds of thousands of dollars in business by recommending you to his or her organization. If they're on your list, chances are much higher that they'll gain the confidence in you to make that recommendation.

3. It's not the number of people that matters, it's each's potential lifetime value as a customer. Currently, the lifetime value of my individual coaching customers exceeds $4,200. The majority of these coaching customers become customers after spending time receiving my newsletters and audio lessons. Therefore, let's say I built a small list of ten people in an engagement, and one of them eventually ended up as a coaching customer. Isn't $4,200 worth bringing out the clipboard for that "tiny" group? Form the habit of building your list every single time.

WHAT YOU NEED TO GENERATE LEADS THE TRADITIONAL WAY

As you know, this book recommends that you look at yourself not only as a speaker but as an expert who speaks and generates multiple income streams from your expertise. This is not the traditional way of landing a speech and getting paid a standard fee. However, you should not throw out the traditional baby with the bathwater. After all, getting a speaking fee from a corporation is another stream of income and can be very healthy. This section describes what you need to have and need to be in order to work with meeting planners and speaker bureaus with great success.

I have been fortunate enough to put on Speaker Champ Camps with Carrie Perrien Smith. She is the president of Soar with Eagles, which is a speaker bureau that has a book-publishing division that focuses on the needs of speakers. Upon deciding to write this book, I immediately thought of Carrie as the person with the most expertise to speak on behalf of what speaker bureaus and meeting planners are looking for when deciding to hire speakers. Carrie agreed to let me interview her for this section, and you'll be wise to heed her advice. Here it goes!

INTERVIEW WITH CARRIE PERRIEN SMITH

Craig: Carrie, let's start from the very beginning. What exactly is a speaker bureau?

Carrie: Craig, speaker bureaus, in general, are different from agents. An agent is focused on finding speaking engagements for specific speakers. An agent's target client is a speaker that he or she might want to represent. A bureau's target client, on the other hand, is a meeting planner who needs to book speakers for events. Speakers are the "product" that the bureaus offer to their clients. While speaker bureaus operate under different business models, most focus on calling on meeting planners. Some bureaus do carry some exclusives—speakers who send all their inquiries and bookings through the bureau. Exclusives are generally pop-culture icons and celebrities who don't want to deal with the details of bookings, contracts, marketing, etc.

With the exception of exclusives, a bureau can book almost any speaker available. Some keep an elaborate database of speakers, and most show a selection of speakers on their website. Just because a speaker isn't listed on their website, it doesn't mean they won't call them. Some bureaus charge the speakers to be listed on their website, because there are site-maintenance expenses.

A bureau can save a meeting planner time and money. When the bureau finds that a meeting planner needs a speaker, they put together a list of speakers to consider that fits the organization's needs—such as budget, topic, demographics, etc. Today, many speakers have online video, so the bureau can send links to the client to view the videos. If hardcopy video or DVD is requested, they send those to their meeting planners. Once the meeting planner makes a decision, the bureau negotiates the deal with the speaker. Once the deal is finalized, the bureau handles the contracts and makes sure that all the needs of the speaker and the hiring organization are met (travel, audiovisual, etc.)

Craig: Great. What does it cost to work with a speaker bureau?

Carrie: Speakers should consider the bureau a marketing expense. Bureaus bring a speaker a nice, warm, gift-wrapped lead that they wouldn't have known about otherwise. The bureau deducts their commission out of the speaker's fee (minus travel). Most bureaus charge 25 percent of the fee. There are a few that charge 20 or 30 percent.

I collect 50 percent of the fee (the deposit) once the contract is finalized, and I take my 25 percent commission at that time. The rest of the fee is due on the day of the event, and I collect that from the client and pay the speaker on that day.

Craig: Carrie, since we are on the topic of fees, let's talk about our fees as speakers. I know I offer fee ranges for local engagements, for multiple engagements, and for nonprofit entities that are less than I offer to my regular corporate clients. However, I always strive to keep the all-important "fee integrity." Can you give us some background on this important topic, whether we're dealing with speaker bureaus or our own clients?

Carrie: Craig, "fee integrity" means that you charge one organization the same fee you would charge another. It also means that you would charge the hiring organization the same fee as you would quote through the speaker bureau. Not every organization has your fee; however, they have things a speaker values that they might be able to offer. These items might cost the organization very little. However, these trades have a monetary value that motivates some speakers to reduce their fee while maintaining fee integrity. These may include the group's mailing list, videotaping, meetings with key decision makers, articles on their website or in their newsletter, an exhibit booth at their conference, memberships, and other avenues for giving that speaker exposure.

Another way speakers maintain fee integrity is to have a fee schedule that addresses different organizations' needs and budgets. I often see an association or nonprofit discount that runs 50 to 75 percent of a speaker's normal fee.

Speakers commonly offer a local fee within a short distance of their home. Mine is 200 miles. Some offer a discount if the engagement is within two hours or within their state. Some speakers reduce their speaking fee if the client buys the speaker's books for the attendees. If an organization books more than one date with the same client, it's common to see the speaker offer discounts of up to 25 percent.

I encounter some speakers or their bureaus that will add my bureau fee on top of their fees but would offer the lower fee to the clients directly (minus my fee). I don't do business with those speakers or their bureaus, because that isn't the way the speaking business works. A bureau should be rewarded for their marketing work, without gouging the meeting planner on cost. There are thousands of speakers, and I can easily move on to another who will do a great job for my client and who understands fee integrity.

Craig: I've heard about some speakers adding that 25 percent bureau fee on top of their regular fee, and I agree that this is no way to do business. That is not fee integrity, and these same speakers will suffer the consequences. Isn't it true that speaker bureaus are good at raising red flags about certain speakers?

Carrie: Absolutely. Associations, meeting planners, and speaker bureaus all talk to each other. It is really awkward when a speaker gets caught offering different fees to different organizations. It's a quick way to get blackballed in the industry.

Craig: Well said. What about spin-off business? I've always been taught to go after spin-off business but to make sure that the business goes through the speaker bureau. After all, that is the bureau's client, correct?

Carrie: That's right Craig. When a bureau gets you in front of an audience, whether you spoke for free or fee, *the speaker bureau owns the client relationship.*

Any future business that comes from that audience needs to go back to the speaker bureau. It's very awkward for a speaker to address that concern when a bureau finds out the speaker didn't honor that industry rule. It's also very sad when the other bureaus find out what happened. There are plenty of speakers who are willing to honor that rule. This is why it's so important to remember to ask someone who contacts you, "How did you hear about me?"

Craig: I came across that very situation years ago. I had worked with a bureau that initiated an engagement for me. However, I thought it fell through, and I honestly completely forgot about them. Then, about a year later, the company called me directly and booked me for two engagements. I asked, "How did you hear about me?" They told me it was initially through the speaker bureau a year earlier. This jogged my memory, and I contacted the speaker bureau to tell them about it. Guess what? They were out of business. However, because I knew the owner of the former bureau, I sent him a check for 25 percent of my revenues. He said, "Thanks, Craig. You didn't have to. The client is yours now." He was very grateful. Is there anything else we should know about fees?

Carrie: Some speakers add their travel allowance into their fee. This gives them the freedom to make their own travel arrangements. An "in-demand" speaker may need to book two one-way tickets as they travel from one speaking engagement to another. That can be awkward to explain to a meeting planner when they are booking your travel. Most meeting planners like one all-inclusive, prepaid price that covers all travel expenses except hotel cost. It makes their budgeting and bookkeeping easier. Keeping an average of your travel expenses will help you determine what amount is right for you.

Craig: Since we are talking about generating leads here, and this is a legitimate income stream, how do speakers get on the radar of these speaker bureaus?

Carrie: On average, only about 10 percent of the most popular speakers' bookings come from a speaker bureau (unless they have an exclusive contract with a bureau). It doesn't make sense for a speaker to invest a ton of time and expense marketing to them. However, it is important to make yourself *easy to do business with*. Remember: a speaker isn't the typical bureau's client. The more time bureaus spend talking with speakers, the less time they have to talk with meeting planners who want to book speakers.

Most bureaus aren't interested in a speaker under $2500. There is a lot of expense in running a bureau, and it takes time to research speakers, draft contracts, negotiate terms, and make sure everyone's needs are met. There are also the costs of maintaining a business to consider, as well. They need to make sure their expenses in handling those functions will be covered by the contract.

Craig: What if you're not up to $2,500 as a speaker yet?

Carrie: Even if you aren't up to $2500, it's okay to make contact with bureaus just to get on their radar. They might be trying to win the attention of a client who has a variety of meetings with different budget needs to accommodate. I have one client that has meetings with speaker budgets that vary from $500 to $50,000. It's best to have what you need to market yourself and avoid being a pest.

Craig: Carrie, since you brought that up, what specific tools do speakers need to market themselves to bureaus and meeting planners?

Carrie: Here are twelve tools for marketing yourself to a speaker bureau or meeting planner:

#1: Be great on the platform. Along with being in front of an audience you've earned the right to speak to, being great on the platform will generate additional bookings (spin-off business) for you.

#2: Be professional and easy to do business with. Be client-focused and have great follow up. Your meeting planner will judge you based on your abilities on and off the platform. Your ability to create a great customer experience off the platform will determine whether you'll be booked again or referred by that meeting planner.

#3: Have a video or audio recording of a live program. Video is preferred, but most meeting planners know that they have fewer options to review speakers in the lower budget ranges. Many meeting planners won't book a speaker without seeing or hearing their live program. If a speaker is just getting started, there is no excuse for not having a live-audio recording. The technology is simple to use and inexpensive.

#4: Have a website with topics, current photos, and video. Your website can make you look like a $30 speaker or a $15,000 speaker. Spend as much as you can afford, and plan your content carefully. There is no more important marketing tool for a speaker today. Make your video or audio recording available on your website as well. That will save you money and time. Meeting planners are growing accustomed to viewing speaker videos on the Internet.

#5: Get professional business cards. You need your picture on them, and it never hurts to have your topics on the card, as well.

#6: Get a professional email address and website domain name. Yourname@yourname.com is perfect. An email that says suzyspeaks@

hotmail.com says you are a new speaker, you don't take yourself seriously, and you speak for thirty dollars. Successful speakers need to build a brand image, and Internet presence is a great way to do that.

#7: Have a professionally produced one-sheet. The one-sheet is a powerful marketing piece. You can print it, but it's also a perfect addition to your website as a PDF file download. Meeting planners can download it to print, email the link to others, or just view it online. It's an important piece in the decision-making process for the meeting planner. It will list your brief bio, tagline or positioning statement if you have one, your topics, and your photo and contact information. The most important thing to remember is to make sure your content is focused on the needs of the client and what you can do for them.

#8: Constantly develop your expertise. Speakers who make themselves the guru on their topic (and market themselves as a guru) garner the highest fees in the industry. They earn the right to speak to certain audiences, because they know that audience and their needs, in addition to their own expertise.

#9: Maintain a reputation for honesty and integrity. Your character accompanies you everywhere—on the platform and off. Audiences hold speakers to a high standard of truth, ethics, and integrity. Make sure you live high values in both your personal and professional life. Audience members have a way of seeing through a smarmy speaker's smokescreen.

#10: Speak on no more than three topics that you deliver better than anyone else. The speakers that make the most money speak on one or two topics. They deliver the same material enough so that they know it well and can focus on the audience and further develop their delivery. They also invest time in continuing to develop their expertise in that one area. This is where the most experienced speakers learn they can work smarter instead of harder. Developing a lot of different speeches can eat up quality time that can be spent on making one or two topics exceptional.

#11: Know whom you've earned the right to speak to and who loves you on the platform. This is lesson number one in marketing yourself. No one else can market you until you know how to market yourself.

#12: Have a killer defining/positioning statement. This is a sentence or two that tells someone what you do, who you do it for, and how your target audience benefits. It's like a mission statement, only a mission statement is meant for the inside of an organization, and the positioning or defining statement is intended to inform those outside an organization. It's like a tagline but a little longer. Here is the one I use for my speaker bureau: "We work with people who organize meetings and book speakers. They trust us to provide the right speaker and create an unforgettable meeting experience." The purpose is to tell someone enough about your business to inspire them to ask for more.

Craig: Carrie, thank you so much for sharing your valuable insights on working with speaker bureaus and meeting planners.

FINAL THOUGHT ON WORKING WITH BUREAUS AND MEETING PLANNERS

As a book publisher who works with speakers, Carrie Perrien Smith is an invaluable contact to have. If you need any of the tools she mentioned (i.e., professional one-sheet, etc.) feel free to proactively reach out to her at www. soarhigher.com. I personally recommend her.

GET COMPENSATED EVEN WHEN YOU SPEAK FOR FREE!

One of the best ways to generate leads is by speaking for free. However, when you speak for free, you should always get compensated. A few years back, a friend asked me to speak to his Rotary Club in Baltimore at eight o'clock on a Saturday morning. Honestly, I could think of nothing I would have rather done less than spend my guarded Saturday morning speaking for free to a tiny group that had never heard of me. Whoa, was I wrong! What I did not realize at the time was that my opportunities were about to explode.

I agreed to speak as a favor to my friend and wound up in front of twenty-four people that Saturday. To my surprise, there were young professionals, seasoned executives, and everyone in between. I gave a short twenty-minute presentation on the art of public speaking, mixed in some relevant stories, and drove home some universal points. Afterward, I shook a few hands and figured that was it.

As a result of that twenty-minute, *free* speech to twenty-four Rotary Club members, I got *four new paying clients*. But it gets better: One of those clients is a federal-government agency that has hired me to speak at their National

Public Affairs Conference in Washington DC. As a result of that conference, the agency has put me on tour doing speaking and training engagements around the country.

In addition, a state-government agency hired me multiple times, too, and—fortunately—these engagements are in Maryland. Thousands upon thousands of dollars in speaking fees have come from that one free speech on a Saturday morning in Baltimore. That's how easy it is to move from free to fee. The best part about it is that *you* could be next. Look up your local Rotary Club, Kiwanis Club, Chambers of Commerce organizations, and other mixed groups, and volunteer to speak at one of their meetings. You will be extremely glad you did.

Why Does Speaking for Free Work?

Why will speaking for free do wonders for you? Because of this undeniable fact about the business of speaking: the best and easiest way to get speaking opportunities is for people to see you speak. This goes back to having your audience members gain confidence and familiarity with you, so that they walk away saying, "We should use that speaker for something in the future." No demo tape, website, or press kit will do as much for you as twenty minutes in front of the right audience. This is, of course, assuming that you leverage it correctly. Let's look at ten ways you can get well-compensated from your free speeches.

Ten Ways to Be Well-Compensated from Every Free Speech You Give

When you get your speaking opportunities, use these ten strategies to pick up all the money and opportunities other speakers consistently leave on the table:

1. **Get referrals.** You are absolutely responsible for letting your audience members know what else you do and the other ways you can help them. Learning to do this seamlessly, without distracting from your presentation, will keep you booked solid and expand your opportunities. For example, I once conducted a full-day seminar for a city-government agency in Washington DC. During the teambuilding program, I began to sense that they appreciated the tools they were getting but didn't quite know when they would have the time to implement them. Finally, I came out and asked, "Do you feel like you're on your heels so much that you won't be able to find time to move forward with these strategies? Do you feel that you're constantly putting out fires?" They nodded their heads in agreement almost to the point of whiplash. Then I said, "I've always been told that planning is the answer. For every minute you plan, you reduce the time it takes to complete something by four minutes. For every hour you plan, you reduce the time it takes to do something by four hours. Imagine what kind of leverage you would have with an entire day of planning. You could get off your heels and actually start moving forward. How would that feel for you?" They liked what they heard.

By the time we finished that workshop, we had a new date set for our planning day, and I was hired as the facilitator. Because I let them know what else I can bring to the table, we expanded our business relationship. People will refer you or rebook you only when they know specifically what else you can bring to the table. Let them know. Don't be shy.

Another strategy you can use is the related-story technique. When I speak to organizations, I always mention a customer with whom I have worked. For example, even if I speak to an organization about presentation skills, I still begin a story in the following fashion:

"Do you know any managers who were moved up into management before they were ready? Have you ever seen someone who was excellent on the front line but terrible in management? Why does this happen? It's probably because managers require a whole new skill set. In fact, you should have seen me working helping this one new manager make a seamless transition into management. After all, it's the foundation for the rest of his management experience. So there we were …"

What have I done with the beginning of this story? Even though I was teaching presentation skills, I told a story to prompt them to think, "Hey, he does management training, too!" Not only that, but I insinuated the importance of having management training and demonstrated what happens when you don't. Having these kinds of stories in your repertoire will get you so much referral business that you'll probably have to turn some away. In that case, hand it over to a speaker you trust. That way the customer is still served, you are still involved, and the reciprocity from this speaker will come back manifold.

2. **Get prospects to sign up for your newsletter** so you can market to them later.

3. **List them** as an audience you have served. One way to build credibility is to have a list of other audiences that thought enough of you to bring you in to speak. Again, this helps raise your prospects' confidence in you.

4. **Record every single speech,** at least in audio, so you can turn these programs into profits. For example, you might do a program on networking and then create an audio CD of the program to sell for $39.95 to future audiences. It does not matter that you are volunteering to speak. Again, nobody has ever listened to an audio CD and then complained, "It's good stuff, but it sounds like he's speaking for free." If the content is good, you should sell it.

5. **Get testimonials** from your audience members. Other than someone actually seeing you in action, testimonials are the best tool for gaining that credibility, confidence, and familiarity with new audiences. The key nowadays is not to simply get the written kind but also the audio and video testimonials as well. You are already recording your speech, so it should not be too much extra effort to record testimonials from your audience members. They will go a long way! Visit www. craigvalentine.com to see how I use these audio and video testimonials as marketing weapons.

6. **Transcribe your recorded speech** and turn it into an e-book or a supplement to a home-study course or training program. I did this with my "Storytelling Home-Study Course." I went to elance.com, hired a transcriber, and had my seven hours of audio turned into an e-book to supplement the home-study course. Likewise, you can leverage your free speeches into audio products and then into e-books (or special reports, manuals, etc.) and sell them for a very handsome profit. People spend hours and hours per week in their automobiles, and right now, your target market should be listening to you. Are they?

7. **Videotape your free speech** and use parts of it for a demo DVD for prospective clients. My first forty-thousand-dollar contract came from me sending a demo tape of a full-length sixty-minute free speech I gave to a Toastmasters district audience years ago. Although the filming was not at a professional level, and all my bloopers and blemishes were left in, the content and connection were good enough to get me hired. Use free speeches as an opportunity to build your valuable video footage. Eventually, you will get professional videographers who can help you leverage your free speech into a full-blown DVD set. You can see Craig's latest demo video at www.craigvalentine.com and Mitch's at www.MitchMeyerson.com, and this can give you ideas for yours.

8. **Sell your products and services** to the audience members right there on the spot. Make sure you get permission from the meeting planners ahead of time, because the cultures in some organizations will not allow for it. On the other hand, if you agree to speak for free at an event, they will usually be more than happy to set you up with a table—and even provide you with a helper—to make your learning resources available for sale.

9. **Provide leave-behinds** that put you ahead. If you provide a well-thought-out, well-constructed, and well-produced "Top Tips List," your audience members will not toss it into the trash can. Instead, they will keep it around and possibly even hang it up somewhere. Whether it is "The Top 10 Tips to Reduce Stress" or the "Top 10 Reasons Sales Presenters Lose the Business," if the content is good and the vehicle (i.e., a magnet, laminated card, etc.) is convenient, your prospects will save it. As a result, it will market your services to

them every day, whether they know it or not. When they realize they need help in that area, whom do you think they will call? Why? They will have confidence in you.

10. Perhaps the best compensation you can get from giving free speeches is your *growth as a speaker*. As a speaker, nothing takes the place of stage time. Feedback from others will help you grow tremendously. In addition, if you tape yourself, you can review it and see how to improve with each and every speech. To this day, I still review every speech I give. In my basketball career, we used to review the tapes of previous games to see how to win the next one. Now, I review audio and video of previous speeches to see how to win over the next audience. You can do the same.

Speaking for Free is Priceless

As you can see, speaking for free is priceless. And when you start leveraging these speeches by getting testimonials, demo DVDs, and new connections, you will rapidly find yourself commanding healthy fees for your future speeches.

Negotiate to Kick New Doors Wide Open

What good are leads that you don't convert? Whether it's an individual or a corporation, you can use the tools you pick up in this section to convert these leads and keep your profits flowing. When you learn to negotiate, a whole new world opens for you. Don't devalue yourself or your experience.

Get what you're worth. Even if I have to be the first one to tell you this, you are worth it! You are worth it! You are worth it!

LEARNING THE HARD WAY

Years ago, a meeting planner from a federal-government agency called and said, "Mr. Valentine, one of our staff personnel saw you speak at an event and recommended you to be the speaker for our National Public Affairs Conference in Philadelphia this summer. We need a one-hour program teaching our public-affairs personnel presentation skills. Are you available— and what do you charge?"

The "charge" question trips up many speakers, and I was no different on that day. I'm almost embarrassed to share this, but I certainly want you to learn from my painful example. I said, "Ms. Johnson, the fee is $4,500. However, because this is a local engagement, I can take off $1,000. And because technically I have spoken to your organization before, I can take another $1,000 off. So your fee is $2,500 for this event." What happened next was absolutely unbelievable: There was a moment of complete silence on the other end of the line. Finally, Ms. Johnson spoke up and said, "Mr. Valentine, we are going to pay you what you're worth. If you normally charge $4,500, that's what we will pay you. As a purchasing agent, I shouldn't be telling you this, but I just can't stand to see you devalue you and your services. You're worth it—so act like it."

When I shared this story to the 2000 World Champion of Public Speaking, Ed Tate, he looked at me wide-eyed and said, "Man, you were going from fee to free!" We laughed, because he was absolutely correct. I have the feeling that if Ms. Johnson let me keep talking, I would have talked myself into giving them the speech for free. I just didn't know any better. After speaking with Ms. Johnson, I felt a combination of embarrassment and gratefulness that she went out of her way not only to make sure I got my full fee but, more importantly, that I received the invaluable lesson. Nobody will value you until you do. In the words of Patricia Fripp, "The first sale is to yourself."

HOW TO NEGOTIATE CORPORATE LEADS

Many times during a speaking event, people will approach you from various corporations, hand you their business cards, and say, "We have an event coming up, and I think you'll be perfect. Can I call you to discuss it?" You get all excited because you know a new opportunity is coming your way. Then, upon discussing the opportunity, they ask, "What do you charge?" What do you say? Do you handle it how I did with Ms. Johnson and talk yourself down from fee to free? Right now, if I asked you what you charge for a keynote speech, what would you say?

By now, you know the importance of having mentors and coaches in your life if you want to get to the next level. Whether it has been basketball, school, sales, speaking, training, or leadership, I have always had great coaches. However, my greatest coach came from the corporate world, and he taught me the art of negotiation. He is the reason that I won Salesperson of the Year for the Mid-Atlantic Region of Glencoe/McGraw-Hill—not because he handed me the awards, but because he handed me the tools I needed to earn them. Al Pagan is by far the best negotiator I have ever met, and, fortunately for me, he shared his wisdom. For years, I said, "Al, you really should write a book called *Pagan's Principles of Negotiation*." He never did. However, he graciously agreed to let me share some of his negotiation wisdom in this book. The same tools he taught me, I now pass on to you. These tools, mixed with some of the strategies I learned elsewhere, will help you actually look forward to this part of the process of getting hired to speak.

TOOLS FOR NEGOTIATION

1. See your goal. Al Pagan lists "knowing your goal" as number one in terms of importance. When I sold textbooks, before I ever walked into a negotiation, I wrote down my goal on a piece of paper. The goal might have read something like the following: "$125,000 with less than 5 percent cost of sale."

Simply having a goal kept me very focused on the desired outcome and let me know when, if necessary, to walk away. In speaking, know the fee you want before you go into the conversation. Whatever you do, keep your goal in front of you so that you don't get lost in the negotiation process.

2. Don't talk fee before you talk value. When someone asks, "What do you charge?" make sure you answer that question with questions. For example, you might say, "Can you tell me more about the event? What are the results you'd like to see come out of it?" They will start verbalizing the desired results, such as the following: "We'd like to get our people to embrace change and stop trying to hold on to the old ways of doing things."

Once they start voicing their challenges and desired results, the fee issue usually takes a backseat. The problem is that most speakers don't ask enough questions. If you become a master questioner, you'll blow open the doors of opportunity and income. Practice your questions so that they become second nature. Once you establish what their pain area is, it's time to take it to the next level. If there is no pain, there is no sale.

3. Ask the most important question in the sales and negotiation process.
Once you hear the concerns about "holding on to the old ways of doing things," it's important to ask the pain-provoking question, "What is that costing you?" There is an old sales saying that you must "make them sick, and then make them well." The point is that you need to get them thinking about what happens if they don't make a change. Again, they're not used to being asked questions, so this is a welcomed conversation for them. People love talking about themselves and their needs. They'll probably say something like the following:

> "It's tearing our team apart. We can't move forward, because we have these few people who are holding back the entire team. Plus, you know that kind of negativity can spread like wildfire."

If there is any way to attach a *monetary value* or *time-loss* to this cost, do it. For example, if I was negotiating with a sales group, I might ask, "How many sales have you lost in the last month because these new reps couldn't compete with the more seasoned reps from the other companies?" If they say, "We lost at least four big ones," I'd ask, "How big?" If they reply, "Each was worth at least $45,000," then I can easily say, "So, you lost $180,000 this month due to this issue?" Then I'd leave it there and simply *let them reflect on their pain.* Compared to $180,000, do you think my fee of $7,500 to fix their problem seems high? Not any more! Even if I helped them close half of the sales, their return on investment would be tenfold. Always remember the following: when they've established their cost, your fee becomes a no-brainer.

Many times, it won't be a cost in terms of dollars and cents. However, they have to at least think about what it's costing them to keep doing business in the same way. When the cost is established, it becomes much easier to quote your fee. Plus, your confidence will be much higher when you quote it.

4. Don't charge for time. Charge for your value. I picked this up from Alan Weiss, author of more than twenty books, including the must-have *Value-Based Fees*. If you charge per hour, you severely limit yourself. Plus, what happens when they reduce your number of hours? All of a sudden, your payment is reduced. Let's look at the following scenario as an example:

You tell your prospect, "My fee for a one-hour keynote is $4,500." What if they come back and say, "Great—we only need 15 minutes. I guess that's $1,500, right?" What do you say? The reason you found yourself in that position is because you based your fee on time. It's not about time, it's about the results they get from utilizing you. If you can help someone gain half of the $180,000 they lost last month from losing sales, who cares whether you teach for an hour, for 15 minutes, or for an entire day? It's about the results.

As a speaker, I suggest splitting your fee into a keynote, a workshop, and a full day of training. It's not about the hours, it's about the vehicle. For example, you might price your vehicles as follows:

Keynote speech: $5,500

Workshop: $7,500

Full day of training: $9,500

What I've found is that offering options gets them to think *how* they will use you instead of wondering *if* they will use you. The question moves from "yes or no" to "how and when."

5. Know how low you are willing to go. As Al Pagan taught me, you must know your absolute bottom price. This gives you some room to maneuver. For example, whenever Al and I did negotiations in the textbook industry, we would get our company's approval in advance for our percentage cost of sale. That way, we knew exactly how much room we could move. If the cost of sale was 7 percent, we knew that we could offer a workbook for each student for a one-year period or offer some additional technology pieces. Either way, we had some flexibility.

In speaking, you might know going in that you'll take a lesser fee if they agree to allow you to sell your products at the event, if they allow you to film it, or if they provide you with a list of all the participants. At times, I have reduced my fee when the organization decided to purchase 100 of my books in advance. We must always remember that our customers have budgets, and sometimes what's not in the training budget is in the budget for materials. Therefore, they might only be able to offer you $4,500 in a training fee but $2000 in the purchase of your product. Just make sure, to keep your fee integrity, you make the same offer available to comparable organizations in like situations.

6. Don't lower your fee without taking away value. Remember, your customer is paying for *value*, not for time. Therefore, if they ask for a reduction in price, it is perfectly within your rights to lower the value they will receive. I know it sounds harsh, but it's critical to negotiations. For example, let's say you've agreed to interview 10 of their personnel, diagnose their selling ills, and create a full-day, tailored training program designed to increase their closing ratios. You've quoted them an investment of $9,500.

They might respond by saying, "That sounds great, but we can only afford to pay you $7,500." At that point, it is perfectly within your rights to say, "I see. The $9,500 includes the 10 interviews and the full-day tailored program. We can nix the interviews and diagnosis and simply deliver a half-day sales training that we've already created. It won't be tailored, and it won't be all day, but your personnel will still benefit from it." What do you think they will usually say in response? They'll say, "Well, we still want you to do the interviews and the diagnosis, so that you find out exactly what we're doing wrong and help us fix it." You say, "Great. That's exactly what you get with this $9,500 program. To whom shall I send the agreement?"

Prospects often want us to reduce the price without reducing what we offer them. That's like walking into a KFC and saying, "I want a bucket of twenty-four pieces, but I want to pay for only six of them." Make sure you understand exactly what your options include, and don't hesitate to cut the package when they ask you to cut the price.

7. **Come to an agreement before sending the agreement.** A few weeks ago, one of the aspiring speakers I work with called and said, "Craig, I need to send in a proposal to this group, and I don't know what I should charge. Can you give me some advice?" I said, "Call them and ask several questions until you can arrive at a verbal agreement first." I saw him a few weeks later, and he said, "Craig, I'm glad you told me to call them. By asking questions, I found out that they do their fees in a different way. Each attendee pays a fee, so I redid my proposal, based on a fee per attendee." He got them to verbally agree on the fee before he sent the proposal.

I normally don't send proposals unless the client and I have already come to an agreement about the following:

- The results they want to receive
- The fee
- The travel and other expenses
- Any other critical pieces of information

Why? It's because *no prospect should ever be surprised* when they receive your written agreement or proposal. You should have discussed it with them first and come to an agreement on the terms.

Al Pagan said, "Negotiations are about relationships and mutual respect." He taught me that the more you build the relationship, the less you have to worry about negotiating, and the more apt you are to create a win-win agreement. A strong relationship outweighs even the best negotiation techniques. The relationship always wins. Therefore, the proposal and agreement become formalities that follow the verbal commitments. Before I send a proposal or an agreement, I clarify our agreement by saying, "So let's go back over what we've agreed to do. We'll do a full day of training on selling …" That partnership makes all the difference in the world.

8. Be willing to walk away. What feeling do you get when you read that statement? I ask because it's important to note that walking away does not mean ruining a relationship. Indeed, you can walk away from a negotiation on great terms. Several times per year, organizations call me and say, "Craig, we had you in here four years ago, and we want you back again this year." Can you see a potential problem here? What I charged four years ago is not even close to what I charge today. Therefore, if they cannot meet my full fee or any of the options I have available, I walk away.

However, because I have built up a network of speakers (which you should consider joining), I can still serve these clients by highly recommending speakers that are willing to do the engagements. My clients win, the up-and-coming speakers win, and I win, because we still have the relationship. That's what negotiation is all about anyway: relationships!

Chapter 8

How to Easily Profit from Back-of-the-Room Sales

In this chapter, you will pick up the tools that you need to make more money in one day than most entrepreneurs make in one month. You will understand exactly how to give presentations and sell loads of your products and services from the back of the room. However, before you get into it, please understand one very important point: *none of these tools will work for you.*

That's an odd thing to declare, isn't it? Why won't these tools work for you? They won't work if you don't have the right *mind-set.* It's the mind-set behind the skill set that matters when it comes to selling anything. Many speakers are self-conscious, embarrassed, and fearful of selling their products and services during their presentations. If you are one of these speakers, unless you change your mind-set, all the greatest sales tools in the world won't help you sell a thing. Let's see if you have the right mind-set for sales. If you don't, let's create it.

ARE YOU BEING CRUEL?

How do I know so much about the inability to sell due to the wrong mind-set? I was once one of these reluctant salespeople. What changed my mind (and my life) was when I gained the following understanding. Brace yourself, here it is: if you don't sell your products and services, you are being cruel to your audience.

A couple weeks ago, I attended a function and witnessed an outstanding poet recite two of her powerful, thought-provoking poems. Afterward, I approached her and told her, "I'd like to purchase your audio CDs." She looked down and said, "I don't have any. I ran out about a year ago and haven't re-upped." I walked away disappointed, feeling cheated. Why? Because as amazing as her poems were, I had no way of taking them home with me. I had no way of remembering everything she said. I had no way of reminding myself of the great truths of which she so naturally spoke. Indeed, I felt cheated.

ARE YOU BEING ARROGANT?

The poet's reluctance to sell her CDs brings another important realization you must have to get into the correct mind-set for selling: if you don't sell your products and services, you are being arrogant.

If you don't sell, then what you're really saying is that your speech is the be-all and end-all. You're saying that your speech is all the audience needs to change their lives and improve their conditions. In reality, they need more. You might have sparked them to make a change, but if they can't take your implementation system home with them, what have you really done? Do you really expect them to remember everything you said? Do you really expect that your forty-five-minute presentation is the be-all and end-all? If you do, that's being arrogant. If you don't, that's being realistic. The reality is that your audience members need a take-home system. Who is better than *you* to offer it? Giving your speech without offering take-home products is like taking a child to the parking lot of an amusement park, getting him excited about all the wonderful rides, and then telling him that you have no tickets and he can't get in. When your audience members are fired up about your speech, give them their tickets so that they can get on their own rides! Don't be arrogant. Don't be cruel. Sell and sell again.

DO YOU KNOW HOW TO SWAP?

I have been in sales for fifteen years and have been selling from the back of the room for nine. One of the reasons I was reluctant to sell as a speaker is probably one with which you can relate: I didn't want to bother or annoy people by "hawking products." Guess what? I have great news for you: You don't have to hawk products. You don't have to annoy people. You don't have to bother people. Why not? Because I have come up with a process called "the SWAP System." SWAP stands for "Selling Without Annoying People." With this system, you'll not only make boatloads of sales, but you'll also keep your reputation as a person with high integrity. After all, the very last thing you want to lose is the confidence others have placed in you. Once you lose that, you lose it all.

The SWAP (Selling Without Annoying People) System includes the following twelve tools you can incorporate into your very next presentation. You'll also find a few quick and valuable SWAP tips. For the purpose of clarity, I provide an example within each explanation, which shows you exactly how I have sold various products and services from the back of the room. Let's step behind the curtain of back-of-the-room sales!

Twelve SWAP System Principles

1. Lay the Groundwork

Seeds grow into sales. Sell from the first words. Most people separate their pitch from the rest of their presentation. This is a recipe for disaster and comes from a lack of planning. A pitch (or offer) is not something you should tack onto the end of your speech. Instead, it's something that starts from your first word. In order for any of these additional eleven tools to work, you must create a fertile ground for them. Do this from the beginning.

Example: I begin 90 percent of my speeches with the story about my coach, Patricia Fripp, and our coaching session in Las Vegas. The foundational phrase to that story is "What got you here won't get you there." Whenever I deliver that line, my audience members nod in agreement. I then say, "It always takes new tools, new strategies, and new ways to take your success (or speaking skills or management skills) to the next level." My audience nods in agreement again.

In the first few minutes of my speech, what have I accomplished? I have started creating the fertile ground in the minds of my audience members. They have just agreed they need *new tools* in order to get to the next level. The

Principle of Consistency suggests that my audience won't agree to this and then act counter to it. From the very first words in my speech, I am putting my audience into the mind-set of lifelong learning. That lays the groundwork for me to sow selling seeds.

What story and point can you present, up front, that lays the groundwork for lifelong learning? When you get your audience members to nod their heads in the beginning, chances are that they'll give you the nod for your products by the end. Remember the following: seeds grow into sales.

2. Interweave the Results

The sale needs to be part of the recipe, not just the icing thrown on top. It's not about a pitch so much as it is about your consistent and strategic seeding within the presentation. Plant seeds throughout. By the time you get to the actual brief pitch, your prospects should be 90 percent across the bridge to purchasing. They will have already made up their minds to purchase something, and now they'll simply need to know what that something will be.

Audiences get annoyed when a speaker drones on and on about a product or service during their pitch. The great part about successfully interweaving is that you won't have to make a long pitch when you get there. In fact, many times people won't even know you've *made* the pitch until it's almost over. If you've interwoven the learning resources throughout the presentation, and then you use the "Then, Now, and How" storytelling sales formula, book a later return flight, because your line will be quite long.

Example: Here are two brief examples of how to interweave the results of specific learning resources:

"Raise your hand if you agree with me. When you are in speaking, you are in sales. Of course you are. You're always selling something, even if it's just an idea. If you don't know how to sell, you don't fully know how to speak. The EDGE sales formula, which comes from my Storytelling Home-Study Course, will help you sell to each person in your audience, no matter what motivates him or her ..."

"I learned that when you read three books on any one topic, you become an expert on that topic, compared to the rest of the country. So I read three books on imagination and creativity. I read *Passion Profit & Power* by Marshall Sylver, *Creative Visualization* by Shakti Gawain, and *The Power of the Subconscious Mind* by Dr. Joseph Murphy. *These* books led to more and more, and the reason why I won the World Championship of Public Speaking is because ..."

I can't tell you how many people have approached me after my presentation to ask, "Craig, what were those three books you mentioned, again? The ones about imagination?" Again, don't cheat your audience members. Give them ways to deepen their knowledge in the areas that interest them. The benefits to you are the following:

- They build confidence in you as an expert
- You plant the seeds that will grow into sales
- You don't have to annoy your audience with a long, tacked-on, inorganic sales pitch

3. Suggest OPP First

OPP stands for "Other Peoples' Products." By "other peoples' products," I mean offerings you have no affiliation with and gain nothing from by suggesting them. You simply refer your audience to these products that they can pick up on their own, sometime in the future. Most speakers don't do this. Wannabe speakers start mentioning their own products right away. Don't do this. It destroys trust. World-class speakers weave other peoples' products into their presentations *before* they ever weave their own. This builds trust, because your audience members think, "Wow, this speaker has my best interests in mind. Most speakers talk about their own products, but this speaker keeps talking about *other* people." This is what I call "the best-interest tool." They truly conclude you have their best interests in mind. And you'd better!

The other huge benefit to mentioning other peoples' products throughout your presentation is that you quickly raise your level of *credibility*. Your prospects think, "She sure has done her research. I'm confident that she knows her stuff."

Example: Before I begin weaving *my own* learning resources, I usually say something like the following:

> "If you really want to take back more control of your time as a manager and stop feeling like you're constantly fighting fires, a delegation log is critical. You can find a great one in Peg Pickering's book entitled *Prioritize, Organize: The Art of Getting It Done*."

In no direct way do I profit directly from suggesting this book. However, I do profit indirectly, because my audience members build confidence in *me*, as they understand that I have their best interests in mind. The more I interweave these resources, the higher my credibility shoots. Notice also that I don't sell the book as the solution. I sell *the results of using a delegation log*, which she happens to have in her book. Here's the system:

- Point to a specific process (i.e., a delegation log)

- Sell them on the results of using it (i.e., take back control of time and stop fighting fires)
- Mention where they can get it (i.e., her book)

4. Build in Pieces but Sell in Packages

Build the value of each particular product or service by interweaving them individually. Then, when you get to your actual pitch, show your prospects exactly how they can get all of these valuable pieces in *one package*. Packages are where the profits are. If you don't sell packages, you'll create a nightmare by trying to process all the sales on the spot, and you'll leave thousands of dollars on the table. When you bundle your offerings, you make a bundle of profits.

Example: When I was with a national training firm delivering management seminars, I used to consistently interweave results that my prospects would get from a goal-setting manual, a teambuilding manual, a time-management book, a recruiting-and-interviewing book, a six-cassette series (yes, we were still using cassettes) on dealing with difficult employees, and a six-cassette series on assertiveness skills. Throughout two days, I mentioned these products (and the results they would get from them) individually and built up their value. When it came time for the pitch before the first break on the second day (usually around 10:30 AM), I put these six pieces together in one nice package. I usually said something like the following:

> "As you can see, separately, these 6 learning resources add up to $279. However, today we have our special Power Package deal, which includes all 6 of these bundled together for the special price of $169. Plus, you can pick up the package today without having any extra shipping costs. I only have 9 of them left, so ..."

The key to the success of the bundle is in building up the value of the individual pieces first, bundling them, and then offering the package at an irresistible price. Your prospects see much more value in the package then they do in each individual piece. When you offer packages, you may have less sales volume, but your dollars per sale will outweigh that drop in a big way. Plus, it makes your offer very simple to explain and your onsite order processing very convenient and easy to perform.

5. Never Sell the Product or the Service

Sell the results. What will your prospects get as a result of using your products or services? Even though the course includes eight hours of audio instruction, a fifty-five-page workbook, and a Storytelling Compass template, I rarely ever mention any of these features during my presentation. Why? Because I am not selling the product, I am selling the results. What are the results of your product? What are the results that organizations will receive when they hire you to speak? Don't sell the two-hour seminar, sell the results. Remember the SIR Formula. Speak In Results.

Example: After using my "Then, Now, and How" story that you read about in chapter six, I translate the story into the following results:

"Just last year, I was able to bottle up this process and put it into a system called 'The Edge-of-Their-Seats Storytelling Home-Study Course for Speakers.' Everything that got me from that embarrassing situation in Michigan to the empowering 92 percent rehire rate I have today is in the program. All the tools that will take you from wherever you are as a speaker to wherever you want to go are in the program. You'll find yourself getting called back time and time again, and that's the easiest way and most fulfilling way to build your business. What took me seven years to learn, you can pick up in seven hours of going through the program. You can quickly rise to become a speaker in high demand."

Have you caught on to what I am doing with my short pitch? As you know, the story is what really sells the product. The story gets the prospects 90 percent across the bridge to buying. The story gets them to feel the results in an emotionally charged way. However, the EDGE sales formula does the rest. Let's revisit this formula here.

Esteem more—Becoming a speaker in high demand is certainly an "Esteem more" result

Do more—Empowerment and building your business are certainly "Do more" results

Gain more—Cutting seven years off your learning curve is certainly a "Gain more" result

Enjoy more—Easy and fulfilling are certainly "Enjoy more" results

When you lay the groundwork, interweave with various resources, suggest other peoples' products first, build up the value of the pieces of your package, and sell the results, you will close a large percentage of your audience members. If done effectively and in front of your ideal customers, you can count on at least 20 percent of them making a purchase.

6. Give It Away

One of the greatest SWAP (Selling Without Annoying People) System principles is *reciprocity*. Give your audience one of your packages. Reciprocity means that if you go out of your way to do something for people, they will bend over backwards to repay you in some way. As people, we can't help it. It's in our DNA to want to respond in kind. Use this principle to your advantage. Go out of your way to give your audience something.

Before I ever even go into my "Then, Now, and How" story about my failed speech in Michigan, I tell my audience, "You're going to get some free prizes today. The prizes will be given based on the premise that being specific leads to being memorable. Therefore, I'm going to ask you questions about one of my stories in order to prove this premise. If you are the first to answer the questions, you get a free prize." Then I give away the first two prizes, which are individual bonus pieces from my home-study course. I talk about each one of them for a few seconds and share the results they will get from them. Remember, build up the pieces, but sell the package.

Example: I'll hold up my book and say the following:

"If you get this question correct, you get this book. Many books on public speaking spend more time talking about the peripherals of the event: what time to get there, what to do with the microphones, and how to greet your audience. This book is different. *The Nuts and Bolts of Public Speaking* gives you one thing: the tools you need to quickly create an entire speech from the ground up. It's a complete, practical, step-by-step system to creating your blockbuster speech. Okay, here's the question ..."

SWAP Tip: Free resources don't annoy people.

Perhaps the greatest benefit of offering these individual pieces for free is that you get to talk about them without annoying people. Remember, you are giving it away. That's not a sales pitch, that's charity! People will listen all day about a product you're giving away! They will get annoyed when you keep describing a product that you're going to sell, but not one that you're offering for free. They want to know all about what they might win. At the same time, you're building up the value of each individual piece before your audience knows you have a package that includes them all. Plus, your audience builds up the desire to have your products.

After I give the first two or three individual pieces away, I go into my "Then, Now, and How" Michigan story and get my audience emotionally involved. After I sell the results (as you can see in point number five), I actually hold up the home-study course to give it away. The audience hums with energetic anticipation.

Example: Here's how I actually give away one entire home-study course and put the *reciprocity* to work for me:

> "What took me seven years of frustration and investments, you can get for free just by answering one question. Here it goes: When Patricia Fripp coached me in Las Vegas, what was my room number?" Immediately, people yell out "437."

I go to the first person to answer and say, "You're absolutely correct, 437 is the answer. This proves my point that being specific leads to being memorable. You remembered my specific room number." I ceremoniously hand the winner the course while everyone applauds. One person won the course, but others built up the lust for it. Once that desire is there, it's difficult to diffuse. They want it, too, and they're willing to invest in it. Now it's time to make that investment irresistible.

SWAP Tip: Relate your pitch to your point. You may have noticed that I'm still teaching when I make my pitch. The premise I use is "being specific leads to being memorable." The prizes reinforce that point. The first story in my entire speech (the Fripp story) is used to reinforce that point. Everything works together to drive that point home. Therefore, the audience is still learning something of great value throughout the offer.

Be Careful about Your Giveaways

I almost found out the hard way the danger of giving away a desirable product. In this case, I planned to prove the premise that "action leads to rewards." Therefore, I lifted my home-study course in the air and asked, "Who wants it?" People began raising their hands and yelling, "I want it!" I simply smiled and waited for someone to take action. The next thing I knew, two ladies ran toward me, from two different angles, with their eyes fixed upon the prize. I thought for sure they were going to collide. They arrived at my product at the same exact time and started to wrestle it from each other. Quickly, I stepped in and said, "Because you both took action, you will both receive a reward." I gave a complete course to each of them. They walked away satisfied, and I finished my speech without injury. However, I was one home-study course shorter than I intended. Using these methods will build up great desire in your audience to have your products. Just make sure you don't go overboard and facilitate an injury.

7. Put the Pitch inside of Your Story

They will be emotionally involved in the story and won't even know your pitch is coming. Reread chapter six for the example of the "Then, Now, and How" formula.

8. Use Urgency and Scarcity

If they don't buy your product today, they probably won't buy it tomorrow. At least, that has to be your mind-set. Think about it: following your world-class speech, will they ever be this fired up again about what you have to offer? All they need is a reason to purchase *now*. This is where scarcity and urgency make their appearance. You can create a sense of urgency by having a "today only" special. In other words, if they don't make the commitment today, they will not get all the bells, whistles, and deep discounts.

Example: After I give away one home-study course, and my audience members build up their desire to have one, here's what I often say to create the sense of urgency so they purchase today:

"By the way, this is available for you today. The price is $297. However, because you've been such a good audience and you've really given me great energy, I'm going to do you a favor and [pause] waive the shipping." This gets a laugh, because they can see from my resource table that I've brought some with me. Therefore, of course there is no shipping. Then I get back into it with the following:

"Seriously, though … today, not only do you get the home-study course, but you also get all three audio CDs that I gave away to our winners. You get five audio lessons immediately sent to you via email, which help you deliver your speech for the greatest impact. Plus, you get my book, so you can create a world-class speech from scratch. Finally, you also get the 165-page e-book on mastering storytelling. Like I said, the price for the course is $297. With all these bonuses, it actually adds up to more than $400. However, for this entire package—today only—take $297 and slash $100 from it. You get the whole thing for $197. I only have ten of them on hand, so this is first come, first serve …"

At this point in my offer, audience members have actually dug into their checkbooks, written checks, and handed them to me while I was still speaking! Why? It's because they have a sense of urgency born from the scarcity. They go from thinking, "Should I buy?" to wondering, "How can I assure myself of being one of the top ten purchasers?" They act quickly, and others follow suit.

The great news for you, at that point, is that the mob mentality often takes over. People are influenced by what they see others doing. If you went to a trade show and saw a multitude of people surrounding one booth while the other booths were empty, what would you likely do? You'd probably walk over to see what's happening in that popular booth. Selling is the same way. When people line up and gather around your resource table, others follow suit. Keep in mind that people don't want to lose out on something of which others are taking full advantage. Create a scarcity, which leads to a sense of urgency.

SWAP Tip: Bring fewer products than you know you will need.

You might ask, "Craig, do you really only have ten courses left, or do you just tell your audience that to create scarcity?" The answer is yes, I really do only have ten courses left. I usually bring fewer home-study courses than I know I'll need. Why? It creates scarcity. Then you can say with complete integrity and honesty that you only have a small number of them left.

The next logical question that I'm sure you have is, "What do you do with the people who want to buy but are not one of the first ten purchasers?" You give them the exact same deal and tell them, "We'll ship it to you, and it will arrive in the next seven days—*and* we'll waive the shipping fee." You don't announce this during your presentation, but you mention it once you run out of materials. This way, your first ten purchasers set the tone by giving you a crowded table, and they leave satisfied because they take the product with them. The next purchasers are still satisfied, because they get the same deal. They just don't get the immediate satisfaction of taking the product home with them from the conference. Everybody's happy, including *you.*

There are times when I bring eleven courses (one to give away) and end up selling forty or fifty. The same will happen for you when you bring fewer than you need. On the contrary, bringing too many products is embarrassing and frustrating. It's embarrassing to look at a speaker's table at the end of a program and see it is still completely full with products. That tells your prospects that nobody wants what you have, and it must not be worthy. It can be frustrating, because you have to repack those products and lug them back home again. When you unpack them at home, they become a reminder of how poorly you did. Ask me how I know this? Live and learn. Perception is reality. Create the demand, and the demand will come. I want my table to be clean and clear.

Pop Quiz: What happens once they take your products home?

What should happen once they take your products home and consume them? Think back to chapter five and the marketing mind-set. Can your product double as a marketing piece? Sure, it can. For example, inside of my Storytelling Home-Study Course for Speakers, I talk of the importance of being able to deliver the story so that audience members feel like they're part of it. To extend this learning, I suggest enhancing their delivery skills and interweave my Edge-of-their-Seats Dynamic Delivery Devices DVD. The point is this: always make sure there is an exact next step for your prospects and customers, no matter where they are on your continuum. To deepen your marketing mind-set, write down these two words, and keep them in a high-traffic area: "Next step?"

Remember that people are motivated by the opportunity for gain and the fear of loss. When you offer a "today only" special and you make it irresistible, prospects will feel like they're *losing out* by not taking advantage of it. This feeling, combined with the hope you inspired by showing them the results, becomes combustible and gets people popping up from theirs chair over to your resource table.

9. Stack Up the Bonuses and Tear Down the Price

In your audience, you'll always have three kinds of people:

People who are prepared to buy

People who are on the fence

People who are not buying, no matter what

I suggest concentrating on the second group (without ignoring the first, of course). The third group already has a worldview they've built up for a lifetime, and you are not going to change that, even if you spend a week with them. However, the second group just needs something that tips the scales and pushes them over the edge to buy. Enter free bonuses! When you stack the bonuses on top of each other, they make the entire offer irresistible. I usually stack the following bonuses with my offer:

An audio-instruction CD for $20

A second audio-instruction CD for $20

A third audio-instruction CD for $20

Five audio lessons via email for $50

My book for $15

My storytelling e-book for $15

Although you don't need to mention the actual prices (I don't) when you're presenting, you can mention the overall price of the package. For example, I say, "With these bonuses included, the entire package adds up to more than four hundred dollars. However, today …" Many times, the bonuses make the sale irresistible, and the prospects that were on the fence eagerly jump over to your side. Sometimes, they want the bonuses more than the actual product! Who knew?

> **SWAP Tip:** The key is *contrast*. Stacking up the bonuses puts you in the perfect position to use the SWAP tip that not only makes your audience tolerate your selling from the platform but has them *thanking* you for it. Once, when I got to the part of my offer about "slashing $100 off the price," the audience members actually broke out into applause! It was as if they were saying, "Thank you very much. We can't believe you're going to offer it so low. Thank you." In truth, I do feel I'm offering it at a low price (i.e., $197 in person); however, like you, I like to over-deliver.

If I first came out and said, "The price is $197," I might have had many more people balk. After all, $197 is still significant. However, by stating $297 first and then piling the bonuses up past $400, all of a sudden, $197 seems like a bargain. That's the power of using *contrast*. State the higher price first. You'll get more on this concept in chapter ten, and you'll see how you can use contrast to create high profits over the web.

10. Give One Exact Next Step

By now, you know the grave importance of giving your prospects one exact next step to take when they come across your marketing communications. Well, guess what? Your speech is a marketing communication. It should influence your audience members to take one specific next step (two at the most).

I have seen wannabe speakers put up PowerPoint slides listing a buffet of products, and then go through each product with a lengthy explanation. Then they close their speeches and expect the audience to choose from the buffet. If the audience members do choose, chances are that they pick a $15 product rather than a $297 package. However, most of the time, these audience members become too confused to choose. As a result, their next step is home. Don't do this to your audience members. Be a world-class speaker, and give them a clear and exact next step. Tell them what to do next, and sell them on why.

Example: When I speak to up-and-coming speakers, the next step is usually my Storytelling Home-Study Course for Speakers. However, I do also suggest my seven-part World Class Speaking Toolkit, which they can get for free by signing up for my newsletter on the spot. Here's the question to which you must have a clear, one-sentence answer before you deliver your presentations: what is the exact next step my audience members should take after my presentation?

11. Put Your Table in Traffic

The placement of your resource table is important. It can mean the difference between closing 20 percent of your audience members and closing 5 percent of them. Money-wise, that's a huge difference. Therefore, I suggest placing your table near the entrance and exit of the room. Make it very visible, and set it up in a place your audience members must walk by in order to leave the room. Some speakers like to put their table in the front of the room and have the products on stage with them as they speak. I attempted that years ago and found it too distracting for the audience members. They sit there thinking, "Uh, oh. He's going to stand up there and talk about those products all day." They get into a non-fertile mind-set before you even say your first word.

Clarify Your Table

When you set up your table, don't make your prospects work too hard. Place your products at eye level, even if it means propping them up on a box or stand. Get stands for at least a few of the products so that your prospects can see them without having to hover over the table and strain to look down.

Finally, treat your table like an extension of you. Use a nice-looking tablecloth or banner. Darren LaCroix called me one day and said, "Craig, do you want to purchase some tablecloths with me? They run about three hundred dollars." I said, "Darren, there are many things I will invest money in, and a table cloth is not one of them." A couple of months later, Darren, Ed Tate, and I conducted a Champ Camp together. They each had these attractive new tablecloths that made their tables look much more professional. I didn't. They sold lots of products. I didn't. There is a correlation. On the spot, I asked Darren, "Hey, where did you say I can get those tablecloths again?" I quickly got onboard and spent three hundred dollars on a banner that includes my name, my company's name, and our logo. Perception is reality. In your prospects' minds, a shoddy table equates to shoddy products and services. *Build* their confidence in you, don't break it. Everything counts.

12. Have a Clear and Simple Order Form

Confused prospects walk away without buying. One of the easiest ways to confuse your prospects is with a poorly designed, ineffective order form. The most common mistake speakers make is offering too many product and service options on one form. Make it simple for your prospects by offering one option (or two at the most) for a package. This empowers you to strategically gear all your interweaving and intentionally guide your prospects toward that one decision. If you try to guide them to too many places, they'll go nowhere except home.

In addition to a clear order form, make sure you can take cash, check, and credit-card payments. The vast majority of my payments come in the form of credit cards. Customers simply fill in the form (see form 8-1) with their credit-card information, sign it, and hand it back to me or my assistants. As soon as I get to my laptop later in the day, I use my shopping cart to process the payments, which go directly into my business bank account. It's simple. If you plan to sell products and services, you must offer credit-card payment as an option, or else you'll leave at least 70 percent of your sales on the table. Visit EasyWebAutomation.com to see how quick and simple it is to set up this payment system. How's that for interweaving?

PART III

*How to Use Virtual
Speaking to Reach
Thousands and Make
Six Figures without
Leaving Home!*

Chapter 9

CREATE MASTERFUL TELECLASSES AND JOINT VENTURES THAT GENERATE PROFITS!

THE DOS AND DON'TS
TO GIVING TERRIFIC TELECLASSES

Have you ever taken a teleclass that was done poorly? Have you ever taken one that was very well-done? Not only have I virtually attended good and bad ones, but I've also *given* good and bad ones. Like any tool, teleclasses can either build the confidence or break the confidence your prospects and customers have in you. If you do like I did by jumping unknowingly into giving teleclasses while trying to grow wings on the way down, you will surely fail. More importantly, this failure will turn away prospects and customers who probably will never give you another chance. That's just the way it is. On the flip side, if you gain an understanding of how to give effective teleclasses and practice with the most effective tools, your prospects and customers will gain so much confidence in you that they will become your biggest fans. One very well-planned and -delivered teleclass will have your prospects and customers saying, "Give me more. What's next? Whatever programs you offer, sign me up!"

Learn from the Best

If you want to build the confidence your prospects and customers have in you and reap the related rewards, doesn't it make sense to learn from those who have been there and done that? Mitch Meyerson has made a solid six-figure income year after year, just off of teleclasses and online courses. As the founder of the Guerrilla Marketing Coach Certification program, cofounder of the Product Factory, and cofounder of The Online Traffic School, he has used the strategies you will learn in this chapter to build these online courses and teleclasses into a very profitable business. You can do likewise, using these proven processes. We'll cover these tools later in the chapter. However, before we learn from Mitch, let me introduce you to one more teleclass expert.

MEET THE QUEEN OF TELECLASSES

Although I do monthly teleclasses and Mitch does entire twelve-week courses using teleclasses, there is someone else who stands very tall when it comes to explaining how to use them. I have been fortunate enough to present in-person Speaker Champ Camps alongside of Karyn Greenstreet. Karyn is the president of Passion for Business LLC, which is a company that helps self-employed people create the business and personal success they want and deserve. Karyn is also the author of the information-packed book entitled *Designing Effective Workshops & Teleclasses*. If there are two people who can give you the most proven and effective advice on using teleclasses to build your business, one is Karyn Greenstreet, and the other is Mitch Meyerson. Let's start with Karyn. I have asked her to take over the next part of this chapter and espouse her gems onto you. Here is what Karyn had to say about the dos and don'ts for designing, presenting, and marketing your teleclasses.

In the Words of Karyn Greenstreet

Three Dos For Teleclasses:

1. **Design your teleclass properly**. Participants need to feel the information is provided in a logical order with clearly defined groupings of information. This also helps you keep on topic and not ramble while teaching a teleclass.

2. **Allow for interaction**. An all-lecture teleclass is excruciatingly boring. Ask participants to share their thoughts and questions. Pose questions to them to bring out salient points in the discussion.

3. **Learn to teach teleclasses properly**. Leading teleclasses is different than teaching live classes, even if you are an experienced instructor. There are some great teleclass-leader techniques you can learn that spice up a class and keep your participants connected and learning.

Three Don'ts for Teleclasses:

1. **Don't go over one-hour.** Studies have shown that people's attention spans begin to waver around forty to fifty minutes. It's better to offer your two-hour teleclass in two one-hour segments than to expect people to sit and listen for two solid hours.

2. **Don't forget to follow up with students.** For free teleclasses, send them your marketing offer within a day after the teleclass. For paid teleclasses, create a course evaluation to get feedback from participants. You can use online survey tools like www.surveymonkey.com to create good course evaluations.

3. **Don't forget that your teleclass is a representation of your brand and your quality standards.** Practice your teleclass before you do it publicly. Ask a small group of people to volunteer to be participants, and teach your class to them first. This will help identify gaps and trouble spots and make your public teleclass a success.

WHERE DO TELECLASSES FIT INTO YOUR MARKETING PLAN?

You can use teleclasses to directly earn income, or you can use them as a marketing tool for future sales. They are often a more efficient use of your time, hour for hour, than providing your services to a single client; they can sometimes earn you up to a thousand dollars per hour of your teaching time. There are three ways to look at teleclasses: as lead-generators, as mailing-list builders, and as moneymakers. Let's look at each.

1. Free Teleclasses as Lead-Generators

Teleclasses are a great way for people to get to know you and to get a sample of the knowledge you're sharing. A free, one-hour teleclass on a small topic is a great way to introduce yourself to your prospective customers. Be very, very careful to include some meaty content into your free teleclass. Participants are getting tired of sales pitches disguised as teleclasses, and they will leave the phone call if they feel they're not getting good, solid information. However, a free teleclass is a marketing event for you. When teaching a teleclass, use subtle comments like "When I was working with a client recently ..." or "I had a student in a class who asked ..." to remind people that they can purchase other services and products from you. A good rule of thumb is: 95 percent content and 5 percent marketing talk when delivering a free teleclass.

In addition, make an offer for the participants to purchase the product or service mentioned in the teleclass. It's wise to offer participants a discount if they purchase your product or service within a specified period of time after attending the free teleclass.

2. Free Teleclasses as List-Builders

One of the major tenets of any good marketing plan is to build your mailing list. When offering free teleclasses, as people register, they are added to your mailing list. Use the auto-responder feature in your shopping cart to allow them to register online, which will do two things for you: automatically add them to your mailing list and automatically email them a confirmation email with the telephone number for the teleclass. This saves you the time of having to email them manually with the class information.

Always *record* your teleclasses, even the free ones. Many people may not be able to attend a live teleclass, but if you offer a recording of the class, they can download and listen to it later. This effectively doubles the amount of people who will sign up for your free teleclass: the people who will listen live and the people who will download the recording later.

Once the recording is complete and on your site, you can ask people to register their email addresses before gaining access to the recording, adding even more people to your mailing list over the coming years without having to teach the class live again. The recording can also be used to give five-minute samples of your teleclass when marketing it. Most teleconference lines come with a built-in recording feature. I have found the quality of these recordings to be too varied for my tastes, so I use a digital recorder (like an Olympus DS-40) connected to my telephone line to get a better-quality recording.

3. Making Money from Paid Teleclasses

Finally, let's talk about making money with teleclasses. There are two ways you can do this.

A. First, offer the teleclass live. When creating a paid teleclass, you have more options available to you about content and length. Many people are willing to pay for in-depth coverage of a specific topic, meeting for one hour a week for up to six weeks. Be careful, however, of making your teleclass series too long. Most people "fade out" of teleclass participation after four to six weeks. If you have a lot of material to cover, it's better to create two four-week classes ("part one" and "part two") than to offer an eight-week teleclass.

B. Second, record your live teleclass, and sell the recordings as downloadable MP3 files. People who have time constraints and can't attend a live class are very happy to purchase and listen to the teleclass recordings. It helps if you divide each hour of recording into two half-hour segments. The typical commute is thirty-seven minutes long, and a half-hour segment is just about the right length for most people's attention span. For instance, you would take a six-hour teleclass recording and divide into twelve half-hour segments.

PROMOTING TELECLASSES

Designing a good teleclass is half the battle. Filling your teleclass seats, but having a poorly designed class, will not lead to repeat business and will damage your reputation as a teleclass leader. Once you design your teleclass, you're ready to start marketing it.

There are many ways to promote your teleclasses, but first, you must write a good course description that talks about the benefits people will get from attending your teleclass. Give participants a *specific list* of what they will learn. Remember, *your course description is your ticket for getting people to register and attend.*

Once you have written your course description, it's time to market your teleclass. Here are some suggestions:

• Send out an email broadcast to your mailing list, announcing the class and telling them how to register. Create a schedule for how often you'll send out this broadcast to your list; people often need to be reminded and prompted before they'll actually register. I have found that your final reminder email should go out to your list within twenty-four to forty-eight hours before the class begins, with a subject line like, "Class begins Tuesday!" or "Last chance to register!"

- Create a strategic alliance with colleagues, and have them send your announcement to their mailing list. Or, have them bring you on as a guest to one of their own teleclasses.

- Put an ad on your own website. Visitors to your website, who aren't already on your mailing list, will see the ad and learn about your offerings.

- Market your teleclass in print media, such as newspapers and magazines.

- Market on the Internet. There are many places you can announce your teleclass:

    www.teleclass.com

    www.planetteleclass.com

    www.cculearning.com

Let's thank Karyn for this wonderful advice on the dos and don'ts of teleclasses. Now, let's dig deeper into using this tool that empowers you to reach thousands of prospects and customers without leaving the comfort of your own home. Hopefully, you'll at least get out of your pajamas, but that's your prerogative.

Mitch's Design

Before we get into the specific ways to turn your teleclass into the gift that keeps on giving, let's address something very important that Karyn mentioned. She said that you must design your course properly for it to be effective. There's nobody better than Mitch Meyerson for designing teleclasses and online courses. Let's go over three specific elements Mitch uses that should definitely be in your teleclasses.

Three Elements for an Outstanding Teleclass

1. One of the best ways to ensure good content is to **interact** by doing some live coaching with a few participants. In Mitch's Guerrilla Marketing Coach Certification Course (www.gmarketingcoach. com), he usually coaches participants on whatever the topic is that week. They get immediate feedback, and the others listening get a reinforcement of the tools they've been learning in the class. Sometimes, due to ego and objectivity, it's actually easier to learn from the feedback others receive than from the feedback you get.

2. Another important element is to have an actual **objective** for each lesson. For example, for class number one, you might have one or two specific objectives, such as the following:

   a. Attendees will be able to construct the opening to a keynote speech that includes the Big Promise and the Roadmap

   b. Attendees will understand steps one, two, and three of a marketing plan

   The key to an objective is to make it measurable. There must be a way for you and the attendees to assess whether or not they hit the mark and achieve the objective. Can they send a text of the opening of their speech? Can they describe the first three steps of their marketing plan? The objective will help your attendees know exactly where you're going with each lesson and hence, with the entire course.

3. Have some exercises? Don't just talk their ears off. Instead, have interaction by having the attendees do some check-ins, role-playing, discussions, questions and answers, and takeaways.

Mitch's Formula

When Mitch leads the Guerrilla Marketing Coach Certification class, he always has the attendees check in each class with the breakthroughs and updates they've had since the previous week's class. Then, during the class, he often puts them on the virtual hot seat, doing role-playing as they portray the role of either the coach or the client, the salesperson or the customer. Finally, at the conclusion of each class, he has them state what their takeaways are for that particular class. In other words, they tell the class what sticks out for them for that evening's class. It's very important to have these takeaways, because they help the other attendees underline ideas they might have missed or skimmed over. This way, each attendee adds value to all the others. For an hour-long class, you probably want the following breakdown that Mitch uses:

- Ten minutes for *check-ins* during the opening
- Forty minutes for *new content* and *activities* during the middle
- Ten minutes for *takeaways* during the end

Obviously, you might not have ten minutes for check-ins if it's a one-time class. However, it's still wise to get an understanding of where your attendees are (i.e., how much do they know?), so that you don't dive blindly into the material.

Turn Your Teleclass into the Gift that Keeps on Giving!

As Karyn mentioned, you can record your teleclasses and sell them to future customers down the line. The real gem with teleclasses is that you can record them once and sell them forever. Plus, these future sales are true profit. They don't require any additional time or costs. You simply record them, post them, and make them available for people who are willing to invest in them.

Let's get real: people are extremely busy, and they cannot always attend your teleclass when you have it. In addition, depending on what time you hold it, your overseas prospects might not attend, because for them, it might be the middle of the night. If you don't make it available later, you will leave thousands of dollars on the table by missing out on the international market. If you do make it available, your teleclass truly will become the gift that keeps on giving.

Use Free Teleclasses to Grow Your List

My colleagues and I once put an advertisement in a magazine, but the ad was not meant to sell anything. Instead, the ad promoted a free teleclass that we were giving on the art of public speaking. Why in the world would we do something like this? Why would we invest good money in an advertisement and not recoup it by selling something? The answer is twofold.

1. We were using the teleclass as a preview call for an upcoming event we were holding in Las Vegas.
2. We were growing our list.

If you think about it, what we did is healthy for long-term results, but many entrepreneurs suffer from short-term thinking. They don't look at the lifetime value of each customer they bring onboard. The lifetime value of my coaching customers is $4,200 per customer. Therefore, over time, I am certainly going to get a great ROI from the investment in the ad.

Most people place advertisements of a product or service, and some viewers purchase from them and others do not. What happens to the people who don't purchase from them? Nothing. Why? Even if they had an interest, there is absolutely no way for the advertiser to follow up with them. This is because the advertisers don't capture the viewers' contact information unless they make a sale. You simply cannot let these people go without having a way to contact them in the future.

We did the opposite of what most do: we invited prospects for free and captured their contact information by requiring it for them to join us on the call. This way, we were able to market to them not just through one "hit or miss" advertisement but *ongoing* as we moved closer and closer to the event. Did it work? Well, consider this. We expected to have one teleclass, and we ended up having six of them! Why? It's because they filled up so fast, we had to keep scheduling more and more. The first call filled up with two hundred seats in about a twenty-four-hour period. Now, we have all these names we can market to for future events. In addition, the event in Las Vegas was a blockbuster and has turned into an annual tradition.

If you plan to market an event in this manner, please understand that you must offer extremely valuable content during the teleclass that makes the attendees want more. Then, instead of tacking on a sales pitch to the end of the class, use an interweaving approach like you learned about in the previous chapter. Throughout the teleclass, mention specific benefits and relevant pointers your attendees will pick up if they join you for the actual event. For example, we made statements like, "There is a definite nine-step process for telling a gripping story that makes an unforgettable point. You picked up two of the points here, and you'll pick up the other seven at the event next month in Vegas." If you plant enough selling seeds along with your valuable content, attendees from the teleclass will become attendees in your live class.

USE THE TELECLASS AS BAIT FOR YOUR FREE TOOLKIT

Another very effective way to use teleclasses to build your list is by offering a free recording on your website for those who sign up for your newsletter or toolkit. Mitch has regularly used the audio that he has with other online marketers in his free toolkit to generate leads on his website. Perhaps your free recording becomes your toolkit. Either way, people will have a strong incentive to join your newsletter list if they know they will immediately receive a sixty-minute, information-packed teleclass. The great benefit to *you* is that you simply use an auto-responder with a link to the teleclass, and the rest is completely hands-off. That's leverage! You can build your list even while you sleep—and with no extra cost to you.

USE JOINT TELECLASSES TO GROW YOUR LIST

A few months ago, I attended a teleclass in which Mitch interviewed Michael Gerber, author of the world-famous business book *The E-Myth*. In order to attend this free call, I had to provide Mitch with my name and email address. What I knew was that I had just increased Mitch's list by one. What I didn't know was that I was one of more than eight hundred people who grew

Mitch's list that day. What takes many businesses months (or even years) to accomplish (eight hundred prospects), Mitch accomplished in fewer than eighty minutes. That's the power of a joint teleclass.

The key is to join with people who have a list or who are at least familiar with the idea of growing one. Mitch has a very healthy list. In fact, he has several of them (different target markets). When you combine forces as such, regardless of whether attendees come to hear Michael Gerber or Mitch Meyerson, both of them can significantly increase their lists. Someone who is not familiar with you, but who is familiar with your joint teleclass partner, soon becomes familiar with you. Just by association, they build confidence in you, too. They arrive at the teleclass already halfway across the bridge to buying into you. Both you and your joint partner build your respective lists. It's a true win-win.

TURN YOUR TELECLASS SERIES INTO A PROFITABLE HOME-STUDY OR E-COURSE

One of the best home-study courses for marketing is called "Creating a Powerful Internet Marketing Strategy to Grow your Business." That, in addition to Mitch's Guerrilla Marketing Jumpstart program, is an absolute must for anyone who has a small business and wants to quickly turn a serious profit. Who is this course by? You guess it: Karyn Greenstreet.

What Karyn knows and what we have to constantly remind ourselves is to *not waste anything*. That means that you should not waste a teleclass (or anything else that you record). Karyn taught a five-week teleclass series and recorded each class. Then, she turned those recordings into five one-hour CDs. She included the workbook she used with the original teleclass participants, packaged it, and made it available for sale for people like me. I bought it and benefited greatly from it. Karyn simply leveraged what she did for those five weeks and turned it into the gift that keeps on giving. It gives to the attendees, and it gives to Karyn, too!

What the original attendees heard over the phone, I heard over the CD player while driving in my car. If you create a program like Karyn did, you'll soon be at a point where you can turn your recordings into MP3s and offer them as an e-course, as well, that we can download straight from the Internet. That way, you won't have to deal with packaging issues and costs. The repackaging options seem endless!

Whatever you decide to do with teleclasses, please remember that you are always either building peoples' confidence in you or *breaking* it. Become a master at using teleclasses to build that confidence. In order to master it, I highly recommend Karyn Greenstreet's teleclass series entitled "Designing Effective Workshops & Teleclasses." You can find out more by visiting her on the web at www.passionforbusiness.com.

Resources for Conducting Teleclasses

1. www.freeconferencepro.com
    Karyn Greenstreet turned me on to this provider. It's great, because you can customize your introduction recording so that it sounds like people are calling your company. For instance, when you call into my teleclasses, I can have the recording say "Welcome to the Communication Factory."
2. www.greatteleseminars.com
3. www.basementventures.com

Now, let's look at a very important strategy that world-class speakers use to reach and teach more people without having to leave home.

JOINT VENTURING FOR PROFITS

As a certified Guerrilla Marketing Coach, I came to understand a fundamental difference in marketing philosophy that will give you huge wins for your business. Jay Conrad Levinson, father of guerrilla marketing, stated the following:

"Traditional marketing practice asks that you look around for opportunities to obliterate the competition. Guerrilla marketing asks you to forget competition temporarily and to scout opportunities to cooperate with other businesses and support one another in a mutual quest for profits."

In a nutshell, learn to *cooperate* with those you may think of as competition. You'll be surprised at the wonderful, mutually beneficial relationships that can come about by joint venturing or partnering with your so-called rivals. Without this shift in your mind-set, your business is limited. With the shift, your opportunities are infinite!

WHAT CAN JOINT VENTURING DO FOR YOU?

When you do joint ventures and partnerships with the right people, here is just a sample of the kinds of results you can receive:

- More speaking engagements than you can possibly handle
- Rapid exposure to your target market

- Exponential growth in product sales
- Opportunities to speak to (and around) the world
- Immense fun working with your partners on a regular basis
- New friends and customers
- A big name in your industry
- Raving fans
- Passive, recurring income
- More top-notch people wanting to joint venture and partner with you
- Profits, profits, and more profits!

As an expert who speaks, the following kinds of joint ventures and partnerships can be very rewarding and profitable for you, and they can help you reach thousands of prospects and customers without having to leave home:

1. Products

There is nothing stopping you from teaming up with another expert and having a bestselling product. In the same way that I partnered with Mitch, you can team up with others on an audio course, a video set, or even a book. The more these products travel, the faster your viral marketing takes off. The next time someone sneezes, your product will be there to wipe their nose.

A perfect example of this is the audio CD entitled Panic to Power. This CD is designed to help people get over their nerves and become better public speakers. At our Get Paid to Speak Champ Camp, we essentially do a joint venture with our attendees. Each attendee gets a copy of the "Panic to Power" audio CD, which includes me, Ed Tate, and Darren LaCroix giving advice and tools for turning panic into power on the platform.

Now comes the best part: each attendee records a section on his or her CD and becomes our "special guest." Therefore, you have a CD with three world champions and our special guest. Guess what this does for our special guests when they sell it? They get extra income and loads of newfound, instant credibility. Guess what it does for us world champions? We get a form of viral marketing. The more our attendees go out and sell these CDs, the more people hear about us. Everyone wins!

2. Teleclasses

This is the perfect vehicle for a joint venture. Again, there is strength in numbers. When Mitch joined up with Michael Gerber on a teleseminar, people stormed through the virtual doors to hear them. As a result, Mitch significantly built his list of prospects. That one joint venture is going to pay off year after year.

The other great thing to remember about the teleclasses is that you can do it once, record it, and make it available forever. Perhaps you want to use it as bait to get more leads. Perhaps you want to sell it and make passive recurring income. Either way, when you team up with the right people, you'll be able to leverage that event for years to come. This is a great way to test your joint venture and see if a possible ongoing partnership might be advantageous.

3. Online Courses

These courses usually consist of an online forum environment coupled with regular weekly teleclasses. Mitch has run more than twenty-three

Guerrilla Marketing Coach Certification classes (of which I am a graduate). These twelve-week, online courses go several miles deep into the subjects of marketing yourself and becoming an in-demand marketing coach for others. The latest class, which I co-lead, attracted customers from all over the globe. See more about this online course by visiting www.wcspeaking.com or www. gmarketingcoach.com . Mitch has also teamed up with Michael Port to create The Product Factory, which helps customers produce their signature product or program in fewer than ninety days. Again, by featuring both Michael Port, author of *Book Yourself Solid*, and Mitch, they can market to each of their lists, which include many thousands of prospects. There is strength in numbers.

What online course can you create with your expertise? If you have expertise in getting out of debt, and someone you know has expertise in investing, can you join forces and provide a more well-rounded solution for your prospects and customers?

4.   Affiliates

Believe it or not, a third of Mitch's income comes from affiliate commissions! To go deeper into how this works, I strongly recommend Mitch's new book, *Mastering Online Marketing*. Affiliates are the close relative of these joint marketing ventures and partnerships. An affiliate is, by far, the easiest way to sell other peoples' products and programs and get passive recurring income without lifting a finger or undergoing risk. Does it sound too good to be true? Well, for once, it isn't. All you have to do is set yourself up as an affiliate and start earning income. This can usually be done completely online.

For example, because I have confidence in Patricia Fripp's products and programs (having purchased many of them myself), I signed up as her affiliate. This means that when people visit my website, link to hers, and purchase something, I get a nice percentage of that sale to keep for making my referral. I did the same thing for Darren LaCroix. Why? I have confidence in the strength of his learning resources. As a result, I set myself up as an affiliate, and people link from my site to his. The first affiliate check I received from Darren was for two dollars and eighty-seven cents. I laughed, because there was a handwritten note from Darren that said, "It's a start!" The next month, my check was a hundred and eighty-three dollars, simply for having an affiliate link on my site. It's another stream of income you should have. If there is someone whom you respect and in whose products and services you have great confidence, you should become an affiliate and profit from it month after month. This is the least risky type of joint venture, as long as you do it with the correct people.

Visit www.wcspeaking.com/affiliates if you are interested in receiving affiliate commission checks from us.

BRAND YOUR JOINT VENTURE

There are infinite possibilities for joint ventures and marketing partnerships, but you must make sure you do one thing: *brand them.* Brand your product, boot camp, teleclass, or whatever you offer. For example, Mitch has many Guerrilla Marketing events, such as the certification program and the Guerrilla Marketing Main Event. Another example is with the other world champions and me. Instead of offering boot camps, we offer "Champ Camps." We have the "Get Coached to Speak Champ Camp," the "Get Paid to Speak Champ Camp," the "Secrets to Storytelling Champ Camp," and many more. "Champ Camp" is our brand. What's yours?

Chapter 10

HOW TO MASTER
ONLINE MARKETING

I was smack-dab in the middle of the Internet boom, and I left the industry immediately before it burst. In the mid to late 1990s, I worked for a small Internet publishing company that gave me an opportunity to attend extravagant events such as the Internet World Conference and the Online World Conference. If you attended, surely you can attest to the lavish surroundings. I always had the feeling that the exhibiting companies were all attempting to outdo each other. Instead of booths, they had two-story houses, each complete with computers, a stage, and often a celebrity. I even met Reggie Jackson in one of the booths as he signed autographs and attracted visitors. He cringed when I shook his hand. I guess holding a bat all those years took its toll. Another company gave a private show featuring Carlos Santana! This was all at the height of the Internet boom, and I always wondered, "Where is this heading?" By now, you know the answer. For many companies, the answer was "out of business."

What happened? Why were so many companies forced to fold up their tents (or indoor houses) and face a harsh reality? In my opinion—and this is just my opinion—the two biggest problems were the following:

1. The companies had fantastic technicians who believed their *craft* would carry them to the top. You can be the best at what you do (technician), but if you don't know how to market it, you won't be doing it for long. If you're the world's greatest speaker but don't know how to market yourself, you'll become the world's biggest waste of talent, because nobody will hear you. Perfecting your craft is not enough. You must become a world-class marketer with your craft. Always remember the following statement that will save you time, frustration, and funds, no matter what industry you serve: You are not in the craft business. You are in the marketing business.

2. These companies confused marketing with money. Putting money ahead of strategy is wasteful. These companies spent millions on building a bigger booth, when they should have spent time on building a better strategy. Metaphorically, these indoor houses were built without a true, solid *marketing* foundation. Henceforth, they collapsed.

Fortunately, these companies did not die in vain. Out of their ashes we are able to snatch the lessons we can use to build our businesses using the Internet. In the rubble of their failures, true profitable processes have emerged that entrepreneurs have been using to generate *leads*, *customers*, and *huge profits* without spending millions.

The King of Internet Marketing: Mitch Meyerson

By now you know that Mitch Meyerson created several online courses designed around marketing and product development. However, he is also the author of several bestselling books, including *Mastering Online Marketing*, *Success Secrets of the Online Marketing Superstars*, *Guerrilla Marketing on the Front Lines*, and *Guerrilla Marketing on the Internet*. (For more information on these books visit www.MitchMeyerson.com.) In other words, when it comes to marketing on the Internet, there is none better. Fortunately for you, many of the tools Mitch uses to build his business online and the strategies he teaches others are in this chapter. By the time you reach the end of it, you'll have the knowledge necessary to avoid waste and attain wealth using the Internet.

This knowledge comes to you in the form of six fundamental, yet critical, strategies for making money online. When you put these six strategies to use, you will be shocked at how inexpensive and simple it actually is to generate wealth using the Internet. Let's look at each strategy in detail.

Six Strategies for Making Money Online

1. Think like a Marketer

Similar to how the past Internet companies thought the biggest conference booth was the best, many entrepreneurs still think the prettiest website is the most effective. Like throwing money at the booths, these businesspeople spend a small fortune putting together what they think is the most attractive website. The problem is that the site doesn't work. What they don't seem to understand is the web is not driven by *prettiness*; it is driven by *content*. People don't search for "pretty," they search for content. They have specific needs, which require specific answers. Nobody in searching history has ever said, "I don't need what's on this site, but I'll stick around because it's pretty."

Laser-Focused Content

We need to be laser-focused with our content so that when people visit our site, they immediately think, "Great. This is exactly what I need. This place is for me." For example, if you are an aspiring speaker and you visit www. wcspeaking.com, you'll feel you are in the right place. If you are a marketing coach and you visit www.gmarketingcoach.com, you'll feel you are in the right place. Why? Because the content speaks directly to your needs.

There are still far too many entrepreneurs using their websites as online brochures. These sites do very little to build relationships, and they don't have a specific purpose. They're just pretty. When you think like a marketer, you make sure you know the *exact next step* you want your visitors to take. That might be signing up for your newsletter, downloading your special report, watching your demo video, calling you, or some other definite next step. The key is having *a clear call to action on each and every page* of your site. For example, when you visit Mitch's www.gmarketingcoach.com site, the strong call to action is to get your free success kit. That's the exact next step Mitch wants you to take.

The Goal Is to Turn Visitors into Regulars

When you think like a marketer, you understand that it is very difficult to get a first-time website visitor to move from cold to hot in one visit. If you have products on your site and wonder why nobody is buying them, it's because of that fact. If you have your speaking fees on your site and wonder why nobody is hiring you, it's because of that fact. As a result, world-class marketers understand that Internet marketing is a lot like dating. Like Mitch says, "You wouldn't ask for marriage on the first date, would you?" Of course not. Chances are that you would ask for a second date. In other words, ask for the next step. I'll extend that analogy a little further and suggest that you even pay for that next date by making it free for them (i.e., newsletter, toolkit, and/or press kit for prospective speaking engagements).

Once the strangers take that next step, you can systematically move them down your sales funnel. This funnel might start with a free newsletter. Once they build confidence in you from your newsletter, they can return to purchase a $19.95 product such as an audio CD. Once they gain even more confidence in you, they can return to purchase a $297–$497 home-study course. Once they build even *more* confidence in you, they can return to invest in a teleclass series or an online course, which might be listed at $2,297.

Do you think it ends there? Once they have demonstrated that they have a wealth of confidence in you, you can provide systematic ways for them to easily spread the word to others. This viral marketing is very contagious, and you'll find yourself with new prospects arriving, already with a built-in confidence in you due to being referred by someone else in whom they place confidence. In a sense, you'll have a new worldwide sales force working for you without being on your payroll.

Think like a marketer. Remember, whatever business you are in, you are actually in the *marketing business*. What's the exact next step you want your strangers, prospects, customers, and fans to take? According the Mitch, here are some of the different types of sites you might want to consider setting up, based on that exact next step:

- **Portal site:** This site is a triage that provides links to your other sites. For example, you might have a site based on your name (www.yourname.com) that introduces visitors to you and then provides links to other websites that are dedicated to specific purposes. As an expert who speaks, you might have a different website for each product that you offer. This is valuable because it keeps your visitors from being confused when they land on those sites.

- **Sales page:** This site is usually dedicated to selling one particular product or service. It often includes a sales letter, complete with testimonials, free bonuses, and a strong close. These sites work well when prospects have already gained confidence in you through some other interactions.

- **Opt-in page:** This site is designed to get your visitor to provide an email address and a name (and possibly more) in exchange for an offering such as a free e-newsletter, toolkit, or special report.

- **Information site:** This site is often what you see when companies use the web as an online brochure. You can use it to provide information about you, your company, and your offerings. Just be sure you have a specific call to action, even on this type of site.

- **Blog:** Short for weblog, this site is usually informal and empowers you to keep a sequence of online posts related to your business. You can use them to provide video and audio clips, and your prospects and customers can subscribe to your feed and receive every post. Blogs are a great way to easily update content, enhance your search-engine rankings, build credibility, generate media exposure, and stay in constant contact with your perfect customers. Here's an example of a blog Mitch runs: www.gmarketingblog.com.

2. Create a Website that is Professional and Clear

Have you ever been to a website that confused you? Perhaps you weren't exactly sure what the company did. Maybe you weren't sure what you were supposed to do once you arrived. Have you ever been to a site that looked so shoddy, you clicked away from it immediately?

What happened to you in these cases is exactly what you want to avoid with your website. If your site is either confusing or amateurish in appearance, visitors will click away from it without giving it another thought or another look. What is it that really makes them click away? It's the lack of confidence your site projects.

You might be the most competent person in your field, but that doesn't matter, because perception is reality. What people perceive is real to them. If you have a shoddy site, you have a shoddy business in the minds of your visitors. If you have a confusing site, your visitors will believe that working with you is confusing as well. Therefore, they will avoid you like the plague. It's not that they're rude; it's just that there are so many other sites and businesses out there. Why should they hang around one in which they have no confidence? If you were selling a house, would you give prospective buyers a tour without first cleaning it up and making it attractive? Likewise, when your website visitors arrive, make them feel at home.

How Can You Avoid Confusing and Deterring Visitors?

I know it's tempting to use one of your website host's templates and throw up a site as soon as possible; however, this will most likely ruin people's confidence in you. Instead, invest in a *website designer* who will, at the very least, give your site a professional appearance. Don't hire someone bent on making it look pretty, but do hire someone bent on making it look *professional.* Then, contract with a good graphic designer to create a logo and perhaps a few other graphics you can use. This might seem expensive, but consider the fact that you can use these graphics on your website, brochures, postcards, letterhead, and everywhere else you can think to build your brand. With that much use, these graphics become quite a bargain. These consistent graphics, such as the logo, build confidence through *familiarity.* When you see the golden arches, do you feel confident about what you'll get from McDonald's?

Next, make sure you give your site *clear navigation.* You should discuss with your website designer just what type of site you want and exactly what you want it to accomplish. If you want it to generate leads, you should have a clear "next step" that tells your visitors exactly what to do. For example, you might have a picture of you, on your site, pointing to an opt-in box telling people to "sign in here." In addition, you might use a video (or audio) of you that influences your visitors to use the opt-in box to get their free toolkit. It's not difficult to do. I use www.instantvideogenerator.com for my audio and video needs. However, you can easily use YouTube to post videos as well.

If you want us to look at your demo video, tell us. Point an arrow toward your video, or use a huge headline that says "See my LIVE presentation now!" The key is to *tell them what to do.* Don't make your visitors guess. Make it clear. Use IKEA as an example. As soon as you walk through their doors, there are arrows on the floor, showing you exactly where to walk. I rarely see people walking in the opposite direction. What is the flow of your site?

Clutter Is a Killer

Unfortunately, over time, most sites become very cluttered and filled with far too much information. This clutter is a killer, because visitors don't know where to go. Confused people leave. Visitors on the web do not have great attention spans. They search for a need and either find it or don't. Therefore, make a conscious effort to keep your site simple, clean, and laser-focused on a specific need. Less is more. You can't make one site all things to all people. Keep it focused. Each site should be designed for one target market. There should be one very clear call to action on each page. If there is more than one call to action, you're asking for confusion and you will get it. Keep it simple. When you know your site's main purpose, you are able to keep it simple. The problem is that most entrepreneurs don't know their site's purpose. What is yours?

3. Build Your List with Strong Opt-In Incentives

If you were being led into any kind of trap, would you want to know about it? Would you want to avoid it? Good, because chances are that you've already been led into a deadly trap with your website. I say "deadly" because it's a trap that kills businesses and leaves their owners wondering why. Chapter seven expressed the importance of building your list and provided you with ways to do so. Your website (along with your shopping cart) can be your greatest tool. However, you must avoid the trap that many business owners fall into. It's the *traffic trap*. Owners keep asking, "How can I build more traffic?" What they should be asking, though, is, "How can I *convert* the traffic when it comes?" Write this down, and keep it in a high-traffic area: "Think about traffic *conversion* before you think about traffic *creation*."

You can receive five thousand website visitors per day and fail miserably with your business. If these visitors come and go without converting, all you've done is left more money on the table than the person who receives four thousand visitors per day. In addition, you've probably lost those visitors forever. What a waste! On the other hand, if you get a hundred visitors per day and convert several of them, chances are that you're on your way to prospering from your site.

Conversion simply means that your visitors take the measurable action you want them to take. It might be purchasing a product, signing up for your newsletter, downloading a report, watching your demo video, or some other measurable action. Ideally, you want them to at least stay long enough to opt in by providing you with their name and email address. The question is, "What do you have in place to get them to take the desired action?" Remember this important point about your website visitors: if you don't get their names and email addresses, then you will probably never hear from them again.

Maybe you *will* hear from them, and maybe you *won't*. Why take that chance? If they are on your site, odds are that they have an interest in what you offer. If you don't have a system to stay in contact with them, they will gladly take their business elsewhere.

Everybody's Doing It

I was so excited watching a musician, under an independent label, say recently in an interview, "I would much rather have your email address than have you buy my CD, because then I can build a relationship with you forever." I wanted to leap out of my seat and scream, "The music industry is getting it!" The biggest asset you can ever have in your business is your list of prospects and customers. Build it while you sleep. Build it while you eat. Build it while you work on other parts of your business. Here are several ideas for you to use your website to build your list:

- **Make an Irresistible Promise**
  Can you offer a free video that helps golfers lower their score? Can you provide a free e-book to help small-business owners get more

customers in one month than they got all last year? Can you give a free forty-five-minute audio lesson that helps sales presenters become the last company standing? What is the irresistible promise you can offer for free? Make sure your promise emphasizes not just what you offer (i.e., free newsletter) but more so what they get (i.e., more customers without more costs). You might ask, "Craig, why should I give it away? Don't I want people to pay for it?" Of course you do, but what happens when you offer it for free? Three valuable results occur:

o   You get their names and e-mail addresses and can market to them ongoing

o   They build confidence in you for what you can do for them

o   They understand that this is only the tip of the iceberg of what you actually know. Due to their confidence in you, they'll gladly dig into their pockets in order to dig deeper into your services.

Be generous with your free offering. Make them feel like they've hit the jackpot! They will keep coming back for more, as long as you show them their next step. Now is not the time to be subtle or shy. Tell them exactly where they should go next.

- **Place a Value on Your Offer**
  People want to know they're getting a great deal. State the retail value of your offering at $97, and then give it for away for free. This helps make the promise irresistible. I once had two audio lessons valued at twenty dollars and failed to pull in many leads. Why? Because the twenty dollars was not enough contrast to make it irresistible.

- **Create a Mini-Course Using Auto-Responders**

  We will cover auto-responders in the next chapter. However, please know that once you set up the mini-course with the auto-responders, it becomes completely hands-off for you. (Mitch did this with his Internet Marketing Toolkit.) Every visitor that opts in will automatically receive each part of your course via email. Once you set up the auto-responders, your system goes to work even when you don't.

- **Create a PDF Downloadable Special Report**

  A special report is a highly focused practical guide that usually runs approximately two to three thousand words. Popular titles for these usually involve "Top 10 Ways …" or "Top 10 Mistakes …" It's a good idea to build your brand with these reports. For example, I can title one of mine "The Top 15 Nuts and Bolts Tools for Captivating your Audience!" Another one might be "The Top 10 Nuts and Bolts Sales Strategies for Residual Income." Get a designer for these special reports, so they look professional and attractive when your prospects print them. Again, perception is reality. Build confidence, don't break it. If your visitors do not like your special report, chances are they won't return. Therefore, spend time creating an offer of immense value. Don't forget to create a link to the next logical step your prospect should take.

- **Create a Downloadable e-book**

  e-books are great because, like special reports, you can embed links that help move your prospect down your sales funnel. When they build confidence in you, they click the next step. If you're not familiar with how to format an e-book, there are several resources available.

However, I suggest searching on www.elance.com to find a person who has created nice-looking, functional e-books in the past. I did this, and it paid off handsomely by saving me time and money.

- **Use Video and Audio**

  Can you show your work in action? For example, if you offer a golf-swing tutorial, can you show it? If you offer public-speaking advice, can you show your demonstration? If you offer financial advice, can you show a process or maybe a chart, graph, or testimonials from a customer? As you know, it's important to tell visitors what to do next, right? Use a video, and tell them exactly what to do. You can say, "Put in your name and email address and you will immediately receive …" You can also use audio to point visitors in the right direction. Audio mixed with good web copy can be extremely influential.

In order for any of these tools to work, you'll need to have access to auto-responders that can handle e-books, audio lessons, and video and can keep track of the different opt-ins you have. By far the best system is called a "shopping cart," and you'll find out much more about this in chapter eleven. You can also visit www.EasyWebAutomation.com to see how it works.

4. Convert Customers with Compelling Copy

Although visitors may land on your site looking for a logical solution, the web copy that engages their *emotions* will lead to their conversion. Writing sales copy is not easy, but it certainly can be learned. First, it is critical to begin with the end in mind and understand exactly what you want your visitors to do on each page. Then, you can write copy that leads them to that exact next step. Because sites tend to get cluttered, I suggest you create a website for every major product or service you offer. For example, you can visit www.edgeoftheirseats.com to see one dedicated sales page for one product. This keeps your copy clean, focused, and results-driven. Now, we'll look at ten guidelines to follow that will put you way ahead of the game in terms of converting customers on the web:

i. **Grab attention with a powerful headline.** When you peruse the newspaper, what do you look for first? Chances are that it's a headline. If a headline does not catch your attention, you won't read the article. Sales copy is the same. If your headline does not grab your visitors, they will not read the rest of the page. You can have the most compelling copy ever written, but guess what? If the headline stinks, your readers will never see that copy. It's a waste. Spend a considerable amount of time creating your headline. One tool I use consistently is the Headline Wizard, which you can find at http://www.headlinewizard.com/. With the Headline Wizard, you can create, in seconds, compelling headlines that get people reading your text. Keep the following statement firmly in mind: the headline's main job is to get visitors to read the first line in the body of your copy.

ii. **Make it scannable.** Write this down and keep it in a high-traffic area: Website visitors don't read websites. They scan them.

Do you read through an entire page of a website when you visit it? We look for what catches our eye. Visitors look for the headline and then begin scanning the page. Your best bet is to use sub-headlines built on benefits to make your page scannable and to break it up into digestible chunks. Visitors should be able to understand the story of what you offer—and what it will do for them—just by reading your main headline and your sub-headlines. Even if they don't read the copy underneath each sub-headline, these benefit-driven sub-headlines should lead them directly into the call to action.

For example, let's say you offer financial-services training geared toward retirees. You might use the following sub-headlines on your page:

- Protect yourself and your family from the unstable economy
- Reward yourself with the life you worked so hard to establish
- You worked for your money; here's how it can work for you.

The key is to use sub-headlines that get visitors to think "Tell me more" rather than "So what?" Here is a formula to remember:

strong benefits = compelling copy = conversions

iii. **Have a clear call to action.** Throughout my fifteen years of sales experience, I have learned that one thing is consistently true: if you don't convert prospects on the spot, you won't convert them off the spot.

In other words, when it comes to the Internet, you'll either get your visitors to take the next step immediately or else their next step will be with someone else. Therefore, it's essential to use tools to get them to immediately convert. This doesn't mean you need them to purchase a product immediately, but it does mean that you need to get them to take you up on your call to action. Otherwise, you will lose them—possibly forever. That's why it's so important to work on *conversion* before *traffic*. Here are two of the greatest tools you can use to get visitors to take the desired next step now:

A. **Urgency.** It is human nature to procrastinate and put things off until tomorrow. The only problem is, when tomorrow comes, we put things off until another tomorrow. Eventually, we forget what we were putting off! You combat this with urgency. Create time limitations for visitors to take action. For example, if you're offering a discount and free bonuses with your product, let visitors know the offer "lasts until December 1" I did this with my Storytelling Home-Study Course and was amazed at my closing ratio at the end of November. This was no coincidence. Sometimes, people won't act until they feel they'll lose out by *not* acting. Time limits emphasize what they'll lose by not taking action now.

B. **Scarcity.** Just as you learned in chapter eight, scarcity taps into the law of supply and demand. How much do you pay for sand on the beach? How much do you pay for a diamond? Which is more scarce? In your web copy, you must find a way to limit the number of products or services, in order to increase the demand and convert browsers. For example, if you are a coach, you can state, "Due to my heavy travel schedule, I can only take on three more new clients for the remainder of this year." This was true for me this year, and it was amazing what prospects were willing to pay to get me to change my mind. Did I mention I'm flexible?

In addition, as a speaker, you can use scarcity by letting prospective companies know that you only have a few dates available on your schedule and that they should attempt to book you at least four months in advance. Let's be real, nobody wants to hire a speaker they think is never busy. Instead, companies have more confidence in speakers they know are being utilized often and for good reason.

If you use workshops and seminars to book individual appointments, like financial services consultants do, you should let your audience members know you only have three possible dates available, and the first ones to sign up get their choice. This alone will increase your closing ratio for appointments. People need to feel a sense of loss for not taking immediate action. They should not think they have all life long to make a decision, or that you are always available and open.

iv. **List compelling benefits.** As you know, benefits answer the question, "What's in if for them?" Far too many entrepreneurs list features and processes, and far too few list benefits. Have you ever seen lists like the following?

"You'll receive ...

- A fifty-page workbook
- Six audio CDs with seven hours of valuable information
- Specialized templates

This is a list, but it's a list of features. Of course people want to know what they're getting, but they first want to know *why* they are getting it. Therefore, it is important to list benefits first and then follow up with features, if need be. For example, if you have a keynote that deals with embracing change, you might list the following benefits:

- Go beyond compliance and create commitment!
- Get more done in one hour than most leaders do in one day
- Increase retention by growing your most valuable resource (your people)

- Cure the StatusQuoaholics™ so your entire team can embrace change
- Become the leader others want to follow
- Avoid the four deadly pitfalls that trap most teams
- Shoot morale through the roof
- Cut out "time-money-energy wasters"
- Produce more with less stress

You can mention benefits within your short paragraphs and, of course, in your sub-headlines. However, a list is effective because it gives your reader a break from the paragraphs and thereby makes the page more readable.

v. **Tell a story.** You know the importance of telling a story in your speeches, but how about in your web copy? Even in web copy, when visitors buy into your story, they buy into your message. When they buy into your message, these visitors will convert. Many times, you can use the same story you use in speaking in your sales copy. For example, in my Storytelling Home-Study Course sales copy, I use the following story. It is the same story I use in my speeches to sell the product.

"Many years ago, an organization in Michigan hired me to speak to a group of three hundred employees. They paid me thirty-five hundred dollars, scooped me up in a stretch limo, took me to a five-star hotel, and wined and dined me. How did I repay them? By giving them a hundred-and-fifty-dollar speech. That's right: I failed miserably. When I finished, the woman who had bragged about me and convinced the powers to hire me could not even look me in the eyes. I have never heard from them again. Fast-forward to today. Today, my rehire rate is 92 percent, and that day in Michigan is far behind me. What made the difference? Well, after many years and many dollars spent, I eventually uncovered a *formula* for creating spellbinding stories from scratch. This formula has changed my speaking destiny, and it will do the same for you …"

Does this story format look familiar? It's the "Then, Now, and How" formula. It's difficult for a visitor to look away from a well-written short story. They want to know how it ends. If you write it using the correct formula, it will end with their conversion!

vi. **Create instant credibility with testimonials.** People want "the truth wrapped up in proof." Besides having someone see you speak or experience your product firsthand, testimonials are the best way to prove your truth. Use them not only on your product pages but also on your homepage. Many speakers know this, but they don't know the right kinds of testimonials to publish. Wannabe speakers use testimonials about their greatness as a speaker. World-class speakers use testimonials about *the results others receive* after utilizing their services. Here are three examples of the kinds of testimonials wannabe speakers use:

"You were *wonderful.* Everyone is *still* talking about you!"

"I was speechless after your presentation. You are an excellent speaker, and you have a lot to be proud of."

"I absolutely loved your presentation in Saint John on Saturday. You were brilliant. I've been attending business and association conferences for fifteen years, and yours was one of the best that I have had the pleasure to see."

Here are three examples of testimonials world-class speakers use:

> "When I got home, doors started opening for me, and literally within a week I had five paid presentations lined up. My business is taking off faster than I would have ever dreamed!"
>
> —*Bonnie Laabs, Professional Speaker,*
> *Founder, B-Inspired*

> "My first day back in my sales territory, I was charged. We broke a district record by selling 154 registrations. Every conference I have been to before has struggled to sell 100. All of us realize that this success was a direct result of our keynote speaker. So ... thanks, Craig, for the help.
>
> —*Bob Sloan, Fall Conference Chair 2001,*
> *President Seaway Toastmasters Cornwall, Canada*

> "We can't thank you enough for your contribution to Chesapeake's event ... you were the highlight of the day and made a significant impact on employee morale. I look forward to working with you again in the near future!"
>
> —*Monique Bell, Marketing/Communications Manager,*
> *Chesapeake Appraisal and Settlement Services Inc.*

All the testimonials above (including the wannabe-speaker ones) are ones I have used in the past. Now I know better. Although we get testimonials like the ones I used as a wannabe speaker, they do not help us convert visitors. On the other hand, the World Class Speaking testimonials do wonders with conversion. You want your visitors to think, "Great, I came to the right place. If I use their services, I will get similar results." The difference between the testimonials for the wannabe speakers and for the world-class speakers is threefold.

A. **Results-driven.** You should use only testimonials that show what others have gained from taking your suggestions or using your processes. Nobody cares how great you are. They do care how great they can become with your help. Only show them the testimonials that prove your truth of helping others improve their conditions. Sometimes, that proof comes in numbers (i.e., 154 registrants) or in intangibles (i.e., impact on employee morale). Whatever it is, make sure it's about *their results* instead of *your* greatness.

B. **Similar to your audience.** It might feel great getting testimonials from celebrities and other influential people. However, your visitors want to know that you can help people *like them*. Chances are that the celebrities were already celebrities before they used your services. Therefore, it's difficult for our visitors to relate. They need proof that what you offer helps people like them. It's best to use testimonials from people and organizations with which your ideal customers can relate.

C. **Credible names, positions, or organizations.** It's not good enough to publish a testimonial and then write "Dave" next to it. We need to know something about Dave. We need to know that Dave actually exists. It's best to publish testimonials that have full names, organizations, and employment positions, if at all possible. Remember:

People want the truth wrapped up in proof.

vii. **Offer a powerful guarantee.** It has been said that a sale is made when the prospect feels the benefits outweigh the objections. One of the biggest objections that prospects have is wondering whether or not the product will work for them. Your job is to put them at ease with this internal questioning, and the very best way to do this is by offering a guarantee.

Many companies give a money-back guarantee on their products and services. This guarantee is usually limited to a timeframe such as thirty days. That's normal, average, and the least a prospect expects. Therefore, in order to stand out and be perceived as a product that truly works, you need to go beyond the thirty-day money-back guarantee. In truth, you need to go way beyond the comfort zone of most companies. Why? I'm sure you know the one-word answer by now: confidence. Here's the guarantee I use for my Storytelling Home-Study Course:

100 percent Risk-Free Guarantee

"Your success in using the 9-STEP FORMULA for crafting spellbinding stories and selling unforgettable points is completely guaranteed. In fact, here's my 100 percent Better-Than-Risk-Free-Take-It-To-The-Bank Guarantee:

"I personally guarantee you will be thrilled with the results this home-study course brings you.

If after a full 6 months you honestly believe I have not delivered on this promise, let me know and I will issue you a prompt and courteous refund. Plus, the free bonus gifts are yours to keep regardless, just for your trouble."

As you can see, not only do I offer their money back for a period of six months, I also urge them to keep the free bonuses, which are valued at $115. If this offer doesn't build their confidence and reduce their risk, not much will.

You might ask, "Craig, isn't it risky to give them a full six months to return it? Won't people take advantage and simply use up the product and then return it for their money back? Don't you have cases in which the prospect sees this as an opportunity to get free bonuses?" The answer to all these questions is the following: it's worth it. Sure, you might have a few snakes who take advantage of you. However, that's going to happen no matter what you do and what kind of guarantee you offer. The bottom line is, if you have a worthwhile product or service, the returns will be very low, and, due to your generous confidence-building guarantee, your profits will be very high.

After a full year of offering this home-study course, guess how many returns I have had? The answer is *one*. That return came from someone who had not even opened the package but simply had the postal service return it. It's unreasonable not to expect returns. Therefore, what should you do when someone wants to return it? And what if they have passed the six-month point and *then* decide they want to return it? The answer is pure and simple: give them their money back. Don't fight it. Don't drag it out. Don't question it. Simply return the money and move on. It's not worth it to find yourself in court or in the Internet's court of public opinion. In today's world, it's not uncommon for a greedy company to find themselves blasted over the Internet with messages that say "don't do business with them." These come from disgruntled customers. It's just not worth it. Honor the guarantee (and beyond), with no questions asked.

Offering a generous guarantee will do wonders for your closing ratio. Prospects that would have just walked away end up walking away *with your product in their hands*. Be creative and generous in what you offer for your guarantee—then you can sit back and watch the orders roll in, day after profitable day.

viii. **Tip the scales with free bonuses.** One of the greatest tools you can use to make sales is *reciprocity*. When you go out of your way to give to other people, they bend over backwards to return the favor. Using free bonuses is an outstanding way not only to tap into reciprocity, but also to make it a no-brainer for your prospects to take action. They should feel like there is no way they cannot act now. Do yourself a favor, and pile up your free bonuses. Let's stick with my Storytelling Home-Study Course as an example. Here are the free bonuses I have offered online:

3 free Bonuses for Ordering by December 1, 2008

A. **Free Bonus Gift #1:** You get five audio lessons delivered immediately via email to help you immerse into all aspects of public speaking and emerge as a world-class speaker! Value: $50

B. **Free Bonus Gift #2:** You get Craig Valentine's 155-page *Edge of Their Seats Storytelling* e-book. This will be emailed to you right away, so you can start learning the storytelling secrets from Craig before you go to bed TONIGHT. Value: $47

C. **Free Bonus Gift #3:** You get the 125-page e-book (from six World Champions) entitled *The Speaking Secrets of the Champions.* Even if you already have the six-audio-CD set, the e-book will help you pick up ideas you may have missed with the audio. You will be able to download this ɪɴsᴛᴀɴᴛʟʏ. Value: $19.95

Together, these three free bonuses are valued at more than $115, but they're all yours, absolutely free, when your order by December 1, 2008.

What do you notice about these stacked-up bonuses? There are four secrets to using the bonuses to make your offer a no-brainer:

A. **Impose a timeframe for the bonuses to be in effect.** The timeframe (i.e., December 1, 2008) together with the free bonuses creates a sense of urgency for your prospects to place their order. People are motivated by a fear of loss and an opportunity for gain. Your prospects don't want to lose out on the $115 worth of products by procrastinating. If your offer is written effectively, your prospects will quickly become customers. It will indeed be a no-brainer.

B. **Use bonuses that are related to the goals of your prospects.** I've often seen marketers selling unrelated items and wondering why they don't work. For example, for my storytelling course, offering free bonuses of coffee mugs is irrelevant. It might be a nice gift, but it does nothing to move my prospect closer to the goal of becoming a world-class speaker. Piling up free, related bonuses makes it a no-brainer.

C. **Offer bonuses that are delivered immediately.** Chances are that your prospects arrived at your website with an immediate need. They don't want to wait long to meet that need. Therefore, anything you can offer them immediately will go a long way in helping them decide to purchase from you. The easiest way to provide immediate help is by using your auto-responders to send out your bonuses as soon as your prospects place their orders. In one auto-responder email, my new customers receive links to the five audio lessons and the downloadable e-books. Knowing they will get immediate help makes their decision to buy a no-brainer.

D. **Build your value without adding to your cost.** The one thing that each of my bonuses has in common is this: they cost me nothing to provide. Sure, the e-books and audio lessons cost me money and time to create. However, those were one-time fees. Currently, they cost me nothing to send out. There are no mailing costs and no time-related costs, because they're sent out automatically! It becomes a complete hands-off process for me, yet it builds significant value in the eyes of my prospects. When you put together your offer, use auto-responders to eliminate the cost for your bonuses while you enhance the value of your overall offer. This also helps to create the contrast you need to make your offer a no-brainer. We'll discuss contrast in point number nine.

ix. **Compare apples to oranges.** How much does an audio CD of one of your favorite musical artists usually cost? Let's say $15. Now, let's multiply $15 times 6, which equals $90. Using this logic, my "Edge of Their Seats Storytelling Home-Study Course for Speakers," which includes 6 CDs, should have a price of $90. How, then, can I justify a price of $297? Does the inclusive manual cost an extra $207? Of course not. My customers are not buying CDs, they're buying better speeches. They're buying what they need to become world-class speakers. If I simply compared apples to apples (CDs and CDs), the price would be $90. However, here's how I use my web copy to compare my course:

> "Many speakers will charge you between $700.00 to $3,000.00 to spend a weekend with them to improve just ONE story. You get to have this program for much longer than a weekend (you keep it forever). Plus, you get more than one great story: you get the PROCESS to create more! You'll have this proven storytelling BLUEPRINT for the rest of your speaking life.

"But, I'm not going to charge you anywhere near $3000.00 or even $700.00. In fact, your total investment for the "Edge of Their Seats Storytelling Home-Study Course" is only $297."

Did I compare apples to apples or apples to oranges? Instead of comparing CDs to CDs, I compared my home-study course to spending a weekend with a speech coach. I could have easily compared it to one of my two-day boot camps that I put on around the United States, which cost $895. Either way, when the prospect sees the true value of what they get, their decision becomes even more of a no-brainer.

Instead of having to pay $3,000.00 plus flights, hotel costs, car rentals, and meals, they can simply take home the same information for a cost of $297—and have that information forever. This is the contrast I referred to in point number eight. The price of $297 alone (or even compared to six CDs) appears high. The price of $297 compared to a boot camp or a weekend with a speech coach appears low. *Contrast makes all the difference.* The key to using contrast is to mention the higher price first. Whether it's on your order form, on the web, or in person, always list the higher price first. List the $3,000.00 first and then contrast that with the $297. When your prospect also sees the bonuses stacked up high without affecting the price, it becomes a true no-brainer.

When I sell this home-study course in person, using the story we discussed in chapter seven, I rarely ever mention what's in the program (i.e., 6 CDs, 165-page manual, 15-page compass). And guess what? Nobody asks. Once they know what they will get by using it, it becomes a no-brainer. They take action. Your prospects will do the same if you compare your apples to oranges.

Secret Tip: It also helps to add the cents column to the higher price. For example, with $3000.00, I include the last two zeros in the cents column. This makes the number appear even larger. However, when I list the $297, I remove last two zeros. This makes the number appear even smaller. I know this is tricky, but if you truly believe in how much your product or service will help your customers, you'll do what you can to get it into their hands. Based on the feedback that I have received, over the last year, about the home-study course, I believe people who regularly make presentations are missing out on a fortune if they don't have it.

x.   **Have a strong postscript.** Yes, postscripts can and should be used in your web copy. Other than your headline, which gets your visitors into the text in the first place, your postscript stands next in importance. Whether it's a speech or a letter, people remember best what they hear (or see) first and what they hear (or see) last. Many visitors go from reading your headline to reading your postscript. Therefore, it's important for you to have one that reinforces the sense of urgency your visitors should have, or at least that reinforces the benefits they will receive. For example, with my home-study course, my postscript reads as follows:

> "PS: Just think! You'll never have to experience the horrors I went through in Michigan. Instead, you'll have the FORMULA that keeps each audience leaning on your every word, begging to see you again. What more could you want?
>
> Invest by December 1, 2008 now to get your three free bonuses."

This postscript reinforces the sense of *urgency* by restating the timeframe (i.e., December 1, 2008), *pushes* them away from the fear of loss (failure like mine in Michigan), and *pulls* them toward the opportunity for gain (audience leaning on your every word). Even if my visitors read only my postscript, what question do you think they will have? They will probably ask, "What free bonuses?" In order to find out, they will scan up into the text, and that's exactly where I want them. Use your postscript to reinforce your offer and to either get your visitors into the text or into the next step toward conversion.

Final Thought on the Ten Web-Copy Tools

Writing web copy is critical to your success as a speaker or entrepreneur. If you utilize these ten tools, you'll find yourself converting more customers and feeling less frustration and stress about the sales conversion process. You'll pull in order after order after order. To write great web copy, I suggest going back to the basics and discovering what true sales copy is all about. There are some classic books on this very topic. Three of my favorites regarding sales copy are the following:

- *Triggers* by Joseph Sugarman
- *Advertising Secrets of the Written Word* by Joseph Sugarman
- *Tested Advertising Methods* by John Caples (and revised by Fred E. Hahn)

I strongly suggest picking these up, digesting them, and watching your profits soar! Now, let's get back to our "Six Rules for Making the Internet Work for You." We just finished point number four, "Converting Customers with Compelling Copy." Now, let's head into point number five, regarding traffic.

5. Have a Plan to Generate Traffic

Did you ever see the wonderful movie entitled *Field of Dreams*? Do you remember the following famous line that was whispered throughout the movie: "If you build it, they will come"? Well, I'm here to tell you something about your website. If you build it, they won't come. That's right, they won't come! No matter how beautiful and how expensive it is, they won't come. Not unless you generate the traffic. The good news is that now that you have a plan to *convert* traffic, you can create a plan to *generate* it. Below are five top ways to get visitors to your website:

A. **Build your email signature.** The e-mail signature is where you virtually sign your name at the end of your emails. This is perhaps the most obvious, yet most neglected or abused, practice for generating traffic. I say "abused," because some email signatures are novels in disguise. They are far too wordy and comprehensive. The result for the receiver is often annoyance. It takes up too much space, especially when the receiver is searching through a trail of emails that were sent back and forth. In addition, you're not going to draw anybody into a link in this way. Instead, provide a short and sweet benefit statement and include a link. Here are two examples:

- Do you want to immediately attract more customers? Click here for *a free* ten-step proven report!

- Click here to see *a free* video on how to motivate even your most difficult employees!

Make sure you use the entire URL (i.e., http://) so that the link is automatic. Then use the link to take your visitors directly to the landing page you promise. Otherwise, you'll break their confidence in you, and they'll leave your site unsatisfied. If they expect to see a report on attracting more customers, that's exactly what they should see after clicking the link. Make sure they land on that exact page.

B. **Write and submit articles.** Entrepreneurs often wonder how they can use search-engine-optimization techniques to get their sites listed high in the search-engine rankings. However, it often seems like a moving target. On the other hand, there is a surefire way to get loads of qualified traffic to your site and to do it with no cost. Write articles about your specialized subject, and submit them to online article banks. If you google "Online Article Banks," you'll find plenty that you can use to submit articles and build traffic.

Here is how it works: You submit an article to the banks and use the resource box at the bottom of the article to include information about you and what you do. Of course, this is the perfect place to list your URL to attract visitors to your site. Once your articles get out on the web and readers start reusing them (with your resource-box information included) the growth of the traffic to your site can be exponential. Moreover, you will start becoming known as the expert you are. Remember, you're an expert who speaks. Ironically, with all these new sites linking to yours, it will actually help your search engine rankings after all!

C. **Publish an e-newsletter.** Entrepreneurs that don't send regular emails to their list are no better off than those who have no list. You absolutely must stay in constant contact with your visitors, and sending out a regular e-newsletter will help you do that. Use this e-newsletter to draw recipients back to your site for more information. If your e-newsletter has value, each time you send one out, other people will find you and subscribe. There is a serious viral-marketing effect to high-value e-newsletters. It's a great idea to add a "tell a friend" link to them to facilitate the growth of your subscriber list.

D. **Use offline strategies.** Just because you want online traffic doesn't mean you shouldn't go offline to get it. Use your business cards, stationary, postcards, letters, specialty gifts, voicemail, and anything else you can think of to post your website and email address. The key is to give recipients a *reason* to visit your site. For example, on the back of my business card, I can state the following:

Create the Ultimate 30-minute Speech! Get your FREE 7-part mini-course today by visiting www.wcspeaking.com

Let's say you speak to managers about managing change within an organization. On your business card, you might include the following:

Get your FREE "Managing Change" toolkit by visiting www.speakingofmanaging.com.

Whether it is your business card, stationary, or voicemail, always give them a reason to visit your website. The lowest barrier to entry is to offer something free. Again, once they build up their confidence in you, they are willing to pay for more.

E. **Establish a pay-per-click campaign.** You can always pay for traffic. Chances are that you've performed a search and have seen the resulting "sponsored links" on the side and top margins. Those spots were paid for, and you can do likewise. You can use Google's AdWords or other pay-per-click campaigns. These campaigns can bring loads of traffic to your site. However, you must be very strategic and careful about using them. A great place to start is by picking up Perry Marshall's book entitled *The Ultimate Guide to Google AdWords*.

Final Thought about Online Traffic

These five ways are by no means an exhaustive list. There are several methods you can use that are beyond the scope of this book. I highly suggest

Mitch's book, *Mastering Online Marketing,* to go a mile deep into these areas. Nobody has ever struck oil by going an inch deep. Dig deep into these online practices, and you'll emerge with vast profits.

6. Use Blogs, Podcasts, and Video Sites to Build Confidence, Traffic, and Profits

By now, you've heard of blogs, podcasts, and video sites such as YouTube. Forward-thinking entrepreneurs embrace these tools first, while others wait around for a written invitation. Woody Allen said "80 percent of success is showing up." In this case, I believe "90 percent of success is showing up—first!" Don't wait to embrace these tools. Wrap your businesses around them and put them to work for you *now.* Let's look at these three tools you can use to build the confidence others place in you.

Blogs

A blog (short for "weblog") is like a public diary that you keep online. You submit entries and allow visitors to comment, thereby making it interactive. Here are seven benefits you get by publishing a blog.

1. **Immediate web presence.** You can literally create your blog, publish it, and make it available to the public within the next fifteen minutes. In addition, you have complete control over the content, which is easy to update. You do not need a webmaster to intervene and charge you for the intervention. Simply get started by visiting one of these top providers of blog platforms:

   www.Blogger.com

   www.TypePad.com

   www.WordPress.com

Go ahead—visit these sites, and see just how easy it is to get started! One solid book on creating blogs is *Blogwild!* by Andy Wibbels. Another is *Secrets of Online Persuasion* by John-Paul and Deborah Micek.

2. **Newsworthiness.** If you want more PR for your business, establish a blog. Many news reporters look to popular blogs for experts in various areas. Your blog helps these reporters perceive you as an expert. In addition, because the search engines look for updates, your newer, relevant blog entries can land high up in the rankings, which makes it easier for everyone to find out about you.

3. **Interaction with prospects and customers.** One of the differences between a blog and a regular website is the level of interaction. With your blog, you invite visitors to make comments. You can then respond to these comments if you want, and this helps you build relationships with visitors and subscribers. Doing so helps them build that all-important confidence in you.

4. **Ongoing contact.** You already know the importance of having constant contact with your prospects and customers. You should update your blog at least twice per week, because this makes your blog *sticky*. In other words, people will return over and over again. In fact, they can subscribe to your blog and receive it via email every time you make a new entry. This is a great way to stay in front of them.

5. **Easy way to write a book.** This is why I think blogs are heaven-sent. You already know the importance of writing every day. Now you have a tool that makes it easy for you to do just that. Picture this: you write each day and publish your writings on your blog. You use the "categories" feature and assign each entry into a category. Let's say

you have ten categories that you begin to fill with entries. Guess what these categories represent? Chapters! Once you have several entries for each category (chapter), you're 75 percent across the bridge to finishing your book. However, that's not even the best part.

What's best about this is that, with each entry, you get comments and feedback. You know what resonates with your readers and what does not. You find what they think about each entry and how you can make it even better. Based on this feedback, you can tweak your entries (offline) and improve them by the time you recreate them for the book. I've read wonderful books by David Meerman Scott (i.e., *The New Rules of Marketing and PR: How to Use News Releases, Blogs, Podcasting, Viral Marketing, and Online Media to Reach Buyers Directly*) and Seth Godin (i.e., *Small Is the New Big: And 183 other Riffs, Rants, and Remarkable Business Ideas*) that at least partially used blog entries during their creation.

6. **Give readers the next step.** You can use each blog entry like a *portal website*. In other words, you can provide links to wherever you want your readers to go next. I suggest that you send them not just to your links but also to the websites and blogs of authors who have related information. Like we discussed in the rules for selling in chapter eight, this helps your visitors trust you more, because they know you have their best interests in mind. Even if you don't benefit directly, you certainly will benefit indirectly. Plus, they will see you as a well-connected expert and as a starting place for their solutions. Of course, you can still provide links to your products, services, and free newsletter, but make sure you mix those with links to places that

don't directly involve you. Don't forget to provide links to products to which you are an affiliate. This is transparent to your visitors, but your resulting checks will be anything but transparent!

7. **Easy to provide audio and video.** Blogs are usually about the blogger's personality as much as the content. Having audio and video on various entries breathes life into the content and makes the visitor more familiar with you. Familiarity builds confidence, and confidence builds your business.

Podcasts

Speakers need to be heard. Hopefully, you are now looking at yourself not just as a speaker but as an expert who speaks. However, you do still speak! Therefore, you need to be heard. One of the best ways to speak to thousands of people without having to leave your home is by delivering a podcast. How much credibility do you perceive subject-matter radio-talk-show hosts to have? Guess what? You can create your own show!

Podcasts are audio or video files that recipients can download into their MP3 players, iPods, computers, or other devices. They can then listen and watch them on their own time. In addition, they can subscribe to your podcast and receive new episodes each time you publish them. Podcasting can differentiate you from the competition, because your energy and enthusiasm will come across, along with your specialized content. Again, recipients will become more familiar with you and build their confidence in anything you offer. Podcasting is often used in conjunction with blogs to create an experience in which the prospect receives text, audio, and possibly video. If you want more information on podcasting, visit these sites:

www.iTunes.com

www.PodcastAlley.com

www.Odeo.com

YouTube

As a speaker, YouTube should not be an option. This is something you *must* utilize, because you have the ability to build a connection using your World Class Speaking skills. *The absolute surest way to get hired as a speaker is to have people see you speak.* If you have masterful platform skills and a solid message, people will hire you once they see you. In the past, the number of people that saw you was limited by the number of people that were physically in the room. Today, that room includes the entire world! Better yet, it's *free*. Put together videos of your presentations, upload them to YouTube, use appropriate keywords based on your expertise, and watch as people find and hire you. Let's look at how you can also use YouTube to market your other products and services.

YouTube allows people to upload, share, and watch videos, free of charge. As a result, forward-thinking marketers are using the site to create videos that grab attention and provide excellent content. Then, at the end of the video, they give an exact next step for their viewers by providing a URL for them to visit. Does this look familiar? In your case, once viewers get fired up about your video, they will take that next step—whether it is visiting your website, viewing your blog, or placing a call to your 800 number.

YouTube works well because visitors can use keyword search terms to narrow down their results and get specific information. This means that you can get highly targeted traffic, rather than freeloaders that can waste your time and energy. The bottom line is that YouTube is another free tool that you can use to market your business, gain the confidence of your prospects, and keep your sales funnel full. Go ahead and visit www.YouTube.com, and see how easy it is to start uploading videos.

Final Word about Making the Internet Work for You

It's now been several years since I walked around those lavish online conferences, wondering what would happen to all those companies. Unfortunately, it is too late for many of them. Fortunately, it is not too late for you to grasp the strategies above and mesh them with your business. Make sure that the Internet does not become the icing on your cake; instead, make sure that it becomes a significant ingredient in your mix. In every way, you have to build your business around it.

Also, please understand that the Internet is anything but static. In fact, it's changing as I write this. For example, Web 2.0 is growing in importance. This is the social-interaction aspect of the web, and there are several tools to help you thrive off of it. Three tools with which you should become intimately familiar are the following:

- **Linkedin** – A networking site for business professionals. Visit www. linkedin.com for details.
- **YouTube** – Video-sharing site. Visit www.YouTube.com for details.
- **wikis** – Sites where visitors can control the content and updates. Visit www.wikipedia.org for an example, and visit www.pbwiki.com for a service provider.

Remember that what got us here won't get us there. Again, 90 percent of success is showing up first. Get on board with Web 2.0.

Chapter 11

HOW TO AUTOMATE SYSTEMS TO RAKE IN MONEY WHILE YOU SLEEP

hen Mitch and I co-lead the Guerrilla Marketing Coach Certification program, we asked our attendees what some of their major business issues were. The number-one complaint we got was that they felt like they were fighting too many fires and not getting enough done. They were on their heels, which made it very hard to move forward. All the strategies they planned to use (writing articles, sending sales letters, tweaking websites, beginning a blog, etc.) had to be put on hold while they took care of *reactive* business ("fires"). In a sense, they felt that they couldn't be proactive. Does this sound familiar to you at all? If so, there is a solution. What is it? Automation!

MITCH'S TOOLS AND STRATEGIES

What I admire about Mitch is that he runs several online courses, writes numerous books (four this year alone), runs a blog, sells products, and writes and plays music, all at the same time, yet he is still able to look forward in a proactive manner to pursue the next great project! How is this possible? Automation. To Mitch's credit, he has shared his ideas and tools with hundreds of marketers and businesspeople and helped us free up our time to stop fighting our fires and start forging our futures. Many of the same strategies that he taught us, you'll pick up in the following section. Let's first dive into what automation helps you do.

AUTOMATION PROGRAMS HELP YOU DO THE FOLLOWING:

- **Save time** – What takes you hours upon hours to do, your automation systems do in minutes. Plus, your systems work even when *you* don't.

- **Thrill your customers** – Customers like to feel important, and they want to be served immediately. They don't want to wait. Your automation systems exceed their already-high expectations.

- **Save money** – What you otherwise would have to spend on employee wages and postage is covered with your automation systems.

- **Speak directly to your market** – A good automation system allows you to easily segment your prospects and customers into separate markets that have distinct needs. As a result, you can tailor your messages to speak directly to each market and have them think, "Wow, this really is for me!"

Here are some of the uses for your automation systems:

- Delivering mini-courses
- Providing thank-you emails
- Confirming purchases
- Processing credit-card transactions
- Providing call-in and code information for teleclasses and webinars
- Delivering e-newsletters
- Sending follow-up information to prospects and customers
- Delivering e-books and audio lessons
- Creating separate lists of prospects and customers
- Keeping track of affiliates
- Tracking orders (old and new)
- Measuring marketing campaigns
- Cross-selling based on the specific product that is ordered
- Helping customers consume your products

Two of the Most Important Uses of Automation:

Mitch says that the two most important uses of automation are the following:

1. Communicating with your market
2. Getting paid online by delivering products to your market

1. COMMUNICATING WITH YOUR MARKET

Let's start with "communicating with your market." One of the most important tools to save you loads of time and money is called the "auto-responder."

Auto-responders

Let's keep it real. Your prospects and customers are already overwhelmed by the amount of information they must sort through every day. How can you provide information that stands out? First of all, as Seth Godin says in his groundbreaking book, *Permission Marketing*, your communications must be "personal, relevant, and anticipated." The question is, who has time to do that? Chances are that you're already busy just trying to keep your head above water; now you have to actually swim somewhere!

Jeffrey Lant, author of *Money Making Marketing*, said that we must reach out to our prospects at least seven times within an eighteen-month period. However, that was back in the 1990s. Nowadays, due to the proliferation of advertising messages our prospects receive, we need to reach out to them much more often and in a personalized manner. Our prospects and customers should hear from us at least once, preferably twice, per month. Those who don't contact their list are no better off than those who don't have a list.

Imagine this, your prospect lands on your website and decides to sign up for your e-mini-course and electronic newsletter. Immediately upon signing up, that prospect receives an auto-responder e-mail with the first lesson of your mini-course. Then, four days later, the prospect receives the second lesson. Four days later, the prospect receives the third lesson, and more lessons are sent until the course is completed.

Toward the end of the course, the prospect has built up so much confidence in you that he decides to order one of your e-books for $29.95. As soon as the prospect makes the purchase, he sees a confirmation of his order and receives an auto-responder link to access his downloadable e-book. A week after he receives the e-book, he gets an auto-responder e-mail from you, pointing out various parts of the e-book that can help him reach his goals. Don't you think your customer will be blown away by such specialized caring and service? He will! However, the best part is that you only need to set this system up once, and you can let it fly for as long as you want. The rest is hands-off. The auto-responders work like clockwork, and your customers receive the excellent service they deserve. As a result, your reputation grows, and so does the number of your new customers.

Let's Look at Ways that Single Auto-Responders Can Help You

As an expert who speaks, you can use *single auto-responders* or *series auto-responders* to your great advantage. Single auto-responders empower you to do the following:

- **Cross-sell per product or service ordered.** You can set up an auto-responder for each and every product you offer through your shopping cart. For example, when people purchase my single audio CD entitled "How to Go from Lackluster to Blockbuster Storytelling," they receive an auto-responder email, several days later, that persuades them to upgrade to "The Edge of Their Seats Storytelling Home-Study Course."

The reason these auto-responders have such a great impact is because they are *specific to each product*. Obviously, the customers purchased my storytelling CD because they are interested in storytelling. Therefore, my auto-responder for that specific product cross-sells them on another storytelling product that goes a mile deep. If, on the other hand, they initially purchased my "Construct your Killer Keynote" CD, they would receive a different auto-responder that markets our "Create your Keynote" Champ Camp. Either way, it's a great feeling to know your auto-responders are always working to cross-sell and upsell your prospects and customers—even when you're off playing golf, being pampered at the spa, or relaxing on vacation.

- **Help people consume a product or service.** This is a piece many marketers overlook, and it costs them greatly. Studies show that most book purchasers rarely read past the first chapter in those books. Purchasers of audio and video materials are often the same. Therefore, it's critical for you to proactively get your customers to *consume* the materials they bought from you. You can do this with auto-responders. For example, you can set up an auto-responder to be sent out fourteen days after customers purchase your e-book. This auto-responder can remind them of their purchase and then point them to a direct page of the book. It might say the following:

  > "Make sure you review the EDGE sales formula before you go into your next sales presentation. It will help you sell your message. You can find it on page forty-six of your *Storytelling* e-book. Remember to print out the chart and use it as you develop your main message. When people buy into that message, you'll likely make the sale."

Pointing them back into the book helps them consume it and build more confidence in you. Plus, it lets them know you really care about the ROI they get from you. I can't tell you how many powerful email responses I get from purchasers who thank me for reminding them of their purchase. It's great for relationship-building, and it gives you a welcomed excuse to stay in contact.

- **Provide teleclass call-in and code information.** When customers purchase a teleclass or telecourse from you, your auto-responder should immediately send them both the telephone number to dial and the code to use to access the call. Immediacy is the key, because customers don't want to worry about tracking down the code information later. They feel a great sense of confidence when they receive the code right away. This, of course, is done through a single auto-responder that goes out with each customer purchase. Can you imagine how much time it would take to do this manually? Especially if you have one to two hundred teleclass attendees? With the auto-responder, it is completely hands-off.

- **Give response for the opt-in list.** Each time visitors become prospects by opting into your offering (newsletter, mini-course, etc.), an auto-responder should go out immediately, confirming their status as a subscriber and *teasing* them on what to expect next.

- **Send promised bonuses.** You learned, in chapter eight, the importance of stacking up the bonuses. You also learned to use bonuses that don't take more time out of your busy schedule. With a single auto-responder, you can include links to all the bonus materials you promised in your sales letter or during your speech.

For example, when customers purchase my home-study course, I provide an auto-responder that includes five links. Each link is to either an audio lesson or an e-book. All of my bonuses are sent out without me having to be involved. I set it up once, and it serves me forever.

- **Provide a special discount code for products and services.** Do you want to make your customers feel special? Then provide them with an exclusive opportunity to get discounts for your products and services. For example, inside of my Storytelling Home-Study Course, I mention a huge discount my customers will get on my Dynamic Delivery DVD. All they have to do is send an email to a certain address. Once they send the email, an auto-responder sends the special code and the URL they need to get the hefty discount. Nobody else knows about the discount or the code, except for those who have purchased my home-study course. This exclusivity makes my customers feel special.

You might ask, "Craig, why do you make them go through the process of sending an email to you? Why don't you simply provide the discount code in the actual content of the home-study course?" First, one very important strategy to use online is called "involvement." You want your prospects and customers to get involved by clicking and taking actions on their part. Then, when you reward them for those actions, it builds a deeper bond. Second, one of the greatest advantages of the web is its *flexibility.* If I put the discount code in the home-study course, I can't change it. However, if I put it in the auto-responder, not only can I change it, but I can also cross-sell other items as well. Finding ways for your prospects and customers to stay in touch with you is very healthy for your profits.

As you can see, a single auto-responder can deepen your relationships and your pockets. Imagine what sequential auto-responders can do. Let's take a look.

Sequential Auto-responders

Sequential auto-responders, which are a series of autoresponders sent out in a specific order, empower you to send out information at designated intervals. For example, the free "7-part World Class Speaking Toolkit" you get at www.wcspeaking.com sends a new lesson every four days. Hence, in twenty-eight days, you will have the tools you need to become a world-class speaker. How much work am I currently doing to give you those tools? None! I already did the work. I created it once, and it serves me and you forever. You can do likewise to automatically serve your list.

What process, system, or course can you put together as bait to get your website visitors or audience members to take the next step you've laid out for them? If you're giving a speech, can you mention your "FREE 5-Part Goal-Buster Sales Course" that they get by signing up for your list? Once they sign up, they'll receive each "part" of the course per the time intervals you designate. For example, they can get "Part 1: Getting Past the Gatekeeper," on day one and then "Part 2: Asking the Right Questions," on day five. Your course can go on for twenty days without you having to lift a finger. By the end of that course, if a small percentage of participants invest in your next step (i.e., seminar, audio CD, home-study course), you'll be making money without spending time. That's a great feeling!

Here are more ways to use sequential auto-responders:

- Multi-part e-courses
- Follow-up reminder messages (countdown) for an upcoming event
- Sending weekly or monthly communications to a membership site
- Newsletter "Weekly Tips"
- Sending individual bonuses to purchasers of your materials

Meeting the Meeting Planners' Needs

When I started in the speaking industry, one of the first efforts speakers made was to get their press kit together. Each time we sent out a press kit, it cost us time and money. Today, you can save time *and* money by having your press kit online. For example, you can have a link for meeting planners to click and automatically gain access to your demo video, your introduction, your handouts, your program descriptions, your downloadable reports, your bio, your downloadable one-sheet, and much more. Once you upload them onto your site, they cost you nothing for the meeting planners to access them. As a result, you no longer have to stop whatever you are doing in order to rush out a press kit with the hopes of getting hired. It all happens automatically. Sometimes I'm 80 percent hired before the potential speaking client ever contacts me. Why? They've received the information they needed, via my website. Here are some specific tools you can use to automatically respond to prospects and customers:

- **Demo videos.** I suggest using a system called "Instant Video Generator," which you can find at www.wcspeaking.com/resources. This program easily adds streaming video to your emails and websites. Therefore, if meeting planners wants to see your demo video, you can either send them to your site or actually send an email with the video linked to it. Either way, the meeting planner will quickly see you in action.

- **Testimonials.** You will likely have testimonials on your demo video. However, that doesn't mean you can't have additional testimonials on your website for meeting planners and other prospects to review. Again, I use the Instant Video Generator for these videos as well. It's completely hands-off, and interested parties can review them without you having to lift a finger.

- **Audio clips.** Just because video is the most desired medium does not mean that you should forget about audio. Let's say you have three different keynote speeches you offer on your website. It is a good idea to have an audio clip from each one of these keynote speeches, so that the prospects and meeting planners can get a taste of what they'll get. If these audio clips pick up the energetic response from your audience members, they'll build confidence in those reviewing them.

In addition, if you have coaching as part of your offering, it's a nice touch to have an audio sample of you doing an actual *live coaching* of a client. The reason this is so effective is because prospects have many questions running around in their minds as they decide whether or not to do business with you. One of the most prevalent questions is "Will I be intimidated?" Surprise! This was definitely a surprise for me. However, by listening to my current customers, I realized the intimidation factor almost kept some of them from taking that next step. If you have actual audio samples of you coaching a customer, your prospects will get a *feel* for your coaching *personality and process* and hopefully eliminate all unfounded objections.

I recommend "Instant Audio" as a user-friendly service that empowers you to add audio to your websites and emails. You can find this at www.wcspeaking.com/resources. You can even leave a message on a voicemail that generates a link you can add to your website or email messages. You have to hear it to believe it! This is great for audio testimonials, as well. Imagine someone being fired up after your presentation. Then you turn to the person and ask, "May I use your words for testimonial purposes?" They will say, "Sure." Then you can say, "I have an 800 number that I'm going to call. It records testimonials. If you simply say what you just told me, that will be great." Then you call the number, record their testimonial, go into your account, pull up the link that is immediately generated, and publish it to your site or to an email postcard. It's that simple!

Note: You can pay one relatively inexpensive monthly fee and get both the audio and video systems. Visit www.wcspeaking.com/resources for information on these systems. Your return on this investment will blow you away!

- **Downloadable one-sheets.** Like Carrie Perrien Smith mentioned in the section on working with meeting planners, one-sheets are still important to your success as a speaker. However, it makes no sense to have to reactively send these one-sheets out, when it's quicker and easier for meeting planners to download them from your site. I still suggest hiring a professional (like Carrie) to design your one-sheet. However, once it's designed, make sure you offer it online as a PDF download. I've also seen speakers have the following items as downloadable documents from their sites:
    - Introductions to their speeches

- o Bios
- o Handouts
- o Sample questions for the media to ask during an interview
- o Sheet of testimonials
- o Client lists
- o Pre-program questionnaires

To create and control PDF documents, I suggest investing in Adobe Acrobat Standard. This program gives you what you need to create, upload, and protect these documents.

As an expert who speaks, you should take full advantage of auto-responders, sequential auto-responders, audio, video, and PDF downloads to provide your prospects and customers with what they need, when they need it. You cannot be everywhere at once, but your systems sure can! Through your automated systems, you can communicate ongoing with your market. Now, let's look at the second part of automation: getting paid by delivering products to your market.

2. GET PAID ONLINE BY DELIVERING PRODUCTS TO YOUR MARKET

If you don't take payments online, forget about just leaving money on the table—now, you're leaving money all over the universe! There's no need to beat around the bush or try to say this carefully, because the bottom line is this: you must be able to take payments online. Why? Because that's the way your customers are going to pay you. When they decide to purchase, they want to be able to push a button and make it so. If you wedge any space or time in between that decision and that action, you'll lose significant sales.

You must also be able to take credit-card payments offline if, as an expert who speaks, you plan to sell products and services at your engagements. Over the past several years of selling products at my speeches, at least 75 percent of the orders have come via credit-card payment. You simply *must* be able to process them.

The Easiest Way to Take Payments Online

The good news is that it's easy to take payments online, if you have the right system. Here's how easily it can work for you. A prospect visits your website and fills in the credit-card information to purchase one of your products for forty-seven dollars. This order gets processed through your shopping cart (complete with merchant account) system and gets deposited into your company's checking account, minus a very small percentage for the credit-card transaction. It's as simple as that, completely hands-off.

What does your customer see? The shopping cart system immediately provides your customer with a confirmation (and receipt), and then shoots them out an email receipt, as well. The order goes into a file on your e-commerce system, which automatically turns this prospect into a customer in your database. Later, you can go back to review your orders and generate reports out the wazoo. If the product they purchased was an e-book or some other kind of download, it automatically gets sent to your customer when the order is placed.

What about Offline?

If you are selling in the back of the room, you can use your e-commerce system to process the credit-card payments you take offline, too. I use an order form for customers to fill out, complete with their credit-card information. I then take that information back to the office to be processed through the same shopping-cart system. With the exception of this one step (entering their information), everything else works exactly the same.

What is this system to which I am referring? It's the www. EasyWebAutomation.com e-commerce system. This one-stop-shop system empowers you to do the following:

- Process credit card payments and send the money directly into your company's checking account
- Send out single and sequential auto-responders
- Take electronic checks
- Instantly add and manage products
- Publish your electronic newsletter
- Sell downloadable products, such as e-books and special reports, automatically
- Track marketing campaigns with ad trackers
- Provide sales reports
- Keep a customer and prospect database
- Build your list
- Build and keep track of affiliates
- Track all of your orders
- Send tailored broadcast emails to each of your target markets
- Provide custom forms to gather market research
- Bundle products

- Calculate shipping and taxes
- Be the employee you always wish you had!

Once you begin using your e-commerce system, you'll wonder how you got along so well without it. Literally within minutes, you can create a service or product and begin selling it online. A few weeks ago, I raised my speech-coaching rate to $2,500 per day. How did I do this? I simply went into my shopping cart system, added a product called "Edge of Their Seats Speech Coaching," and typed in "$2,500" under the price. I saved this new product, and the system immediately created a link that I sent to those whom I had decided to coach. This took all of three minutes. My customers used the link to purchase the coaching, and my new rate was fully in effect. That's how easy using the e-commerce system is. Whether you get EasyWebAutomation.com or another system, make sure you get one that allows you to do all you've read here. Otherwise, you're not getting the best.

FINAL THOUGHTS ON AUTOMATION

In order to communicate with your market and get paid to deliver products to them, you need the right system. You can do it piecemeal and get an auto-responder system over here, a merchant account over there, a shopping cart to the north, a database system to the south, a customer contact management system to the east, and a reports generator to the west. Or you can do the smart thing and get everything in one place and for one cost. Go to the one-stop shop. In Mitch's opinion, the very best system you can use is through www.EasyWebAutomation.com. This system is by far the best employee you will ever have. It never gets sick. It never complains. It never takes an hour off. Yet, what it does is amazing almost beyond comprehension. I seriously don't know what I would do without it. Neither will you. Visit EasyWebAutomation.com and see how easy it is to free up your time and earn nonstop income by automating your business.

BUILD AN INFORMATION EMPIRE!

A s a speaker, you know to tell your audience what you're going to tell them, tell them, and then tell them what you've just told them. Well, here we are at the end of this resource, so let's quickly review where we've been. You've learned how to

- Avoid the seventeen mistakes most speakers make
- Structure a world-class speech
- Develop content for a world-class speech
- Deliver a world-class speech
- Create a focused marketing plan for great profits
- Tell a superb story that sells your message, products, and services
- Generate leads in the traditional and nontraditional ways
- SWAP (Sell Without Annoying People) from the back of the room
- Develop and market teleclasses as well as profit-producing joint ventures
- Use the Internet to build your business
- Automate your systems to rake in money while you sleep or play

So now what? I've saved the most important idea for last. Everything you create starts with this very next point. I'd venture to say, if you consistently act on this next and final idea, it will change your life. You will have a newfound, deeper level of security, profits flowing to you from many angles, and the peace of mind that comes from the ongoing self-expression of your creative genius. The starting point for your career is the ending point for this book. Read it. Follow it. Profit!

Your Final World Class Speaking Point

A few years ago, I made a commitment that changed my future and my fortune as an entrepreneur. If you make a similar commitment, I have no doubt that you will get similar, if not better, results. Here is the commitment statement that I made for myself:

I, Craig Valentine, will write at least 747 words every day.

Today, my commitment is still to write 747 words per day. You might ask, "Craig, why 747?" Well, let me answer your question with a question. When you think of the numbers 747, what comes to mind? For most people, it's an airplane. That's the point. I know the following truth: the more I write, the less I fly. My products fly *for* me. Don't get me wrong; I have nothing against flying. However, at the time of this writing, I have a five-year-old daughter, a three-year-old son, and an amazing wife. The point is that I don't want to become one of those extremely successful businesspersons who does not know his kids. *World Class Speaking* is not just about building immense profits through your presentations; it's also about keeping first things first and living the kind of life *you* want. Just as Mitch has decided to speak to thousands without being stuck in long lines and strip-searched at airports, you, too, can create the lifestyle that you desire by making and sticking to your commitment. Writing has made all the difference for me, and it will do the same for you. Let's look into this deeper.

How Does Writing Build Your Empire?

Writing is at the *root* of all your products and services. It's where you give birth to your ideas and nurse them to health. As they grow, these ideas branch out into many different products and services. Here is a list of twenty-one profit-producing ways your writings can easily manifest:

1. Keynote speeches
2. Training sessions (workshops and seminars)
3. Teleseminars
4. Coaching processes (in person, online, and over the phone)
5. Books
6. Special reports
7. Manuals
8. Audio CDs
9. DVDs
10. Home-study courses
11. Downloadables
12. Templates
13. Webinars
14. Boot camps
15. Consulting services
16. Newsletters
17. Audio postcards

18. Website content
19. Blogs
20. Podcasts
21. Online courses

The Key to Securing your Future

When you are offering your expertise in all—or at least several—of these formats, rest assured that you are building an information empire. While you sleep, prospects from around the entire world will pay for these products and services. Once they taste one and gain *confidence* in you, they will be back for seconds, thirds, and fourths. When you multiply this by hundreds, and perhaps *thousands*, of customers, you will find your profits blossoming daily. Your reputation will spread, too, which will attract many speaking engagements. This is exponential growth! More importantly, these profits will be rooted in a stable foundation, because you'll have multiple income streams. If one crumbles, you can lean on the others for support. That's *World Class Speaking*.

Are you willing to make the commitment? Do it today. Fill in the following blanks and immediately start planting the seeds that will grow your fruitful future. Most people live on "get set." Don't do that. Instead, take your marks, get set, and *go* for it *now*. That's what world-class speakers do. Are you a world-class speaker?

"I, _____, will write at least _____

per day, every day."

GET YOUR FREE 7-PART WORLD CLASS SPEAKING TOOLKIT (VALUED AT $97)

Plus a special offer for the readers of this book!

www.WCSpeaking.com

For more information on Craig Valentine
Visit www.CraigValentine.com

For more information on Mitch Meyerson
Visit www.MitchMeyerson.com

BUY A SHARE OF THE FUTURE IN YOUR COMMUNITY

These certificates make great holiday, graduation and birthday gifts that can be personalized with the recipient's name. The cost of one S.H.A.R.E. or one square foot is $54.17. The personalized certificate is suitable for framing and will state the number of shares purchased and the amount of each share, as well as the recipient's name. The home that you participate in "building" will last for many years and will continue to grow in value.

Here is a sample SHARE certificate:

THIS CERTIFIES THAT
YOUR NAME HERE
HAS INVESTED IN A HOME FOR A DESERVING FAMILY
1985-2005
TWENTY YEARS OF BUILDING FUTURES IN OUR
COMMUNITY ONE HOME AT A TIME
1200 SQUARE FOOT HOUSE @ $65,000 = $54.17 PER SQUARE FOOT
This certificate represents a tax deductible donation. It has no cash value.

YES, I WOULD LIKE TO HELP!

I support the work that Habitat for Humanity does and I want to be part of the excitement! As a donor, I will receive periodic updates on your construction activities but, more importantly, I know my gift will help a family in our community realize the dream of homeownership. **I would like to SHARE in your efforts against substandard housing in my community!** *(Please print below)*

PLEASE SEND ME _____ SHARES at $54.17 EACH = $ $_____

In Honor Of: _____

Occasion: (Circle One)   HOLIDAY   BIRTHDAY   ANNIVERSARY

        OTHER: _____

Address of Recipient: _____

Gift From: _____ *Donor Address:* _____

Donor Email: _____

I AM ENCLOSING A CHECK FOR $ $_____ PAYABLE TO HABITAT FOR HUMANITY <u>OR</u> PLEASE CHARGE MY VISA OR MASTERCARD *(CIRCLE ONE)*

Card Number _____   Expiration Date: _____

Name as it appears on Credit Card _____   Charge Amount $ _____

Signature _____

Billing Address _____

Telephone # Day _____   Eve _____

PLEASE NOTE: Your contribution is tax-deductible to the fullest extent allowed by law.
Habitat for Humanity • P.O. Box 1443 • Newport News, VA 23601 • 757-596-5553
www.HelpHabitatforHumanity.org

Printed in the United States
140619LV00002B/74/P